Seeing
Judaism
Anew

Seeing
Judaism
Anew

Christianity's
Sacred
Obligation

EDITED BY MARY C. BOYS

A SHEED & WARD BOOK

ROWMAN & LITTLEFIELD PUBLISHERS, INC.

Lanham • Boulder • New York • Toronto • Oxford

A SHEED & WARD BOOK

ROWMAN & LITTLEFIELD PUBLISHERS, INC.

Published in the United States of America
by Rowman & Littlefield Publishers, Inc.
A wholly owned subsidiary of The Rowman & Littlefield Publishing Group, Inc.
4501 Forbes Boulevard, Suite 200, Lanham, Maryland 20706
www.rowmanlittlefield.com

PO Box 317
Oxford
OX2 9RU, UK

British Library Cataloguing in Publication Information Available

Library of Congress Cataloging-in-Publication Data

Seeing Judaism anew : Christianity's sacred obligation / edited by Mary C. Boys.
   p. cm.
  "A Sheed & Ward book."
  Includes bibliographical references and index.
  ISBN 0-7425-4881-3 (hardcover : alk. paper) — ISBN 0-7425-4882-1
(pbk. : alk. paper)
  1. Judaism—Relations—Christianity. 2. Christianity and other religions—
Judaism. 3. Judaism (Christian theology) I. Boys, Mary C.
  BM535.S328 2005
  261.2'6—dc22   2004027866

Printed in the United States of America

♾™ The paper used in this publication meets the minimum requirements of
American National Standard for Information Sciences—Permanence of Paper
for Printed Library Materials, ANSI/NISO Z39.48-1992.

To Charles and Margaret Obrecht

In gratitude

for your dedication to Christian-Jewish relations

and for your hospitality to our Christian Scholars Group

Contents

XII.
CHRISTIAN-JEWISH RELATIONS AFTER
THE SHOAH: HISTORICAL REFLECTIONS

Preface

F OR OVER thirty years, the various participants in what is presently called the Christian Scholars Group on Christian-Jewish Relations have studied the complexities of the biblical, ethical, historical, liturgical, and theological interconnections between the living traditions of Judaism and Christianity. Its members have included some of the most influential North American Christian researchers and writers in the field—a field that emerged in the aftermath of the Shoah and blossomed with the formal repudiation by many churches of perennial anti-Jewish claims and teachings.

The Center for Christian-Jewish Learning at Boston College is honored to be the present sponsor of the Christian Scholars Group. This center is dedicated to the multifaceted development and implementation of new relationships between Christians and Jews that are based not merely on toleration but on full respect and mutual enrichment. The building of new, positive relationships between Jews and Christians requires sustained theological research like that undertaken by the Christian Scholars Group and its members. Its continuing work contributes uniquely to the renewed Christian theological engagement with the distinct yet related Jewish community of faith.

This collection of essays provides a snapshot of the current "state of the question" from the Christian side of the Jewish and Christian relationship. It also invites other Christians to ponder the fuller implications of the rapprochement between the two communities that has been underway for several decades.

The Center for Christian-Jewish Learning at Boston College thanks each of the contributors, the editorial committee, and especially editor Mary C. Boys for this important volume.

Philip A. Cunningham,
Executive Director

Ruth Langer,
Associate Director

A Sacred Obligation: Rethinking Christian Faith in Relation to Judaism and the Jewish People

A Statement by the Christian Scholars Group on Christian-Jewish Relations

September 1, 2002

Since its inception in 1969, the Christian Scholars Group has been seeking to develop more adequate Christian theologies of the church's relationship to Judaism and the Jewish people. Pursuing this work for over three decades under varied sponsorship, members of our association of Protestant and Roman Catholic biblical scholars, historians, and theologians have published many volumes on Christian-Jewish relations.

Our work has a historical context. For most of the past two thousand years, Christians have erroneously portrayed Jews as unfaithful, holding them collectively responsible for the death of Jesus and therefore accursed by God. In agreement with many official Christian declarations, we reject this accusation as historically false and theologically invalid. It suggests that God can be unfaithful to the eternal covenant with the Jewish people. We acknowledge with shame the suffering this distorted portrayal has brought upon the Jewish people. We repent of this teaching of contempt. Our repentance requires us to build a new teaching of respect. This task is important at any time, but the deadly crisis in the Middle East and the frightening resurgence of antisemitism worldwide give it particular urgency.

We believe that revising Christian teaching about Judaism and the Jewish people is a central and indispensable obligation of theology in our time. It is essential that Christianity both understand and represent Judaism accurately, not only as a matter of justice for the Jewish people, but also for the integrity of Christian faith, which we cannot proclaim without reference to Judaism. Moreover, since there is a unique bond between Christianity and Judaism, revitalizing our appreciation of Jewish religious life will deepen our Christian faith. We base these convictions on ongoing scholarly research and the official statements of many Christian denominations over the past fifty years.

We are grateful for the willingness of many Jews to engage in dialogue and study with us. We welcomed it when, on September 10, 2000, Jewish scholars sponsored by the Institute of Christian and Jewish Studies in Baltimore issued a historic declaration, *Dabru Emet: A Jewish Statement on Christians and Christianity*. This document, affirmed by notable rabbis and Jewish scholars, called on Jews to re-examine their understanding of Christianity.

Encouraged by the work of both Jewish and Christian colleagues, we offer the following ten statements for the consideration of our fellow Christians. We urge all Christians to reflect on their faith in light of these statements. For us, this is a sacred obligation.

1. God's covenant with the Jewish people endures forever.

For centuries Christians claimed that their covenant with God replaced or superseded the Jewish covenant. We renounce this claim. We believe that God does not revoke divine promises. We affirm that God is in covenant with both Jews and Christians. Tragically, the entrenched theology of supersessionism continues to influence Christian faith, worship, and practice, even though it has been repudiated by many Christian denominations and many Christians no longer accept it. Our recognition of the abiding validity of Judaism has implications for all aspects of Christian life.

2. Jesus of Nazareth lived and died as a faithful Jew.

Christians worship the God of Israel in and through Jesus Christ. Supersessionism, however, prompted Christians over the centuries to speak of

Dr. Peter C. Phan
Ignacio Ellacuria, S.J., Chair of
    Catholic Social Thought
Department of Theology
Georgetown University
Washington, DC

Dr. Jean-Pierre Ruiz
Associate Professor and Chair
Department of Theology and
    Religious Studies
St. John's University
Jamaica, New York

Dr. Franklin Sherman
Associate for Interfaith Relations
Evangelical Lutheran Church
    in America
Allentown, Pennsylvania

Dr. Joann Spillman
Professor and Chair
Department of Theology
    and Religious Studies
Rockhurst University
Kansas City, Missouri

Dr. John T. Townsend
Visiting Lecturer on
    Jewish Studies
Harvard Divinity School
Cambridge, Massachusetts

Dr. Joseph Tyson
Professor Emeritus of
    Religious Studies
Southern Methodist
    University
Dallas, Texas

Dr. Clark M. Williamson
Indiana Professor of
    Christian Thought,
    Emeritus
Christian Theological
    Seminary
Indianapolis, Indiana

Introduction

Mary C. Boys

In September 2002 twenty-one Christian scholars, Protestant and Catholic, released a statement that includes these sentences:

> We believe that revising Christian teaching about Judaism and the Jewish people is a central and indispensable obligation of theology in our time. It is essential that Christianity both understand and represent Judaism accurately, not only as a matter of justice for the Jewish people, but also for the integrity of Christian faith, which we cannot proclaim without reference to Judaism.

This book expands upon our statement and explores its implications by bridging the realm of scholarship and the life of the church; it also seeks to bridge the longstanding divide between Jews and Christians. Our statement is far more than an intellectual exercise; we wrote it because each of us cares passionately about a vital and vibrant Christianity that does justice to its complex and profound relationship with Judaism. Our book arises from that same commitment, as we seek to develop the assertions expressed in "A Sacred Obligation."

We write primarily for Christian readers, many of whom are instinctively aware of the deep bonds between Jews and Christians and find their faith enriched by a deeper understanding of Christianity's relationship to Judaism. Many Christians, however, lack awareness of the centuries of Christian disparagement of Judaism that has had tragic consequences for

Jews and tainted Christian theology and self-understanding. This topic, while the subject of many books and articles, is only beginning to gain wide public interest; we have written our book with this larger public in mind. We hope, of course, that other scholars will read this book, and we also welcome Jewish readers.

Because we have written with a broad audience in mind, we have done our best to express complicated matters in as clear a fashion as possible, minimizing the accouterments of scholarly writing. Accordingly, we have kept the chapters relatively brief and the language accessible. Readers will note cross-references to the various chapters; we all read each other's chapters in draft form and want to show connections between them.

Our book takes its shape from our statement "A Sacred Obligation." Our goal is to explain why rethinking Christian theology—that is, how we might understand our faith—is not only necessary but a "sacred obligation." So our book forms a kind of pathway through the many topics and ramifications of Christian attitudes toward Jews. We begin with a chapter on the Holocaust (the Shoah) by Eva Fleischner. This is fitting because recognition of Christian complicity in that tragedy led to the realization that something was terribly wrong in the church's relationship with Jews. In particular, post-Holocaust reflection has uncovered "the teaching of contempt" for Jews and Judaism that has been a persistent virus in Christianity over the ages.

In seeking to eradicate this virus, we have looked especially to a renewed understanding of the scriptures. The chapter by Mary Boys develops a basic premise of "A Sacred Obligation": God's covenant with the Jewish people endures. Joseph Tyson contributes complementary chapters that situate the life and death of Jesus in their historical context; his latter chapter has particular relevance in the wake of the controversy sparked by Mel Gibson's film *The Passion of the Christ*. Celia Deutsch follows with a chapter analyzing a passage from the Acts of the Apostles (10:34, 37–43, read on Easter Sunday in churches that use the lectionary) that accuses the Jews of putting Jesus to death by "hanging him on a tree." Then Jean-Pierre Ruiz shows how understanding the situation of the followers of Jesus in the Roman Empire offers insights into texts such as Romans 13:1 ("Let every person be subject to the governing authorities") and Revelation 2:9 ("those who say they are Jews and are not but are a synagogue of Satan"). Two chapters continue this biblical focus through feminist concerns. Mary Boys examines certain Christian feminist claims that convey anti-Jewish notions, and Deirdre Good reviews the contributions Jewish feminists have made to the study of the New Testament and early Christianity.

These chapters correspond to the first three points of our statement and provide readers with ways of interpreting texts characteristic of contemporary biblical scholarship. In particular, they situate Christian origins in their complex context, thereby illumining the complicated and conflictual process by which Christianity and Judaism eventually parted ways.

Our book then turns to the fourth and fifth points of "A Sacred Obligation." Peter Pettit and John Townsend contribute a chapter that traces Jewish thought after the destruction of Jerusalem in 70 C.E. through the leadership of the rabbis—a development all too few Christians are aware of. Walter Harrelson's chapter invites its readers to reconsider how they understand the relationship between the Testaments.

The chapters by Peter Phan and Clark Williamson address how we might understand salvation (point 6), a topic encapsulated by the controversial question "Can only Christians be saved?" Complementing their work are chapters by Philip Cunningham and Joann Spillman arguing that Christians should *not* seek the conversion of Jews (point 7).

We turn then to implications for Christian liturgy, the subject of point 8. John Merkle shows how the teaching of contempt has been incorporated into the church's worship; he suggests a deeper understanding of Jewish approaches to God offers a more profound grasp of our own liturgical life. Rosann Catalano offers an intriguing reading of a passage from Mark's gospel, that of the tearing of the curtain of the Temple after the death of Jesus. Then Norman Beck argues for the importance of more adequate translations of the Bible, particularly as texts become a part of worship in churches that use the lectionary.

Michael McGarry takes up the vexed question of Israel—the land and nation-state—in his chapter explaining our ninth assertion, "We affirm the importance of the land of Israel for the life of the Jewish people." John Pawlikowski's chapter develops our final point about working with Jews for the healing of the world; he identifies both common commitments and points of tension in this task.

A final set of chapters concludes the book. Franklin Sherman and Eugene Fisher situate the official statements of Christian denominations and ecclesial bodies since 1947, and Alice Eckardt offers a view of the work of the Christian Scholars Group since its inception in 1969 as the Israel Study Group.

Many churches have officially rejected the allegation that God cursed Jews forever because they crucified Jesus, and this rejection is a significant step in repairing the relationship between Christianity and Judaism. Official statements, however, do not suffice to repair the damage this idea has inflicted on Christian self-understanding, let alone what Jews have suffered because of it.

It is our hope that this volume will contribute to the growing Christian awareness of our sacred obligation to understand our faith in ways that do justice to our relationship with the Jewish people—an understanding that will also deepen our appreciation of our commitments as Christians.

As editor of this volume, I wish to express my thanks to the members of the Christian Scholars Group for their chapters, each of which went through numerous drafts. I extend my gratitude as well to the hard-working editorial committee: Rosann Catalano, Philip Cunningham, Joseph Tyson, and Clark Williamson. Our group has benefited immensely from the sponsorship of the Institute for Christian and Jewish Studies in Baltimore and, more recently, from the Center for Christian-Jewish Learning at Boston College. On behalf of the Christian Scholars Group, I extend thanks to both institutions.

We dedicate this volume to Charles and Margaret Obrecht of Baltimore, whose gracious hospitality to our Christian Scholars Group has enriched many a discussion. Charlie and Peggy's passion for just relations between Christians and Jews exemplifies what it means to live the sacred obligation that is the subject of our book.

PART

Introductory Essay

1

CHAPTER

The Shoah and
Jewish-Christian Relations

Eva Fleischner

I N WRITING "A Sacred Obligation," the statement that is the
inspiration for this volume, we in the Christian Scholars Group
acknowledged "with shame the suffering [that a] distorted portrayal [of Jews as accursed by God] has brought upon the Jewish people."
Although we made no specific mention of the Shoah (Holocaust), we were
keenly aware of the terrible legacy of Christian preaching and teaching that
provided the ground on which the "venomous plant of hatred for the Jews
was able to flourish," as the Catholic bishops of France wrote in their 1997
"Declaration of Repentance."

A Hebrew term for catastrophe, "Shoah" refers to the systematic, deliberate murder of nearly six million Jews by the Nazis. Many prefer "Shoah" to
"Holocaust," because the latter originally referred to the most sacred of sacrifices in biblical Israel.

No statistic can convey even remotely the horror of the genocide that
exterminated one-third of the world's Jews for no other reason than that they

were Jews. The Nazis murdered millions of other victims as well, whether those they branded racially inferior (e.g., Roma [Gypsies], Poles, the disabled) or politically undesirable (e.g., homosexuals, Jehovah's Witnesses, Communists). Yet only Jews had been vilified by Christians for centuries; only Jews were targeted for extinction precisely as a people in order to make the world *Judenrein*: free of Jews. As Elie Wiesel has said, "Not every victim was a Jew, but every Jew was a victim."[1]

Two aspects of the Shoah distinguish it from other genocides. First, a powerful, "civilized" nation used advanced technology to destroy human beings whom the state deemed "unworthy of life." Second, the killers sought to dehumanize their victims before killing them, destroying their spirit and soul before annihilating their bodies.

Only the testimony of those who experienced the Shoah—whether they survived or perished—can convey to the world something of the horror. Perhaps no words of witness are as powerful as this paragraph from Elie Wiesel's memoir of his internment in Auschwitz, *Night*:

> Never shall I forget that night, the first night in the camp, which has turned my life into one long night. . . . Never shall I forget that smoke. Never shall I forget the little faces of the children, whose bodies I saw turned into wreaths of smoke beneath a silent blue sky. . . . Never shall I forget these things, even if I am condemned to live as long as God himself. Never.[2]

The overwhelming evil of the Shoah calls into question many religious commonplaces. Rabbi Irving Greenberg articulates this most radically: "No statement, theological or otherwise, should be made that could not be credible in the presence of the burning children."[3]

The Pivotal Role of the Shoah in Christian-Jewish Relations

Voices such as Wiesel's and Greenberg's began to resonate in postwar Christian circles. The churches began at long last to reconsider and repent of their anti-Jewish teaching, a repentance that requires building a "new teaching of respect." It is a complex and challenging task to root out distortions of Judaism that have become so intertwined with Christian self-understanding. However difficult, our group of scholars considers it a "sacred obligation," fundamental to a just relationship with Jews and to the integrity of Christianity. And at the heart of this sacred obligation lies Christianity's confrontation with the Shoah. It took the Shoah—the cries of survivors, the quiet witness of rescuers, the analysis of historians, the voices of writers, the creativity of artists, and the leadership of a few religious scholars—to awaken the churches to their complicity. It is the Shoah that shattered Christian smugness, revealing the depths of Christianity's anti-Judaism and engendering rethinking of its relationship with the Jewish people.

Thus, the Shoah is pivotal to Jewish-Christian relations in two quite different ways. It casts a new and searing light on the past: the nearly two millennia of Christian anti-Judaism. Yet the rethinking to which it has given rise is the principal factor in the dramatic change that has occurred in the relationship between the two faith communities. I explore both perspectives in this essay. In order to appreciate the revolutionary character of the changes we must be aware of what went before. It is a history familiar to Jews, but virtually unknown to most Christians.

Christian Anti-Judaism

Many contemporary historians and theologians, Christian as well as Jewish, argue that Christian anti-Judaism contributed directly to the Shoah. The church, Rosemary Radford Ruether wrote in the 1970s, "must bear a substantial responsibility for a tragic history of the Jew in Christendom, which was the foundation upon which the political antisemitism and the Nazi use of it was erected."[4]

How could this have happened? How could Jesus' gospel of love have been turned into the teaching of contempt? After all, Christianity had begun as a Jewish movement. Jesus was a devout Jew, as was his mother, as were all his first followers. We know from the Acts of the Apostles that the disciples kept the Jewish times of prayer in the Temple even after the resurrection. Certainly, disagreements and tensions existed between Jesus' followers and other Jews about the interpretation of Torah. Such differences, however, were typical of first-century Judaism, as Joseph Tyson explains in his chapter, "Jesus—A Faithful Jew," in this volume.

By the late first century, however, tensions had increased, particularly in the aftermath of the Jewish War against Rome (66–70 C.E.). Some Jews apparently regarded Jesus' followers as heretics, dangerous to the fragile stability Judaism enjoyed under the Roman Empire. As the Christian community became more Gentile in composition, it became less able to understand the inherently Jewish terms of the debate. After the failed Bar Kochba revolt against Rome in 135, Christians increasingly distinguished themselves from Jews, often doing so in terms that disparaged Judaism. This "identity construction," which Celia Deutsch speaks of in this volume in "Ancient Rivalries and New Testament Interpretation," gave rise to the "teaching of contempt," a term coined by historian Jules Isaac. Isaac, who survived the Shoah because he was hidden by a Catholic member of the French underground, Germain Bocquet, documents the ways in which the teaching of contempt came to permeate Christian preaching, liturgy, and teaching.[5]

Over the centuries the teaching of contempt has been the cause of immense suffering for the Jewish people. Without question, it has contributed to hostility toward and violence against Jews in many times and places, not simply in Nazi Germany. While this teaching is today repudiated by many major Christian churches, vestiges still linger. The teaching of contempt remains an open wound in the life of the church.

The Teaching of Contempt

During what is often called the age of the "apologists"—the second through fifth centuries, when Christian leaders argued the legitimacy of their beliefs—Christianity increasingly portrayed Jews as rejected and cast aside by God because they had not recognized Jesus as Messiah. They characterized the ancient covenant as now null and void (see Mary Boys's "The Enduring Covenant" in this volume). The apologists interpreted the Roman destruction of Jerusalem and its Temple as punishment for the crucifixion of Jesus; they viewed this devastation as the visible and tangible evidence of God's rejection of the "old" people of God. A new people of God, the Christian church, had taken its place. This belief, which was to sink deep roots in Christianity and which helped the church to define itself, has been a main source of contempt for Jews and discrimination against them. This "replacement theology" is often termed "supersessionism," the supplanting of one people by another.

Late in the second century, Melito, bishop of Sardis (d. 190), added a particularly toxic dimension to supersessionism: the accusation of deicide. His logic is that according to Christian belief Jesus is God; therefore, in crucifying Jesus the Jews had killed God. "God has been murdered; the king of Israel is slain by an Israelite hand" ("Homily on the Passover"). Similarly, Justin Martyr says in his *Dialogue with Trypho*: "Tribulations were justly imposed upon you, for you have murdered the Just One." Note that the apologists level their accusation not only at Jesus' Jewish contemporaries, but at all Jews everywhere in every age. Yet, as Augustine argues in his *Reply to Faustus the Manichean,* there is a reason for continued existence of the Jews (a confusing fact for the church): in their exile, Jews remind the world of what happens when human beings reject God.

However shocking these views may sound to Christians today, they remained relatively harmless as long as Christianity was a powerless, minority religion in the Roman Empire. The situation changed drastically, however, in the late fourth century, when Emperor Theodosius I (379–395) made Christianity the empire's official religion. Christianity took on the trappings of Rome's temporal power. Now theological views began to be translated into legislation, a process that gained momentum and persisted through the Middle Ages and beyond, into the twentieth century. From the (regional) Council of Elvira in Spain (ca. 304) to the Fourth Lateran Council (an ecumenical [universal] council) in 1215, a body of anti-Jewish laws developed, ranging from the prohibition of intermarriage to the imposition of special clothing and a badge, foreshadowing Nazi antisemitic legislation.

Indeed, in many respects Hitler had little left to invent in the Nuremberg Laws, which the German parliament passed in 1935. The main legislative tool for excluding Jews from society, the Nuremberg Laws segregated Jews, prohibited them from marrying non-Jews, made them ineligible for employment, and ultimately deprived them of all human rights. Hitler completed the process begun by the church centuries earlier. He added, however, one unprecedented, critical step: genocide.

The Churches and the Shoah

The Shoah cannot be solely attributed to the anti-Jewish teachings of Christianity, however contemptuous those were. The Third Reich's genocidal policies, complemented by the romantic myth of the German *Volk* and theories of race "science," resulted in the unparalleled destruction of the Jewish people. Without doubt, the teaching of contempt fertilized the soil in which Hitler's genocidal antisemitism flourished. "Christianity was not a sufficient condition for the Holocaust, nevertheless it was a necessary condition" for it, writes Holocaust scholar John Roth.[6] A few examples illustrate Roth's point.

- In 1941 Archbishop Conrad Gröber of Freiburg (Germany) issued a pastoral letter in which he blamed Jews for the death of Christ. He added, "The self-imposed curse of the Jews, 'His blood be upon us and upon our children' [Matt 27:25] has come terribly true until the present time, until today."[7]

- Also in 1941, Marshal Pétain, head of the Vichy government in France, asked Léon Bérard, Vichy's ambassador to the Vatican, to find out the Vatican's reaction to the anti-Jewish laws the Vichy regime had enacted. Bérard reported that he had not heard any misgivings in Rome concerning the persecution of Jews. "In principle, there is nothing in these measures which the Holy See finds necessary to criticize."[8]

- In 1942 Rabbi Michael Dov-Ber Weissmandel (of Slovakia) went to Archbishop Kametko to plead for his intercession on behalf of Slovakian Jews, who were about to be deported. The rabbi did not know as yet about the gas chambers, but he stressed the dangers of starvation and disease to which the victims would be exposed. The Archbishop of Nietra replied: "It is not just a matter of deportation. You will not die there of hunger and disease. They will slaughter all of you there, old and young alike, women and children, at once—it is the punishment that you deserve for the death of our Lord and Redeemer, Jesus Christ—you have only one solution. Come over to our religion and I will work to annul this decree."[9]

The record of the Protestant Church of Germany is no better. The majority of German Protestant Christians (known as "German Christians") supported Hitler, who appointed Bishop Ludwig Müller as their head. As early as 1934, Müller said that Christianity did not grow out of Judaism: "There is no bond between them, rather, the sharpest opposition." Even the "Confessing Church," comprised of Christians who courageously and unambiguously opposed Hitler, did not mention Jews in its statement of opposition to Nazism, the Barmen Confession of 1934.

The Rescuers

Jan Karski, the Polish diplomat who was the subject of a biography subtitled, *How One Man Tried to Stop the Holocaust*, told an interviewer that "Jews were abandoned by governments, by church hierarchies, by societies, but they were rescued by individuals, following the Lord's law of love—love your neighbor."[10] The same could be said of Christianity: Jews were abandoned by the churches, but not by individual Christians.

Although the churches as institutions largely failed Jews, some Christians in every country of occupied Europe risked their lives to save Jews. The dangers were enormous—severe punishments were meted out, including death—but some nonetheless took the risk of helping Jews because they recognized in them their brothers and sisters. We shall never know how many rescuers there were. Whatever their number, they were a tiny minority among the millions who were bystanders or collaborators. Despite their minority status, they loom large as signs of hope. They prove that individuals can make a difference, and that good can overcome evil. The State of Israel honors them with the title "Righteous among the Nations of the World." Visitors to Yad Vashem (the Holocaust Memorial in Jerusalem) can walk down the "Avenue of the Righteous" lined with trees planted in tribute to those who saved Jews during the Shoah. In the saying often attributed to the sage Hillel, "Whoever saves one life, it is as if he [or she] had saved the entire world."

To illustrate, let me recount three of my encounters with French Catholic rescuers during a research project I conducted between 1985 and 1987. I met Fr. Albert Gau, then in his seventies, in the beautiful medieval city of Carcassonne, where he still lives. One of the projects in which Fr. Gau was involved during the war was the opening of a restaurant (ostensibly run by a woman he knew) that served as a front for rescuing Jews and other refugees from the Germans. I asked him if he had the support of his bishop. Hesitantly, he answered, "Yes, up to a point." One day the bishop called him: "My dear Father, this is getting too dangerous for us all. I must ask you to stop." That very night Fr. Gau's doorbell rang. There stood a Jewish woman, "pregnant, very pregnant." He welcomed her, and then proceeded to phone the bishop: "Bishop, I have a pregnant Jewish woman here. You told me to stop, so I'll send her over to your place. You have plenty of room." The bishop responded: "Please, please keep her!" So Fr. Gau kept her for the night and then enabled her to be admitted to a maternity ward. Her child was born, and they both lived. And Fr. Gau continued his rescue work.[11]

When I met Rolande Birgy, she was walking with a cane; she was in her seventies. As a young woman during the war she had spent much time in the French Alps, finding homes for Jewish children until she could get them across the border into Switzerland. It was important to her to make sure that the families hiding the children would respect their Jewish faith. Finally, one day the police caught up with her and she was jailed. A police-man, puzzled by this attractive young woman who kept risking her life, came to see her in prison. The policeman asked, "Why on earth do you help those Jews?" Birgy replied with what was obvious to her, "Because I am French, and Catholic!" Perplexed, he retorted, "But you surely know that the Jews killed Christ?" "My dear sir," Birgy responded, "let me tell you something: Anyone who has had any catechism at all should know that it wasn't the Jews who killed Christ, but our sins!" The policeman replied sheepishly, "I guess you are right."

We have here, incidentally, an example of both the teaching of contempt and the overcoming of it.

As I began my research in France, one name kept coming up. "Have you met Germaine Ribière yet?" interviewees would ask. "She was at the heart of things, her testimony is crucial." Cardinal Henri de Lubac told me, "We used to call her our Joan of Arc."

A small incident on the occasion of our first meeting gave me an important clue to this woman's character and approach to life. At her suggestion, we had arranged to meet for noon Mass and then to have lunch together. We were walking to the restaurant, engrossed in conversation, when she suddenly interrupted herself: "I am worried about this little girl, I wonder if she has lost her mother." I had noticed, vaguely, a little girl in front of us, about two years old, but had not really "seen" her. Germaine had seen, and worried. As it turned out, the mother was close by, walking ahead of the child. As I came to know Germaine in the months that followed and learned of the extraordinary things she had done during the war—crisscrossing France, going back and forth between France and Poland, infiltrating the Gestapo—I realized how consistent she is. She is Germaine Ribière because she notices a little girl who may be lost and in need of help, in the middle of peacetime Paris in 1985, just as the Jews needed help during the war.

New Beginnings

As the world gradually came to grips with the death camps, the churches were forced to confront the role Christianity had played in making the Shoah possible. This has led to serious soul-searching and, in many cases, to a conversion of heart and repentance. Many churches issued statements refuting the charge of deicide, repudiating antisemitism, and repenting of their complicity in the Shoah, as well as outlining changes in Christian theology vis-à-vis Judaism. Other chapters in this volume examine these important documents, which have led to revolutionary changes in Christian self-understanding (see the chapters by Alice Eckardt, Eugene Fisher, and Franklin Sherman in this volume).

The documents from the churches effect change as they are embodied in institutional structures and the production and dissemination of resources. Among numerous exemplars:

- Many Christian textbooks have been thoroughly revised so that they provide a more accurate account of Judaism.
- Jewish scholars teach courses in Christian colleges and seminaries. (A Jewish New Testament scholar, Professor Amy-Jill Levine of Vanderbilt University's Divinity School, is currently the book review editor of the *Catholic Biblical Quarterly*).
- The Secretariat for Ecumenical and Interreligious Affairs of the National Conference of Catholic Bishops publishes resources and serves as a coordinating center for dialogue.
- The Judaeo-Christian Institute of Seton Hall University (West Orange, New Jersey), founded by pioneer John Oesterreicher, has educated scholars and lay people since the 1960s.
- The National Catholic Center for Holocaust Education of Seton Hill University (Greensburgh, Pennsylvania) has conducted annual education programs for Catholic teachers for the past eighteen years, both in Israel and in the United States.
- The National Christian-Jewish Workshop, convened from 1971 through 1998, has played an important educational role in various cities throughout the country. Efforts are underway to continue this event.
- Christian theologians, often in collaboration with Jewish scholars, continue to rethink Christianity's relationship with Judaism. The present volume is one of the fruits of this effort.

Various symbolic actions contribute to awareness of the changing relationship between Jews and Christians. Pope John Paul II's visit to the synagogue in Rome in 1986 and cordial relationship with its chief rabbi, Elio Toaff, underscore the new equality and mutual respect between Judaism and Christianity. Even more dramatic was the pope's visit to Israel in March 2000. Among its memorable moments were his visit to Yad Vashem and meeting with Shoah survivors, and his placing a prayer in the Western Wall begging God's forgiveness and pledging commitment to forging "genuine brotherhood with the people of the Covenant." Of this latter gesture, the *New York Times* commented: "It was a searing image that many Israelis said signaled a new era in Jewish-Christian relations" (March 27, 2000).[12]

The Task Ahead

The churches cannot eradicate nineteen centuries of anti-Jewish teaching and preaching quickly or easily. Despite significant progress—what one Jewish observer called "the major success story of the twentieth century"— vestiges of anti-Judaism remain, particularly in preaching and worship. The selection and interpretation of scripture readings, especially during Holy Week and the Easter season, are in urgent need of reform. This has become all the more evident in recent controversies surrounding interpretation of the Passion accounts in the gospels. Most Christians have no idea of the recommendations various churches have made in the past forty or so years that offer crucial context for understanding the death of Jesus in its fuller historical and theological setting. Worrisome as well is the resurgence of antisemitism, both in Europe and North America, often fueled by the tragic conflict in the Middle East (see Michael McGarry's "The Land of Israel in the Cauldron of the Middle East" in this volume). As efforts continue to make this "new era" a lasting reality, it is good to remember that the past forty years of extraordinary progress have not been without problems and setbacks. Yet nothing has turned back the clock.

In conclusion, let me mention one of the most hopeful events of recent years: the promulgation by Jewish scholars of *Dabru Emet* (Speaking Truth). This statement first appeared as a full-page advertisement in the *New York Times* on Rosh Hashanah 2000 (September 9). The four authors and some 250 rabbis and scholars who signed it expressed the conviction that Judaism needs a theological understanding of Christianity. Intended as a response to the radical changes that have taken place in the churches and a recognition of Christianity's efforts to build a positive relationship with Judaism, *Dabru Emet* is a sign that these efforts have begun to bear fruit. In turn, our "A Sacred Obligation" may be seen as an ecumenical Christian response to *Dabru Emet*.

More than ever before in our troubled, tragic history, Jews and Christians are committed to relating to one another as equal dialogue partners in a mutual effort to understand, respect, and learn from one another. This is important not only as a matter of justice to the Jewish people and of the integrity of the Christian faith, but for the sake of our divided world. May relations between Jews and Christians flourish, so that we will be a sign of hope that those who were once enemies can reconcile.

Notes

1. Wiesel's memorable phrase appears, among other places, in the "Report to the President [Jimmy Carter] of the President's Commission on the Holocaust," September 27, 1979, iii. Wiesel uses it in his cover letter to President Carter in forwarding the commission's report: "While not all victims were Jews, *all* Jews were victims, destined for annihilation solely because they were born Jewish." I thank Mr. Ralph Grunewald for assistance in locating this citation.

2. Elie Wiesel, *Night* (New York: Bantam Books, 1982), 32. First published in English in 1960 by Hill and Wong.

3. Irving Greenberg, "Cloud of Smoke, Pillar of Fire," in Eva Fleischner, ed., *Auschwitz: Beginning of a New Era?* (New York: KTAV, 1977), 23.

4. Rosemary Ruether, *Faith and Fratricide* (New York: Seabury, 1974), 184.

5. Jules Isaac, *The Teaching of Contempt* (New York: Holt, Rinehart and Winston, 1964).

6. John Roth, "What Does the Holocaust Have to Do with Christianity?" in Carol Rittner, Stephen D. Smith, and Irena Steinfeldt et al., eds., *The Holocaust and the Christian World: Reflections on the Past, Challenges for the Future* (New York: Continuum, 2000), 6.

7. Cited in Guenter Lewy, *The Catholic Church and Nazi Germany* (New York: McGraw-Hill, 1964), 294.

8. Cited in Michael R. Marrus and Robert O. Paxton, *Vichy France and the Jews* (New York: Schocken, 1983), 201.

9. Cited in Greenberg, "Cloud of Smoke," in Fleishner, ed., *Auschwitz: Beginning of a New Era? Reflections on the Holocaust* (New York: KTAV, 1977), 11–12.

10. Catholic News Service, cited in an obituary of Karski in the *Denver Catholic Register*, August 2, 2000, at www.archden.org/dcr/ archive/20000802/ 2000080204wn.htm.

11. For this and the following two stories see Eva Fleischner, "Can the Few Become the Many? Some Catholics in France Who Saved Jews during the Holocaust," in Yehuda Bauer et al., eds., *Remembering for the Future*, vol. 1 (Oxford: Pergamon, 1989), 232–47.

12. Richard Boudreaux and Tracy Wilkinson, "Saluting 3 Faiths, Pope Departs Holy Land," *New York Times* (March 27, 2000).

Further Reading

Barnett, Victoria J. *Bystanders: Conscience and Complicity during the Holocaust.* Westport, CT: Praeger, 1999.

Cohn-Sherbok, Dan, ed. *Holocaust Theology: A Reader.* New York: New York University Press, 2000.

Fleischner, Eva, ed. *Auschwitz: Beginning of a New Era?* New York: KTAV, 1977.

Phayer, Michael, and Eva Fleischner, *Cries in the Night: Women Who Challenged the Holocaust.* Kansas City, MO: Sheed and Ward, 1997.

II

PART

God's Covenant with the Jewish People Endures Forever

2
CHAPTER

The Enduring Covenant

Mary C. Boys

T HE TERM "covenant" slips easily off the lips of Christians. It is a term that is often used casually, and its meaning is usually taken for granted. Yet an accurate understanding of our relationship with Jews and Judaism depends on probing its meaning and functions.

Covenant—an agreement between two parties in which at least one of those parties promises under oath to do something (or to refrain from doing something)—is a central term in the Bible. It is one of the fundamental metaphors for Israel's relationship with God (see the chapter by Philip Cunningham in this volume). It establishes the basis of peoplehood. By the initiative of the transcendent God, a people is bound to the Divine and to one another. Jesus recapitulates this divine initiative at the Last Supper, taking the cup and saying, "Drink from it, all of you; for this is my blood of the covenant, which is poured out for many for the forgiveness of sins" (Matt 26:27–28).[1]

Covenant is at heart a call and response. Yet it has many variations, some of which are evident in differing emphases in the covenants with Moses (Exod 19–29) and David (2 Sam 7). Each of the texts on covenant

17

is a complex tapestry, including accounts of early covenants (e.g., with Abraham [Gen 15] and Noah [Gen 9:8–17]).

The classic formulation is the Mosaic covenant: "If you obey my voice and keep my covenant, you shall be my treasured possession out of all the peoples" (Exod 19:5). Yet the call is typically shrouded in mystery, as the imagery in Exodus 19 of the covenant at Sinai evokes. God comes amidst a "dense cloud" (v. 9); Sinai is shrouded in a thick cloud, and there is thunder and lightning (v. 16): "Now Mount Sinai was wrapped in smoke, because the Lord had descended upon it in fire; the smoke went up like the smoke of a kiln, while the whole mountain shook violently" (v. 18). The response was to be one of obedience: the people were to live in a way that would witness to the justice and mercy of the God who had heard their groaning (Exod 2:24). The Ten Commandments (or "Ten Words") frame the response.

Yet the response often fell short. The Hebrew prophets in particular provide vivid accounts of God's loving overtures and the people's rejection. The prophet Isaiah, for example, characterizes Israel as God's beloved vineyard (Isa 5:1) and as God's "dearest" (Isa 44:2).[2] Despite God's tender care, the vineyard yielded only wild grapes (Isa 5:2); God had expected justice, but saw bloodshed; had anticipated righteousness, but heard only the outcry of the oppressed (Isa 5:7). The prophet Isaiah depicts God as "weary" of the shallowness and hypocrisy of sacrifices and worship; the people's hands are "full of blood." Isaiah lays out the covenant obligations starkly:

> Wash yourselves; make yourselves clean;
> remove the evil of your doings from before my eyes;
> cease to do evil,
> learn to do good,
> seek justice;
> rescue the oppressed,
> defend the orphan,
> plead for the widow. (Isa 1:16–17)

Even as the Hebrew prophets indicted their people for failing to live out their responsibilities as a people bound to God and one another, they portrayed the inexhaustible fidelity of God. Jeremiah speaks of the Holy One as renewing the covenant with God's people and making it new. This covenant, he says, will be inscribed on their hearts: "I will put my law within them, and I will write it on their hearts; and I will be their God, and they shall be my people" (Jer 31:33).

Those from whom we have the Dead Sea Scrolls, sometimes referrred to as the "covenanters" of Qumran, saw Jeremiah's promise fulfilled in their community. Luke's version of the Last Supper, in which Jesus speaks of the *new* covenant of his blood (Luke 22:20), seems also to lay claim to the promise in Jeremiah 31. The writer of the Letter to the Hebrews goes further, presenting Jesus as the "mediator of a better covenant, which has been enacted through better promises" (Heb 8:6). Citing Jeremiah 31 (in the Greek translation known as the Septuagint), the author of Hebrews concludes: "In speaking of 'a new covenant,' he has made the first one obsolete. And what is obsolete and growing old will soon disappear" (Heb 8:13).

Is the "Old" Covenant Obsolete?

The texts in Hebrews 8 in particular presage what became a long and bitter controversy: Did the "new" covenant of Jesus cancel all previous covenants? Who belongs in this covenant relationship? Have Christians replaced Jews as a people covenanted with God? Or might we image God as bound in covenant with more than one people—and, if so, what might this mean for the relationship of Christians and Jews?

Questions such as these reveal that the term "covenant" is not easily contained, especially in Christian theology, where it functions as a sort of centripetal force in attracting related understandings: the relation of the "Old" and "New Testaments," the pattern of promise and fulfillment, and the meaning of salvation and of mission. This is evident in our statement "A Sacred Obligation," in which the claim that God's covenant with the Jews endures is foundational to several of our ten statements (particularly numbers 1, 6, and 7). In fact, our statement is indebted to the realms of both theology and church, where there is *new* thinking about the covenant, perspectives that radically affect the entire nexus of issues connected to covenant.

When this new thinking is juxtaposed with the trajectory begun in the Letter to the Hebrews, a dramatic reappraisal is evident. Its significance reveals itself only when we analyze the logic of the church's longstanding assertion that it has come to possess Israel's covenant.

Ours Is the Covenant!

Many of Christianity's early apologists, intent on explaining and defending their neophyte movement, argued that the covenant that had once belonged to the Jews had now been given to Christians. Yet their claims must be situated in the context of a time in which Christianity was a fledgling religion, an illegal and insecure minority in the Roman Empire that needed to justify itself both to the Greco-Roman religious world and to Jews.

To many Greco-Romans, Christians must have seemed a strange lot. They claimed continuity with Israel, even to be the *new* Israel. They retained Israel's scriptures and asserted they had inherited its covenant. Yet, they had abandoned to one degree or another the very practices commanded in those scriptures: circumcision, dietary laws, festivals, and observance of the Sabbath. In the late second century, the philosopher Celsus observed the differences between the teaching of Jesus and that of Moses, and he wondered if God had given "contradictory laws to this man from Nazareth." "Who is wrong?" Celsus asked, "Moses or Jesus?" "Or when the Father sent Jesus had he forgotten what commands he gave to Moses? Or did he condemn his own laws and change his mind, and send his messenger for quite the opposite purposes?" (Celsus, *True Doctrine*, 7:18).

The apologists also had to justify Christianity vis-à-vis Judaism, which was well established and respected and undergoing its own process of transformation as it adapted to the loss of the Temple and Jerusalem. In retrospect, it is clear that Christianity's inextricable connection to Judaism complicated its theological differences: The closeness of the traditions, perhaps best imaged as a sibling relationship, made the disagreements all the more powerful.

For example, over against the more authoritative Jewish tradition, Christians asserted that *their* interpretation of the scriptures was the correct one—even as they used some of the same exegetical techniques. In the course of his "dialogue" (mid-second century) with his Jewish colleague Trypho, Justin Martyr cites many biblical passages that he sees as pointing directly to Christ. He asks, "Are you acquainted with them, Trypho? They are contained in your Scriptures, or rather not yours, but ours. For we believe them; but you, though you read them, do not catch the spirit that is in them" (*Dialogue of Justin, Philosopher and Martyr, with Trypho, a Jew*, ch. 29). Thus, Justin follows the author of Hebrews in claiming:

> For the law promulgated on Horeb is now old, and belongs to yourselves alone; but this is for all universally. Now, law placed against law has abrogated that which is before it, and a covenant which comes after in like manner has put an end to the previous one; and an eternal and final law—namely, Christ—has been given to us, and the covenant is trustworthy, after which there shall be no law, no commandment, no ordinance. (*Dialogue*, ch. 11)

In Justin's thinking, Christians have become "the true spiritual Israel," "led to God through this crucified Christ" (*Dialogue*, ch. 11).

The Letter of Barnabas (early second century) excoriates Jews, holding them responsible for the death of Jesus (*Let. Barn.* 5:11–13; 6:7; 7:5; 8:2; 12:5). It argues against those (presumably Christian) who claim that the covenant is both theirs and ours. Rather, "those people lost it completely [or finally]" by "turning to idols" (*Let. Barn.* 4:6–8). Barnabas's distinctive argument is that because of their sin the Jews were never truly covenanted with God—always it was God's intention that the covenant should belong to Christians alone.

Early church writers such as Justin and Barnabas believed that in Christ a new era had arrived in which Judaism would give way to Christianity. Certain events appeared to reinforce this conviction. The Temple lay in ruins after its destruction by the Romans in 70 C.E., and Jerusalem had become a Roman city, Aelia Capitolina, after 135 C.E. So history seemed to confirm what Christian theology suggested: Judaism had been unfaithful to the covenant, and, consequently, it was punished by the loss of both the Temple and Jerusalem.

Origen (ca. 185–254 C.E.) is explicit: the Jews had committed "the most impious crime of all when they conspired against the Savior" of humankind in the "city where they performed to God the customary rites" that symbolized profound mysteries. "Therefore," he concludes, "that city where Jesus suffered these indignities had to be utterly destroyed. The Jewish nation had to be overthrown, and God's invitation to blessedness transferred to others, I mean the Christians, to whom came the teaching about the simple and pure worship of God" (Origen, *Against Celsus* 4.2.3).

A Lethal Logic

The early Christian apologists established a trajectory of thought that has a long—and tragic—legacy in the church: to Christians belong the blessing and the covenant because of the infidelity of the Jews. And that infidelity is, above all, Jewish responsibility for the crucifixion of Jesus of Nazareth.

Thus, we see a new and lethal logic at work: in killing Jesus Christ, "the Jews" have proven their faithlessness to God. God, consequently, has not only punished them by allowing the destruction of the Temple and the loss of Jerusalem, but given the "invitation to blessedness"—the covenant—to the Christians. The apologists' logic altered the prophetic critique in which infidelity had primarily to do with injustice. Now there was but one injustice: the crucifixion of Jesus. Indeed, we might say that from the time of the apologists until recently the belief that "the Jews" bear responsibility for the death of Jesus was the linchpin in assertions that God had ended the covenant with the Jews.

Because perspectives on the covenant are inextricably linked to interpretations of the death of Jesus, any reconsideration of the context in which those narratives were authored affects our understanding of the covenant relationship of Jews and Christians (see Joseph Tyson's chapter "The Death of Jesus" in this volume). Only in the latter half of the twentieth century did the churches begin to reappraise their teaching about Jewish involvement in the crucifixion. So the lethal logic of the apologists lasted until recently— and still lurks in the thinking of some Christians.

A "Covenant Never Revoked"

Contemporary rethinking of covenant is grounded in large measure in the churches' recognition that the Jewish people, whether past or present, cannot be held accountable for the death of Jesus. The International Council of Christians and Jews, meeting in Seelisberg, Switzerland, in 1947, issued the earliest repudiation of the charge of Jewish guilt in its "Ten Points." Four of the points involve recommendations about interpreting the death of Jesus, including the admonition: "Avoid presenting the Passion in such a way as to bring the odium of the killing of Jesus upon all Jews or upon Jews alone."[3] In the United States, the House of Bishops of the Episcopal Church issued a statement in 1967, "Deicide and the Jews," that states: "The charge of deicide against the Jews is a tragic misunderstanding of the inner significance of the crucifixion."[4]

Similarly, the 1965 decree from the Second Vatican Council, "Nostra Aetate" §4, reads:

> Even though the Jewish authorities and those who followed their lead pressed for the death of Christ, neither all Jews indiscriminately at that time, nor Jews today, can be charged with the crimes committed during his passion. It is true that the church is the new people of God, yet the Jews should not be spoken of as rejected or accursed as if this followed from Holy Scripture. Consequently, all must take care, lest in catechizing or in preaching the word of God, they teach anything which is not in accord with the truth of the Gospel message or the spirit of Christ.[5]

Although a modest document in itself, *Nostra Aetate* inaugurated a wide-ranging reappraisal within Catholicism of Christianity's relationship with Judaism, as Eugene Fisher explains in his chapter in this volume. The growing ecumenical spirit among Christian denominations meant that the council's refutation of deicide affected many Protestant traditions (and, to a lesser extent, Orthodox Christian traditions). Theologians and historians from the various denominations, such as James Parkes, Franklin Littell, Roy Eckardt, and Edward Flannery, deepened awareness of the issues (see Alice Eckardt's chapter in this volume).

That this reassessment of the death of Jesus impinged on thinking about covenant is evident in a speech by Pope John Paul II in 1980, referring to Jews as "the people of God of the Old Covenant, never revoked by God, the present-day people of the covenant concluded with Moses."[6] In 1987, John Paul II made a similar reference to Jews as "partners in a covenant of eternal love which was never revoked."[7] Both references continue to be widely cited, but are given no further explication in papal documents. Yet once such a reversal of thought appears in papal speech—without, of course, any indication that centuries of Christian teaching and preaching had presented the covenant with the Jewish people as cancelled—commentaries and developments follow. "A Sacred Obligation" is one such commentary, jointly authored by Protestants and Catholics.

The negative formulation (covenant "never revoked") invites reflection on the positive meaning: If God is faithful to the covenant with Israel, then what? This question remains open. To assert that the "old covenant" has not been revoked carries little import if there is no theological reason for the existence of Judaism after the coming of Jesus Christ.

A panel of scholars in the Evangelical Lutheran Church in America framed its understanding of the relationship of the covenant in a more positive way, in the second of eight "Talking Points on Jewish-Christian Relations." "Covenants Old and New" points to the importance of the term "covenant" for Christianity. A covenant is far more than a legal contract. Guaranteed by divine faithfulness, "a covenant brings a promise that helps to define the life of God's people":

> From ancient Israel to our own day, Jews have lived in covenant with God as well. This is seen not only in the circumcision of Abraham and his offspring, but also, for example, in the kingship of David, the gift of the Torah at Sinai, and the appearance of the rainbow in the heavens. Israel's prophets were the ones who proclaimed God's faithful intent

to establish a new covenant with the people, a living covenant "written on their hearts" (Jer. 31:33), even embodied in a "new heart" (Ezek. 36:26). *This would not have to supersede the existing covenant understandings, but in continuity with them it would renew and extend Israel's hope and confidence in God's loving commitment.* ("Talking Points on Jewish-Christian Relations," emphasis added)

☞

So we now live in the new covenant established by God in Jesus Christ, joined in continuity to those who have already been made God's people in the covenant of Sinai, and rejoicing with them that God's covenant, new and old, is a gift that is "irrevocable" (Rom. 9:4, 11:29) ("Talking Points on Jewish-Christian Relations," emphasis added).

This "Talking Point" ends with a citation from Paul (Romans 11:1): "I ask then, has God rejected his people? By no means!" Of particular note is the way in which the "new covenant established by God in Jesus Christ" joins Christians "in *continuity* to those who have already been made God's people in the covenant of Sinai" (emphasis added). This continuity becomes a cause for celebration, because God's covenant, whether "new" or "old," is a "gift that is 'irrevocable.'"

Irrevocable Covenants in Continuity

To claim that God's covenant with the Jewish people endures forever is an act of faith in God's fidelity. What kind of a God would betray divine promises? Or, if a people's infidelity causes God to cancel covenants, then do not the many acts of Christian infidelity offer God abundant opportunity to cancel our covenant?

It is imperative that we who are Christian challenge the lethal logic of making Jews of all times responsible for the death of Jesus and thereby concluding that Jewish infidelity caused God to reject them and instead enter into a covenant relationship with Christians.

Yes, both Jews and Christians are unfaithful in many ways to the God who demands justice and righteousness, but God's steadfast love endures forever. God is still calling amidst the mystery of life, still at work in both our communities inscribing divine teaching in our hearts. We must listen—and respond.

Notes

1. Luke 22:20 speaks of the "new" covenant.
2. What translators render as "God's dearest" is in Hebrew *Jeshurun*; it is also found in Deut 32:15 and 33:5, 26.
3. Text in Helga Croner, ed., *More Stepping Stones to Jewish Christian Relations: A Stimulus Book* (New York: Paulist, 1985), 32–33.
4. Text in Helga Croner, ed., *Stepping Stones to Further Jewish-Christian Relations* (London: Stimulus Books, 1977), 87.
5. "Declaration on the Relation of the Church to Non-Christian Religions" ("Nostra Aetate"), in Austin Flannery, ed., *Vatican Council II: The Conciliar and Post-Conciliar Documents,* vol. 1, rev. ed. (Collegeville, MN: Liturgical, 1984), 741.
6. Text in Eugene J. Fisher and Leon Klenicki, eds., *Pope John Paul II: Spiritual Pilgrimage; Texts on Jews and Judaism* (New York: Crossroad, 1995), 13–16.
7. Text in Fisher and Klenicki, *Pope John Paul II* ("Talking Points on Jewish-Christian Relations"), 105-9.

Further Reading

Boys, Mary C. *Has God Only One Blessing? Judaism as a Source of Christian Self-Understanding.* A Stimulus Book. New York: Paulist, 2000.

Lohfink, Norbert. *The Covenant Never Revoked: Biblical Reflections on Christian-Jewish Dialogue.* New York: Paulist, 1991.

Mendenhall, George E., and Gary A. Herion. "Covenant." In David Noel Freedman et al., eds., *The Anchor Bible Dictionary.* Vol 1. New York: Doubleday, 1992, 1179-202.

Sloyan, Gerard. *The Crucifixion of Jesus: History, Myth, Faith.* Minneapolis: Fortress, 1995.

Wilson, Stephen G. *Related Strangers: Jews and Christians, 70–170 C.E.* Minneapolis: Fortress, 1995.

3

CHAPTER

Jesus—A Faithful Jew

Joseph B. Tyson

AN UNDERSTANDING of Jesus is indispensable for those who wish to comprehend the relation of Christianity to Judaism and the Jewish people. Despite the fact that a movement emerged from him that later and gradually separated from Judaism, Jesus himself lived and died as a faithful Jew.

This fact—that a movement emerged from Jesus and later separated from Judaism—has led many believers and scholars to portray Jesus in ways that distinguish him from other Jews of his time and often show him as opposed to Judaism. To support this false portrayal, interpreters usually point to three factors: (1) his teachings opposed Jewish teachings; (2) his teachings opposed Torah; and (2) his death was due to Jewish opposition. In this chapter, I analyze and challenge the first two factors; in the companion chapter that follows, "The Death of Jesus," I take up the third factor. First, however, it is necessary to make a few general comments.

A consideration of Jesus of Nazareth is essentially a historical enterprise. That is, it asks questions about events. Events occur at specific times and places and involve human beings. If it is the case that Jesus lived among other people at a certain time and in a certain geographic location, as Christian creeds confess, it should be possible to make historical statements about him in the same way that we make historical statements about Alexander the Great, John F. Kennedy, or Indira Gandhi. Christian thought frequently distinguishes between the Jesus of history and the Christ of faith. The classic Christian creeds affirm Jesus' humanity and divinity and so encourage both historical study, which is necessarily confined to his humanity, and theological reflection, which considers both his humanity and his divinity. In this chapter we are interested in the Jesus of history.

But the study of the historical Jesus is plagued by many difficulties. Nearly a century ago Albert Schweitzer showed that historical scholars tend to portray Jesus in ways that harmonize with their own contemporary cultures.[1] The temptation has generally been to portray Jesus in our own images and as embodying our ideals. The study of Jesus has been compared with looking down a well that reflects the image of the viewer. We expect to see Jesus, but we see our own reflections. Even if we do not portray Jesus in our own images, we tend to emphasize those characteristics that make him appealing to ourselves and our contemporaries.

In addition, historians do not have extensive source materials on which to draw for a study of Jesus, and the writers of these sources did not share the interests of modern historians. Although the gospels in the New Testament contain genuine information about what Jesus did and said, they emerged from communities of believers, who were usually far more interested in articulating their faith in Jesus as Lord and Christ than in historical matters. The believers remembered some of what Jesus said, but they did so selectively. Sayings that were applicable to the believers were remembered; sometimes they were altered; almost always they were interpreted in ways meaningful to the believing communities. The gospels stand at the end of a long process of oral development, during which the sayings and the accounts of Jesus circulated and changed. As a result the gospel writers had the task of arranging these individual sayings and accounts in some meaningful way, putting them together in order and providing plausible but not necessarily accurate settings. Sometimes they did not agree on the order and the settings. The Gospel of John, for example, locates the narrative about Jesus' disturbance in the Temple early in the life of Jesus, while Matthew, Mark, and Luke place it during the last week of his life (see John 2:13–25; Matt 21:12–17; Mark 11:15–19; Luke 19:45–48). Furthermore, the authors of these gospels could not avoid following their own theological impulses in composing their books. As a result, although the gospels frequently agree on Jesus' teachings and acts, they sometimes disagree at significant points, as we shall see in the examination of Jesus' teachings and in the narratives about his death.

Students of Matthew, Mark, and Luke have noted the great amount of duplication among these gospels, which are generally referred to as the synoptic gospels. The most likely reason for this duplication is that Matthew and Luke independently used the Gospel of Mark as a source and simply adopted most of the material in it. Narratives that appear in all three of these gospels, often with substantially the same words, may confidently be accounted for in this way. For example, the narrative in which Jesus heals a man with a shriveled hand (Mark 3:1–6) also appears in Matthew 12:9–14 and Luke 6:6–11. But Matthew and Luke also have narratives and teachings which were not in Mark, some of them almost identical in their wording. An example is the Lord's Prayer in Matthew 6:9–13 and Luke 11:1–4. It is probable that Matthew and Luke made use of a source in addition to Mark; this source provided them with extensive material. This source is usually called "Q" (an abbreviation for the German word *Quelle*, meaning "source"). Of course both Matthew and Luke each had some narratives and sayings that the other gospel writers did not have, and they integrated these materials with what they drew from Mark and Q. There are other plausible explanations of the relationship among these gospels, but the two-document hypothesis, which is sketched here, is the theory that is used by most scholars today. In this theory, Mark is the earliest of the New Testament gospels, and Mark and Q are the major sources for Matthew and Luke.

Problems of history and sources require us to have sound methods to study the historical Jesus. Although there is currently a great deal of debate about methodology, a few basic principles have emerged. Space does not allow a discussion of the criteria used by modern scholars, and readers should refer to John P. Meier's excellent treatment of this important topic.[2] The important point is that we must be cautious in our use of ancient texts and careful to maintain strict historical criteria for our study.

We should note, however, that scholars who carefully use historical criteria do not all come to the same conclusions about the historical Jesus. Some regard Jesus as mainly a social reformer, providing by his life and teachings the foundations for an ethical society. Others see him as one who proclaimed a new age, initiated by divine action but resulting in a reformed human society. This debate will undoubtedly continue, because our sources allow for diverse interpretations. Since I lean toward the understanding of Jesus as proclaiming a new age, I intend here to follow that line of interpretation. The list of further resources following my chapter includes scholarly books on many sides of this issue.

Jesus' Proclamation of the Kingdom of God

The new age that Jesus proclaimed is referred to in our gospels as the "kingdom of God," or the "imperial rule of God." The Gospel of Matthew sometimes speaks of it as the "kingdom of heaven," apparently making use of a Jewish substitution for the divine name. Whatever the term, Jesus' proclamation would have been clear and meaningful to a Jewish audience at his time. It evokes expectations that we identify with Jewish apocalypticism, a form of thought and writing that focuses attention on events approaching the end of time, when God will vanquish evil. This form of thought is expressed in Jewish texts, some written before and some after the time of Jesus. It often included an expectation that God would bring in the kingdom through a Messiah. Of course, not all Jews accepted apocalypticism or expected a Messiah, and many regarded it as unimportant, but it would at least have been understood by most Jews of Jesus' time.

Apocalypticism frequently made its appearance at a time when the Jewish people were being oppressed by outside forces, and it spoke to the victims of oppression by providing assurance that God would bring this bad time to an end and create new possibilities for human existence. The Revelation of John in the New Testament is a familiar apocalyptic writing that fits almost exactly the literary form of earlier Jewish apocalypses.[3] The gospels also include similar apocalyptic images (see, for example, Mark 13). For the most part, Jesus in the gospels does not talk in terms of the fantastic images we find in Revelation, but he speaks frequently of the kingdom of God as coming in the future. Again, not all first-century Jews accepted apocalypticism, but most of them would have understood the basic meaning of Jesus' proclamation of the kingdom of God.

The Gospel of Mark actually summarizes the teaching of Jesus as the proclamation of the kingdom of God: "Now after John was arrested, Jesus came to Galilee, proclaiming the good news of God, and saying, 'The time is fulfilled, and the kingdom of God has come near; repent, and believe in the good news'" (Mark 1:14–15; see also Matt 4:17). There are good reasons to think that Mark's summary is a faithful representation of the heart of Jesus' message. Not only is it found here in the earliest gospel, but it is found in other layers of the gospel tradition and is represented in sayings and parables throughout the gospels.

It is probable that Jesus expected a dramatic intervention of God to come without warning and in the very near future. It is within this context that issues about Torah observance should be considered. Mark's summary statement (Mark 1:14–15) says that Jesus' proclamation of the kingdom was followed by a demand for repentance. The demand is part of the fabric of the synoptic presentation of Jesus' teachings. It is intimately related to the proclamation of the kingdom, because if the kingdom means judgment, the appropriate response is to repent. People are called upon to prepare themselves for the coming judgment by repenting and thereby reforming their lives. But they do not hasten the coming of the kingdom by repenting or delay it by refusing to repent. The kingdom simply comes, just as a seed planted in the ground grows into a plant (Mark 4:26–29). Jesus announces the coming of the kingdom as a fact, and he demands repentance as the appropriate response to this impending fact.

The repentance demanded by the impending kingdom involves a radical decision. The coming of the kingdom means the end of all usual values, so people must decide between the values of the present and those of the future. They must not store up earthly treasures or try to hold on to wealth (Matt 6:19–21). A camel can go through a needle's eye with greater ease than a rich person can get into the kingdom (Matt 19:24; Mark 10:25; Luke 18:25). On any scale of values, however, the kingdom is worth the sacrifice. A prudent merchant who deals in fine pearls and finds one of very special value sells everything in order to purchase it (Matt 13:45–46). Someone who finds a treasure in a field sacrifices everything in order to purchase the field (Matt 13:44). Repentance means rejecting those things associated with life as usual and changing everything that might hinder a full acceptance of the kingdom. It may even be necessary for some to cut off a hand or a foot or pluck out an eye (Mark 9:43, 45, 47; Matt 18:8–9). The possibly hyperbolic character of this last saying strengthens the sense that the kingdom is worth any sacrifice.

Jesus and Torah

It is within the context of Jesus' announcement of the kingdom of God that we can best examine his teachings about Torah. Repentance means not only turning away from something but also turning toward something, namely toward obedience to the demand of God. But what does God demand? It is clear that for Jesus and his Jewish contemporaries God's requirements were to be found in Torah. Although many readers of the New Testament understand that the Hebrew word *torah* means "law," its basic meaning is "teaching" or "direction." When applied to God's teaching, as it is in first-century Judaism, it effectively signifies divine revelation, initially recorded in the first five books of the Hebrew Bible. So Torah is the revealed teaching of God that includes ethical and cultic requirements.

Despite the fact that Jews in the time of Jesus were in basic agreement that Torah was God's revealed teaching, there was wide diversity in the interpretation of its meaning in specific cases. A later chapter in this volume will examine this diversity and explore the range of interpretive options that circulated among Jews at the time of Jesus. The main point to note is that at the time of Jesus there was no such thing as a rigid Jewish orthodoxy. So the question is not that of determining whether Jesus' teachings were characteristically Jewish, but rather of asking how these teachings might have been perceived within a wide range of familiar Jewish perspectives.

At this point we meet a significant difficulty, because the gospels in the New Testament do not agree in regard to Jesus' teachings about Torah. Contrast, for example, the two passages in table 3.1. The passage in the left column from Mark shows us a Jesus who would reject some of the laws of purity and the dietary laws. The second, from Matthew, claims that Jesus was very conservative on issues of Torah observance.

Jesus could hardly have abolished the dietary laws, as Mark says he does, and at the same time have claimed not to do so, as Matthew says he does. The two sayings represent the extreme possibilities for interpreting the teachings of Jesus. They probably also represent the convictions of two communities of Christians, one group holding firmly to Torah obedience, as in Matthew, and the other rejecting some aspects of it, as in Mark. Note that the sentence "Thus he declared all foods clean" (Mark 7:19) is grammatically a statement made by the gospel's narrator and thus not the word of Jesus. It is probable that the authentic position of Jesus vis-à-vis Torah is not to be found in either of these extreme statements but rather in the many controversy stories, dialogues, and parables in which Jesus' position is more carefully nuanced.

Narratives in which Jesus debates with other Jews, especially Pharisees, remind us of the diversity of interpretation in first-century Judaism. These controversy stories are probably typical of dialogues that occurred among various groups of Jews at the time, and we may see examples of similar debates in the Mishnah, a second-century Jewish text (see the chapter by Peter Pettit

Table 3.1

Mark 7:18–19	Matt 5:17–19
He said to them, "Then do you also fail to understand? Do you not see that whatever goes into a person from outside cannot defile, since it enters, not the heart but the stomach, and goes out into the sewer?" (Thus he declared all foods clean.)	"Do not think that I have come to abolish the law or the prophets; I have come not to abolish but to fulfill. For truly I tell you, until heaven and earth pass away, not one letter, not one stroke of a letter, will pass from the law until all is accomplished. Therefore, whoever breaks one of the least of these commandments, and teaches others to do the same, will be called least in the kingdom of heaven; but whoever does them and teaches them will be called great in the kingdom of heaven."

and John Townsend in this volume). Jesus' interpretations in these controversy stories do not imply that he was un-Jewish—quite the contrary.

The gospels contain a number of incidents that tell of controversies about Sabbath observance. In them Jesus consistently makes the point that regulations about the observance of Sabbath are secondary to considerations of human need (see, for example, Matt 12:1–8; Mark 2:23–28; Luke 6:1–5; Matt 12:9–14; Mark 3:1–6; Luke 6:6–11). Jesus also distinguishes between more and less important commandments in Torah. He severely attacks Pharisees for "straining out a gnat and swallowing a camel" (Matt 23:24; Luke 11:42). Quoting from Deuteronomy 6:4–5 and Leviticus 19:18 (the *Shema*, so called because the Hebrew text begins with this imperative, meaning "listen" or "hear"), Jesus declares the greatest commandments to be the love of God and the love of one's neighbor (Mark 12:28–31 and parallels). His Golden Rule (Matt 7:12; Luke 6:31) is intended as a summary of Torah, a summary also found as a teaching of the Jewish sage Hillel, who lived in the generation before Jesus.[4]

Jesus also intensified the observance of some commandments by adding to them. The dialogue between Jesus and the rich ruler (Matt 19:16–22; Mark 10:17–22; Luke 18:18–23) contains some major themes to be emphasized when thinking about Jesus and Torah. The ruler first asks Jesus about

4

CHAPTER

The Death of Jesus

Joseph B. Tyson

IN THE HISTORY of Christian-Jewish relations nothing has
been more contentious than the death of Jesus. Shortly after the
surrender of Jewish forces to Rome and the destruction of the
Temple and Jerusalem in 70 C.E., Christians explained that these losses were
God's punishment of Jews for their failure to accept Jesus as Messiah and
for their role in putting him to death. The Gospel of Matthew, written after
70 C.E., depicts this blame of Jews for the death of Jesus in this well-known
passage: "Then the people as a whole answered, 'His blood be on us and on
our children!'" (Matt 27:25). This verse is the infamous "blood curse" that
has echoed down through the centuries of Christian-Jewish relations. This
and other portrayals in the New Testament were used in medieval Europe
to justify pogroms, riots, and acts of violence and oppression against Jews.
Roots of the Nazi persecution of Jews in 1933–1945, referred to by the
Hebrew term "Shoah," can be found in Christian teachings about Jews and
the death of Jesus. Irving Greenberg reports that in 1942 a Slovakian rabbi
called upon the local archbishop and pleaded for Catholic help in resisting
the Nazi policy of deporting his town's Jews:

Since the rebbe did not yet know of the gas chambers, he stressed the dangers of hunger and disease, especially for women, old people, and children. The archbishop replied: "It is not just a matter of deportation. You will not die there of hunger and disease. They will slaughter all of you there, old and young alike, women and children, at once—it is the punishment that you deserve for the death of our Lord and Redeemer, Jesus Christ—you have only one solution. Come over to our religion and I will work to annul this decree."[1]

As it turned out, not even conversion to Christianity was sufficient to save the Jewish victims. It is appalling that an archbishop of the church was able to explain the unimaginable horror of the Shoah as the punishment twentieth-century Jews deserved for the death of Jesus in the first century. Fortunately, after the end of World War II the Roman Catholic Church and most Protestant churches strongly disavowed such sentiments, as the chapters in this volume by Franklin Sherman and Eugene Fisher document.

The death of Jesus is such a volatile issue that it deserves a serious examination in terms both of the gospel presentations and of the history to which they point. In what follows, I presume familiarity with the accounts in the gospels and emphasize the major themes to be found in these narratives. There are many places in these narratives where the gospels disagree with one another, but they are in basic agreement that the death of Jesus was the result of a judicial verdict and that he died by means of crucifixion. Three major themes or tendencies govern the way they tell the story.

One tendency in all of the gospels is that of placing major responsibility for Jesus' execution on the Jews rather than on the Romans. In Mark and Matthew, the Jewish council conducts the initial trial at night, convicts Jesus of blasphemy, and acts as prosecutor before Pilate, the Roman governor.[2] In all of the canonical gospels, when Pilate offers to release Jesus, the crowd calls instead for the release of Barabbas, a convicted prisoner (Matt 27:15–26; Mark 15:6–15; Luke 23:18–25; John 18:39–40).[3] In Matthew, Pilate washes his hands as a symbolic act, declaring that he has no responsibility in the proceedings. He says, "I am innocent of this man's blood; see to it yourselves" (Matt 27:24). By contrast, the Jewish people in attendance accept responsibility not only for themselves but for their descendants (Matt 27:25). The Gospel of John goes to great lengths to show the guilt of the Jews. Pilate repeatedly declares Jesus' innocence and attempts to release him (John 18:38; 19:4, 6). The Jews, however, insist that their law requires Jesus' execution, and they threaten to charge Pilate with insubordination if he refuses to crucify Jesus (John 19:12).

A second tendency in the gospels is to stress the injustice of Jesus' opponents in prosecuting an innocent man. Mark calls attention to disagreement among the witnesses against Jesus and expressly declares their testimony false (Mark 14:57–59). Matthew describes Judas' suicide as an act of remorse at the realization that he had betrayed an innocent man (Matt 17:3–5). In the midst of the Roman trial in Matthew, Pilate's wife warns him to have nothing to do with this innocent man (Matt 27:19). In Luke, Pilate and Herod both declare Jesus to be innocent, and in John, Pilate makes repeated declarations to this effect (see Luke 23:4, 14, 15, 22; John 18:38; 19:4, 6). Luke lists specific charges of which Jesus is accused and shows Jesus to be innocent. For example, in Luke 23:2 Jesus is accused of opposing payment of Roman taxes. In Luke 20:25, however, when questioned about taxes, Jesus says, "Then render to Caesar the things that are Caesar's, and to God the things that are God's" (see Matt 22:21; Mark 12:17). Luke also says that Jesus was accused of claiming to be Christ, a messianic king, although in Luke's gospel Jesus never makes any such claims; rather he speaks of the coming of God's kingdom.

A third tendency that is discernible in the gospels is to call attention to scriptural predictions about Jesus' suffering and death. The theme of prophetic and scriptural fulfillment is notable throughout Matthew and plays a role in the report of the trial in that gospel. Matthew expressly calls attention to prophetic fulfillment in connection with Jesus' arrest (Matt 26:54, 56) and in the story of the purchase of the potter's field (Matt 27:9–10). Peter's denial (Matt 26:69–75) is a fulfillment of Jesus' own prediction (Matt 26:34). Luke includes few explicit references from the Hebrew Bible in the trial narratives, but in chapter 24 the risen Jesus interprets the scriptures to his disciples so that they are able to understand the divine necessity of his suffering and death (see Luke 24:26–27, 45–46). Moreover, scriptural passages probably influenced the narratives in subtle ways. For example, the silence of Jesus before some of Pilate's questions may have been inferred from reading a scripture such as Isaiah 53:7, where the suffering servant is pictured as silent in the face of oppression (see Matt 27:12, 14; Mark 15:4, 5; John 19:9). The hearing before Herod in Luke 23:6–12 (only in Luke) may have been influenced by Psalm 2:2, "The kings of the earth set themselves, and the rulers take counsel together, against the Lord and his anointed." In Acts 4:25–28, Luke himself calls attention to this scripture and its connection with Jesus' trial.

Despite the many differences among the gospels in their handling of the details, their passion narratives are shaped by these three major themes. The use of these themes has created a number of difficulties in understanding the history that may lie behind our texts. In Matthew and Mark, for example, the Jewish council convicts Jesus of blasphemy but makes no effort to carry out the usual penalty for blasphemy, namely, stoning (see Lev 24:10–16). Instead, they take Jesus to the Roman governor and charge him with the Roman crime of royal pretension, the usual penalty for which is crucifixion. In John the Jews demand Jesus' execution first on the basis of Jewish law, then later on the basis of Roman law. The fact of a Passover amnesty—as in Matthew, Mark, and John—cannot be verified in contemporary non-Christian records and is brought into the narratives in a peculiar way. Although Pilate tries to use it as a device for securing Jesus' release, he presents as an alternative a person who is already convicted of sedition, that is, a person on an entirely different legal footing. Add to this the picture of the Roman governor acting totally under pressure from subject peoples. He is presented as convinced of Jesus' innocence and anxious for his release, as holding the power of life and death in his hands, but as succumbing to the insistence of the people he governed, even though they offered no evidence for their charges.

When we recognize that the gospel writers left no signs that supporters of Jesus were present to serve as eyewitnesses of these trials, we are forced to conclude that the narratives are governed almost entirely by the three themes that were dealt with above. The tendency of the gospel writers to place major responsibility for Jesus' death on the Jews has probably created most of the difficulties in the narratives about the trial.

One of the synoptic gospels, the Gospel of Luke, deserves special consideration in connection with Jesus' trial. Although the third gospel shares with the others (and the Gospel of John as well) the three themes discussed above, there are some unique elements in it. The framework of Luke's narrative (22:47–23:25) is comparable to those in Matthew and Mark, but there are significant differences. Luke has no night meeting of the Jewish council but one the morning following Jesus' arrest. The council does not examine witnesses or hear evidence but questions Jesus directly. He is asked if he is the Messiah and Son of God, and he gives evasive answers to both questions. Afterward the council takes Jesus to Pilate and brings three charges against him: perverting the nation, opposing the payment of Roman taxes, and claiming to be a king (Luke 23:2). The Roman governor is initially reluctant to hear the case, and, when he finds that Jesus is a Galilean, he sends him to be examined by Herod Antipas, tetrarch of Galilee (Luke 23:6–12). This examination seems inconclusive, and Jesus is returned to Pilate, who reaffirms his verdict of innocence. Then Luke tells of the crowd's demand for the release of Barabbas and for the crucifixion of Jesus and of Pilate's capitulation to their demand.

Clearly, Luke's account has been overlaid with themes he shares with the other gospel writers, but it appears to rest on materials that give the narrative a somewhat different spin. We should note two things in particular. (1) In Luke the status of the Jewish council is clearly subordinate to that of the Roman governor. The Jewish body looks initially into charges against Jesus but conducts no trial. (2) In Luke the charges against Jesus are political in nature. The charges are that he perverted the nation (that is, he attempted to turn it away from the alignment that Rome thought proper), that he spoke against Roman taxation, and that he claimed to be a king. Although Luke was convinced that Jesus was innocent of all three charges, he nevertheless reported them. Luke's presentation is not without historical difficulties, but it creates fewer such problems than the other gospels do.

The actual facts surrounding the death of Jesus are so thickly clouded over by tradition and by gospel accounts that we cannot expect easily to sort them out. Nevertheless, it is helpful to keep in mind certain fundamental points:

1. Rome held supreme political power in the land of the Jews. From the year 6 C.E., this power was exercised in Judea by governors directly appointed by the Roman emperor. Although they left some matters to native courts, the Roman governors had ultimate judicial authority in their realms. They had the right of capital punishment over all persons under their jurisdictions, even over Roman citizens. They had complete financial and legislative control in their areas.

2. The Roman governor at the time of Jesus, Pontius Pilate, is described by the first-century Jewish historian Josephus as especially insensitive to Jewish concerns. Josephus tells of one occasion when Pilate ordered his soldiers to display the emperor's image in Jerusalem, thereby violating the biblical command to avoid images and deliberately offending his Jewish subjects (Josephus, *The Jewish War*, 2:169–74; *Antiquities of the Jews*, 18:55–59). He also diverted certain Temple funds to the building of an aqueduct (Josephus, *Jewish War*, 2:175–77; *Antiquities*, 18:60-62). Another first-century Jewish writer, Philo, says that Pilate was recklessly arbitrary and that his administration was marked by "the briberies, the insults, the robberies, the outrages and wanton injuries, the executions without trial con-

stantly repeated, the ceaseless and supremely grievous cruelty" (Philo, *On the Embassy to Gaius*, 302).[4]

3. We know that crucifixion was customarily used by Romans as a penalty for crimes against the state. It was the typical method used by them for executing slaves, rebellious foreigners, hardened criminals, and political prisoners. Punishment by crucifixion resulted in an ignominious death, and Roman governors used it as an effective deterrent against any challenges to their authority. It was carried out in public, and frequently large numbers of people were crucified at the same time. Although it had been used as a form of Jewish execution almost two centuries before the time of Jesus, it seems to have ceased as a Jewish practice before the time of Herod the Great (37–34 B.C.E.). In Jesus' time, the typical Jewish method of execution was stoning; the typical Roman method was crucifixion.

4. Early Christian literature, including the letters of Paul and the gospels, is unanimous in asserting that Jesus was crucified.[5] This is probably the most certain historical fact relating to Jesus: he died by crucifixion.

5. Although the gospels are not unanimous in dealing with the charges against Jesus before the Roman judge, they imply that he was accused of political crimes, including royal pretension. This charge appears implicitly in all the gospels and explicitly in Luke and John. All four gospels tell of a placard placed on the cross that identified Jesus as "King of the Jews" (see Matt 27:37; Mark 15:26; Luke 23:38; John 19:19). This placard means to identify the one being crucified and to announce his crime, royal pretension, to all observers. The gospels also imply that the basis for this charge was the association of Messiahship with royal power. The connection is probably to be seen in Jesus' authoritative proclamation of the kingdom of God. "Kingdom" is a political term, and a proclamation such as that made by Jesus would, in some quarters, seem politically dangerous. Only a few decades after the time of Jesus, Jewish Zealots were proclaiming the kingdom of God, and there was no uncertainty about the political dimensions of their preaching. Roman governors frequently dealt with suspected Jewish revolutionists, and they dealt with them harshly. So Jesus was probably regarded by Pilate as a revolutionary because of his preaching of the kingdom of God.

6. We know that, from time to time, Roman governors made use of existing groups in their provinces to assist them in keeping order. In some cases, they probably used native courts to conduct preliminary investigations of suspected criminals. The Jewish council, led by the high priest, who served under the direction of the Roman governor, would have been one of those assisting groups.

7. Although the gospels frequently depict Jesus in controversy with Pharisees, this group of Jews is notably absent in the trial narratives. The unanimity of the gospel writers is notable at this point. The coalition of Jewish leaders who are allied against Jesus in the passion narratives is described in various ways in the gospels, but it always includes the high priest and the chief priests, and never any Pharisees (see Matt 26:57; 27:1; Mark 14:53; Luke 22:52, 66; John 18:14).

If we put all these items together, we come to a conclusion with a high degree of probability: Jesus was put to death under the authority of the Roman governor, Pontius Pilate, for an alleged violation of Roman law. It is probable that the charge against him was political in nature, similar to the specific charges listed in Luke 23:2 and reflected in the placard on the cross. What we know about Pilate would lead us to believe that he would not have been careful to investigate thoroughly the charges against Jesus and certainly not reluctant to impose the appropriate penalty. Remember Philo's words: Under Pilate there were "executions without trial constantly repeated." Jesus' would have been one of those executions. It is also likely that some Jewish priestly leaders assisted the Romans in the apprehension and investigation of Jesus, in something like the proceedings described in Luke 22:66–71.

The gospels in the New Testament were written several decades after the events they narrate. Their authors look back on the horrifying events of 70 C.E., when the Jewish rebellion was suppressed by Roman troops, the city of Jerusalem was invaded, and the sacred Jewish Temple was destroyed by fire. Those Jews and Gentiles who accepted Jesus as God's special revelation began to interpret these disasters as God's punishment on those Jews who did not accept Jesus. These attitudes colored and shaped the gospel narratives in more profound ways than did the simpler historically rooted story of the death of Jesus. For these reasons, the narratives in our gospels tend to blame the Jews for the death of Jesus. The result in Matthew and Mark is an unlikely set of narratives in which Jesus is tried twice, once for the religious crime of blasphemy and once for a political crime. Here as much blame is placed on Jewish leaders as is possible: even in the Roman trial, the Jewish leaders are the prosecutors, and the Roman governor, who had the power of life and death over all his subjects, simply crumbles under their pressure.

But the gospel records do not totally obscure the probable history. Even though they are shaped and partially obscured by the themes discussed above, some probable events are discernible: Jesus was crucified; he was accused of violating Roman law; he was put to death on orders of the Roman governor, Pontius Pilate. The role of Jews in the death of Jesus was minimal and limited to a few leading priests acting on behalf of the Romans. Thus, it is historically inaccurate to claim that Jews were responsible for Jesus' death.

By way of summary, historical study of Jesus shows that the following statements are highly probable: (1) Jesus' teachings about the kingdom of God were characteristic of other forms of Judaism at his time; (2) Jesus' teachings about Torah included his own interpretations, but they acknowledged the place of Torah as God's revealed will; (3) Jesus' death was not brought about by Jewish opposition but rather by Roman political oppression.

Notes

1. Irving Greenberg, "Cloud of Smoke, Pillar of Fire: Judaism, Christianity, and Modernity after the Holocaust," in Eva Fleishner, ed., *Auschwitz: Beginning of a New Era? Reflections on the Holocaust* (New York: KTAV, 1977), 11–12.

2. In Matthew and Mark, the charge of blasphemy appears to depend on the answer Jesus gave to the question of the high priest, asking if Jesus is Messiah (Matt 26:63; Mark 14:61). The Mishnah (Sanhedrin 7:5) defines "blasphemy" as pronouncing the divine name, a violation of Exodus 20:7. There is, however, evidence that the term was used more broadly, to include any speech that would insult the majesty of God. In any event, Leviticus 24:10–16 requires stoning as the punishment for blasphemy, and it is evident that Jesus was not stoned to death.

3. Although Luke does not refer to it, the other gospel writers say that Pilate made this offer in connection with a customary Passover amnesty (see Matt 27:15; Mark 15:6; John 18:39).

4. *Philo* X, translated by F. H. Colson and G. H. Whitaker (Cambridge: Harvard University Press, 1981).

5. Paul frequently refers to Christ as crucified (see, e.g., 1 Cor 1:13, 23; 2:2, 8; 13:4). 1 Corinthians 2:8 refers to the "rulers of this age," arguably Romans, who crucified "the Lord of glory." In 1 Thessalonians 2:14–16, Judean Jews are blamed for the death of Jesus, but these verses are probably a post-Pauline interpolation into this letter.

Further Reading

See suggestions listed under the previous chapter, "Jesus—A Faithful Jew."

IV

P A R T

Ancient Rivalries Must Not Define Christian-Jewish Relations Today

5

CHAPTER

Ancient Rivalries and New Testament Interpretation: An Example from the Acts of the Apostles

Celia Deutsch

"A SACRED OBLIGATION" speaks of rivalries that influenced the writing of the gospels. The gospels recount disputes between Jesus and various opponents. Other texts echo or even describe later debates between followers of Jesus and others, whether Jewish or Gentile. Sometimes those later disputes are read into the life of Jesus himself and influence the gospel narrative. For example, the bitterness of Jesus' pronouncement of woes against the scribes and Pharisees in Matthew 23 reflects the rivalry between Matthew and other Jewish teachers at the end of the first century even more than it does the controversies between Jesus and the Pharisees during his lifetime.[1] And John's references to Jesus' followers being expelled from the synagogue reflect the experience of John's community at the end of the first century or the beginning of the second rather than events during the first generation (see 9:22; 12:42; 16:2).

A literalist reading of the text—what Philip Cunningham describes in his chapter in this volume as disinterest in the circumstances in which a biblical book was written, the perspectives prevalent at the time, or the text's literary styles and purposes—thus contains the risk of actually misinterpreting it. As a consequence, too often ancient stereotypes are perpetuated. For example, scribes and Pharisees are construed as legalistic, lacking in concern for the deeper meaning of God's word or for the people whom they teach. John's gospel is misunderstood as reflecting a uniform policy of expulsion of Jesus' followers from the synagogue during Jesus' lifetime and shortly afterward.

In contrast, readings that distinguish the layers of the controversies reflected in these materials yield new riches and challenge stereotypical interpretations, lest we continue them in our time. I will show this by using Acts 10:34–43 as a case study in understanding ancient rivalries.

The Acts of the Apostles, attributed to the evangelist Luke, plays a central role in contemporary Christian understandings of the death of Jesus. In recent years scholars, clergy, and educators have given close attention to the interpretation of the Lenten and Holy Week readings and the ways in which the interpretation of those texts might reinforce age-old stereotypes of Jews and Judaism. However, too little attention has been paid to the readings of the Easter season in which Acts features so prominently. The attribution of Jewish responsibility for Jesus' death so often repeated in Acts makes the correct understanding of this book as important as that of the passion narratives.

Acts 10:34, 37–43 is the first reading of Easter morning. Denominations using the lectionary hear this proclaimed:

> Then Peter began to speak to them. . . . That message spread throughout Judea, beginning in Galilee after the baptism that John announced: how God anointed Jesus of Nazareth with the Holy Spirit and with power; how he went about doing good and healing all who were oppressed by the devil, for God was with him. We are witnesses to all that he did both in Judea and in Jerusalem. They put him to death by hanging him on a tree; but God raised him on the third day and allowed him to appear, not to all the people but to us who were chosen by God as witnesses, and who ate and drank with him after he rose

from the dead. He commanded us to preach to the people and to testify that he is the one ordained by God as judge of the living and the
dead. All the prophets testify about him that everyone who believes in
him receives forgiveness of sins through his name.

The passage is a terse summary of preaching in Acts by Peter, Stephen,
and Paul. Their preaching depicts the innocent Jesus as murdered by parties explicitly or implicitly Jewish, whether "inhabitants of Jerusalem" or
leaders. Their preaching does not end with the death of Jesus, but proclaims
his resurrection from the dead and the commissioning of the apostles to
preach and bear witness. The Easter lection, as in some but not all instances,
associates Jesus' death and resurrection with forgiveness of sins and fulfillment of prophecy. It assigns responsibility for Jesus' death solely to Jews;
there is no mention of the Romans. Reference to the prophets emphasizes
the guilt of those who should have recognized Jesus: the Jews. They should
have known, Luke implies. Mention of the prophets also raises a question
about who interprets correctly the ancient scriptures; it implies that the Jews
responsible for Jesus' death failed to understand prophecy. For Luke, accurate interpretation is related to belief in Jesus and thus belongs to those who
follow the "Way."[2]

Certainly such summaries, read on Easter and throughout the Easter
season until Pentecost, tend to reinforce in the very act of proclamation the
same stereotypes as the Lenten and Holy Week readings. However, examining this lection from Acts 10 in its literary and historical contexts allows
readers to understand more deeply what was at stake for Luke and his community in retelling the story of the first generation of believers: forming
their identity vis-à-vis the venerable tradition of Judaism and the power of
imperial Rome.

Peter, Cornelius, and Boundaries

Acts 10:34–43, the passage from which the first reading of Easter morning
is drawn, occurs at the end of a story that is programmatic in Luke's work
of showing the development of the Gentile mission and demonstrating how
the gospel spread from Jerusalem to Rome.[3] The narrative suggests tensions in Luke's community about how to include Gentile members in the
Way and how much Jewish ritual law they should be expected to observe.
The story reflects rivalry between the followers of Jesus, both Jews and
Gentiles, and those Jews who do not accept Jesus as Messiah. At stake is

the very identity of the new movement, caught up in what sociologists today call "identity construction."

A significant clue to the formation of identity in Luke's community occurs in the exchange between Peter and Cornelius in the verses of chapter 10 prior to the Easter lection. The chapter opens in Caesarea, the headquarters of the Roman procurators. Cornelius, a centurion, is a "devout man who feared God," who helps to support "the people" (i.e., the local Jewish community) and prays constantly "to God." In other words, he is a Roman soldier, a noncommissioned officer in the occupying army, who worships Israel's God and has established a positive relationship with the local Jewish community. He, a Gentile sympathetic to the Jewish community, has a vision in which an angel instructs him to send men to fetch Simon Peter from Joppa.

Meanwhile, Peter is at prayer at Joppa. He falls into a trance and has a vision in which the heavens open and something like a sheet descends, bearing "all kinds of four-footed creatures and reptiles and birds of the air" (10:12). A heavenly voice instructs Peter, "Kill and eat." He protests that he has never eaten anything ritually impure. The voice addresses him a second time, "What God has made clean, you must not call profane" (10:15). Peter is perplexed by the vision, but Cornelius' men have arrived and ask for him. When they have delivered their message, Peter, a Jew concerned about ritual purity and food laws, invites the messengers into the house as his guests (10:17–23).

We thus see boundaries being crossed. Former lines of distinction no longer hold. A Roman Gentile has a vision, sees an angel, and receives heavenly instruction. Peter, a Jew, receives a vision in which he is told that God considers nothing unclean. Peter the Jew receives the pagan centurion's envoys as his guests and, it is implied, his equals. Thresholds are being crossed, both literally and metaphorically.

The following day, Peter goes to Caesarea, accompanied by Cornelius' men as well as some of the "believers," a group that includes "circumcised believers" (10:45).[4] Peter, received by Cornelius, points out the anomaly of a Jew associating with a Gentile, "but God has shown me that I should not call anyone profane or unclean" (10:28).[5] Luke thus reveals the deeper significance of the Joppa vision: just as all food is "clean," so too all people are "clean." All are to be included in the new Way, Jew and Gentile alike.

Cornelius summarizes his vision and subsequent request that Peter come to his home in Caesarea. Peter then delivers the speech in 10:34–43, much of which is read on Easter Sunday morning. In the full text Peter begins with the words—omitted in the lectionary—"I truly understand that

God shows no partiality." Even as he speaks, the Holy Spirit falls on those listening, both Jews and Gentiles (v. 44), thus demonstrating God's inclusion of unbaptized Gentiles. Luke emphasizes this by noting the amazement on the part of Jewish believers "because the gift of the Holy Spirit had been poured out even on the Gentiles" (v. 45). Gentiles speaking in tongues and praising God convince Jewish believers of the authenticity of the outpouring of the Spirit (v. 46). The scene concludes with the baptism of the members of Cornelius' household.

The initial transgression of boundaries is enacted by individuals. But that initial transgression of boundaries represents more than the actions of two individuals, however important. The vision about clean and unclean food represents the issue of inclusion. "Clean" and "unclean" signify not only food but also the inclusion of the Gentiles—"God shows no partiality" (10:34b). This is exemplified in the conversion of Cornelius and his household.

The outpouring of the Holy Spirit on "all who heard the word" (10:44) includes the unbaptized members of Cornelius' household as well as Jewish believers. It precedes the baptism of Cornelius and his household. The boundaries breached by Cornelius and Peter open wide to include the communities under their leadership, the household of Cornelius and the Jewish believers. Jews and Gentiles who previously did not associate are brought into a new way of being together, united by the word, the outpouring of the Spirit, and baptism.

The Matter of Context

The meeting between Cornelius and Peter provides a crucial context for Acts 10:34–43. Luke depicts Cornelius the Roman convert in dramatic contrast to the Jews responsible for Jesus' death. The latter have not understood their own prophets. In Luke's narrative, however, Cornelius is not the first Gentile to be brought into the new community. There is the Samaritan mission in 8:4–8. In that same chapter, Philip baptizes an Ethiopian—we are not told whether he is Jewish or Gentile—who has come to Jerusalem to worship (8:26–40). But the story of Cornelius presents the first outpouring of the Spirit on Gentiles. With the conversion of Cornelius we see explicit communal implications. An entire *Roman* household is brought into the membership of the believers. People previously represented as forbidden to associate with one another now are shown together in table fellowship, drawn by the hearing of the word, by the outpouring of the Spirit, by baptism, and by the gift of repentance.

The inclusion of Gentiles as well as Jews in the one community of believers is at the heart of Luke's narrative in Acts. The Cornelius-Peter incident and its sequel in the debate in Jerusalem (Acts 15:1–29) address fundamental issues of identity. To the question of what makes a disparate community one they answer: the Word, outpouring of the Spirit, baptism, and repentance. To the question of how Jews and Gentiles associate, they answer that table fellowship is permitted because what God has made clean cannot be deemed unclean. The story of Cornelius that establishes the context for that first reading of Easter morning represents a turning point.

The ramifications of this movement in the narrative will play out over the course of Acts. Paul will be sent to the Gentiles, though preaching in synagogues. Jewish believers will come into conflict over the question of the necessity of circumcision of (male) converts (15:1). A meeting of apostles and elders will settle the question with the decision that Gentile converts are required only to "abstain only from things polluted by idols and from fornication and from what is strangled and from blood" (15:20). In other words, circumcision will not be required, while it will be necessary to observe a minimum of food laws. The reference to sexual morality is both a literal and a metaphorical allusion to idolatry. Easing of the requirements of Jewish ritual observance will facilitate the inclusion of Gentiles among the new people.

James' words, proclaiming the agreement in Jerusalem, specifically refer to the Cornelius story: "Simeon has related how God first looked favorably on the Gentiles, to take from among them a people for his name. This agrees with the words of the prophets" (15:14–15). Luke implies that a new people is being created, a people of "believers," both Jewish and Gentile. That new people is the fulfillment of the prophetic word, and the correct interpretation of that word now resides in the new community.

An Accusation

Luke's portrayal of this new people, however, has a shadow side, one that has had tragic consequences over the centuries. Luke has Peter, as well as Stephen and Paul, declare unrelentingly that Jews are responsible for Jesus' death.[6] Luke underscores Jewish culpability by minimizing Roman involvement. In Peter's speech to Cornelius, there is no reference to the Romans, and Cornelius' status as a Roman centurion signals Luke's willingness to view Romans in a favorable light.

References to Jewish responsibility for Jesus' death occur in summaries of the teaching of the new Way. Several other elements occur in these passages to indicate the nature of the speeches as summary statements. In all but 7:52, the death of Jesus is counterposed with the resurrection. Other motifs include repentance (2:38; 3:19; 5:31–32), forgiveness of sins (2:38; 5:31; 10:43; 13:38), witness (2:32; 3:15; 5:32; 10:39; 13:31), the prophets (3:18–25; 7:37, 42, 48, 52; 13:27, 40), and the Holy Spirit (2:43; 5:32; 10:38, 44, 45). The theme of witness suggests the missionary function of these summaries and their function as vehicles of persuasion. The recourse to the prophets suggests the need to explain the disgraceful death of Jesus and to legitimate the new Way as a movement in continuity with an earlier tradition. It indicates as well the rivalry between communities concerning the ownership and interpretation of sacred texts, a rivalry that intensified in the second through fifth centuries.

Rival Layers

Thus, in looking closely at Acts 10, we discern layers of meaning with a double-sided character. On the one hand, we find the summary of the community's experience of forgiveness and new life, grounded in the witness to the resurrection. The conversion of Cornelius demonstrates that that message is for all who would join the company of "believers," Gentiles equally with Jews. This new Way is in fulfillment of the prophets and thus in continuity with the ancestral Way of Judaism. Yet, on the other hand, we hear in Peter's speech a blunt accusation that the Jews put Jesus to death by "hanging him on a tree." How is it that Peter makes no mention of the power of imperial Rome, symbolized by the Roman prefect governor, Pontius Pilate?

Identity construction lies at the heart of both layers. In a traditional society where innovation is suspect, a new movement receives legitimacy by claiming continuity with antiquity. The infancy narratives of the first volume of Luke's work are peopled with characters who embody the ideal of Judaism. They indicate the continuity of the new Way with the ancestral religion. And in Acts, even members of the Jewish leadership acknowledge the possible legitimacy of the new Way (4:16; 5:33–39). The infancy narratives in the gospel, the leaders' words in Acts, and the appeal to the scriptures—that is, the Hebrew Bible—represent the same claim; these strategies imply that the new Way alone interprets the text correctly.

The claim to continuity with tradition and thus to authority made particular sense in the Lukan project. Luke wrote for two audiences at the end of the first century or the first half of the second: (1) his own community, a diverse Mediterranean group that was predominantly Gentile but probably also included Jews, and (2) a non-Christian Gentile audience for which Rome was the ruling power.[7] In that context, threatened by civil unrest, social order was a primary concern. Ancestral religions and the state cult were principal ways in which social and cosmic orders were maintained.

The imperial government expected conquered peoples both to participate in the state cult and to maintain their ancestral religions. Jews as monotheists had been exempted from participation in the imperial cult, while continuing their own practice under the rubric of Judaism as an ancestral religion. Luke needed to demonstrate to his audience that the Way did not constitute a new and therefore suspicious innovation that might pose a threat to the social order. Suggesting its continuity with the past implied that the Way shared Judaism's nature as an "ancestral religion," and thus its legitimacy.

It seems that some in the Roman establishment associated the Way with civil disorder. Rome often perceived small groups, voluntary associations such as the *Christianoi* (Christians) and diaspora Jewish communities, as sources of social unrest. Jews, moreover, had engaged in a series of hostile actions and revolts against Rome throughout the first century and well into the second. The Christians' leader, after all, had been crucified—a Roman punishment reserved for those guilty of sedition, among other crimes. So, while needing to establish the legitimacy of the Way as an ancestral religion by demonstrating it to be Israel's heir and the interpreter of its scriptures, Luke also needed to establish that his community was *not* the same as *those* people, the Jews who were not among the believers. His community included such respectable people as the centurion Cornelius and well-born matrons (17:12). Paul himself was a Roman citizen (22:28–29) who attracted the sympathy of the client ruler Agrippa (26:27–32). Luke was arguing that the Way would prove no source of unrest, in contrast to the unbelieving Jews who provoked civil disturbance.[8]

Luke framed Peter's speech to Cornelius and his household in the context of instruction for his community. It was a summary statement that displayed an assertion of identity around the events of the death and resurrection of Jesus, forgiveness of sins, the fulfillment of prophecy (i.e., the sacred text), and the outpouring of the Holy Spirit. Furthermore, that identity blurred ethnic boundaries: Peter the Jew and Cornelius the Roman became fellows as thresholds were crossed. While claiming continuity with the ancestral religion Judaism and asserting its right as authentic interpreter of the sacred text, the new people were distinct from those Jews who did not believe in Jesus. Members of the Way were no threat to civil or cosmic order.

Certainly the proclamation of the death and resurrection of Jesus, forgiveness of sin, prophetic witness, and the claim to inheritance of the sacred text provided Luke's audience with a key articulation of the emerging community's self-understanding. The repeated assertion of Jewish responsibility for Jesus' crucifixion functioned not only as a strategy of identity construction—demarcating followers of Jesus from those Jews who did not believe in him—but also as a means for the community to position itself in relation to the Roman Empire. All of this says something about the dynamics of identity construction and ancient rivalries in relation to Acts and Peter's speech to Cornelius read on Easter morning.

But we hear that text read in other, very different contexts. Christian identity construction in this third millennium involves dealing with our history vis-à-vis Jews. As our introduction to "A Sacred Obligation" confesses: "For most of the past two thousand years, Christians have erroneously portrayed Jews as unfaithful, holding them collectively responsible for the death of Jesus and therefore accursed by God." "A Sacred Obligation" challenges us to think about new ways in which those summary statements in Acts about the death and resurrection of Jesus, accompanied by the community's claim to be the rightful inheritor of the scriptures, can function in our time. In particular, how might our proclamation of, and preaching about, such texts in the lectionary manifest a spirit that respects those who have paid a terrible price for assertions of Christian identity that blamed "the Jews" for the death of Jesus? How might contemporary interpretations of Acts reflect reverence for Jewish readings of the prophets?

Luke could not have foreseen the tragic consequences of his exculpation of the Romans and assignment of blame to Jews. Yet in his layering of Acts 10, he invites Christians to contemplate contemporary ways of crossing the thresholds of class and ethnicity.

Notes

1. Compare Luke 11:39–52.

2. For examples of the word "way" to designate the new movement, see 9:2; 19:9, 23; 22:4; 24:14, 22; "way of salvation" in 16:17; "way of the Lord" in 18:25; and "way of God" in 18:26.

3. Joseph B. Tyson, "The Gentile Mission and the Authority of Scripture in Acts," *New Testament Studies* 33 (1987): 624–30.

4. For examples of Luke's use of "believers" to denote those who follow the Way, see also Acts 13:34; 16:1, 15.

5. Actually, there was considerable close association between Jews and Gentiles, even in the land of Israel; see Seth Schwartz, *Imperialism and Jewish Society, 200 B.C.E. to 640 C.E.* (Princeton, NJ: Princeton University Press, 2001). Luke is trying to emphasize the point that the new people brings together two distinct groups.

6. Acts 2:22–23, 36; 3:13–18; 4:10, 27–28; 5:30; 7:52; 10:38–43; 13:27–30.

7. See Stephen G. Wilson, *Related Strangers: Jews and Christians 70–170 C.E.* (Minneapolis: Fortress, 1995), 56–71.

8. For example, Acts 17:10–15; 21:27–28; 23:7, 19; 24:5, 19.

Further Reading

Fredriksen, Paula, and Adele Reinhartz, eds. *Jesus, Judaism, and Christian Anti-Judaism: Reading the New Testament after the Holocaust.* Louisville, KY: Westminster / John Knox, 2002.

Tyson, Joseph B. *Images of Judaism in Luke-Acts.* Columbia: University of South Carolina Press, 1992.

———, ed. *Luke-Acts and the Jewish People: Eight Critical Perspectives.* Minneapolis: Augsburg, 1988.

6

CHAPTER

Ancient Jewish-Christian Rivalries in the Shadow of Empire: The Tensions of the Past as Lessons for the Present

Jean-Pierre Ruiz

Entangled in the Empire

The Apostles' Creed, an ancient profession of Christian faith that remains in use among many Christian churches today, testifies to the large-looming shadow Roman imperial power cast over first-century Judaism and early Christianity by affirming that Jesus "suffered under Pontius Pilate." This statement, all but taken for granted by the many millions of Christians who

59

recite it when they gather for Sunday worship, suggests that we cannot understand the world in which Christianity emerged without taking account of the pervasive influence of Rome.

Biblical scholars are increasingly using the tools of postcolonial interpretation to facilitate a clearer understanding of the forces that were at work in the first-century Mediterranean world, a setting in which the pervasive power of the Roman Empire affected every dimension of life. Postcolonial interpretation had its beginnings in literary studies, emerging in the latter part of the twentieth century among the former subjects of the British Empire. In the wake of independence from Britain, writers from the former colonies established their own voices in what amounted to a process of intellectual decolonization. This led to their self-conscious reflection on the impact of colonization and on the relationships between colonizers and the colonized.

Applied to biblical studies, postcolonial interpretation reminds us that the European empires of the nineteenth and twentieth centuries had their precursors in ancient empires. Therefore, much of what has been learned about the dynamics of imperial power as it operated in recent centuries can be used to sharpen our focus on the world in which the Bible took shape. Reading through the lenses of postcolonial interpretation, biblical scholars recognize that the Bible itself is a collection of documents that emerged from various colonial contexts: Egyptian, Persian, Assyrian, Hellenistic, and Roman. These scholars see in biblical texts issues such as nationalism, identity, and ethnicity that have arisen in the wake of colonialism.[1]

Postcolonial criticism addresses the impact of empire on its subjects, listening closely to what can be recovered, reading between the lines to recover the voices of the colonized that might not otherwise be heard. Biblical scholars who employ postcolonial criticism approach ancient texts with a number of questions:

- How do those on the margins look at the "world"—a world dominated by the reality of empire—and fashion life in such a world?
- How does the center regard and treat those on the margins in the light of its own view of the "world"?
- How do biblical texts regard and represent "the other"?[2]

It would be short-sighted to limit our attention to Pontius Pilate, who from 26 to 36 C.E. served as the fifth governor of the Roman province of Judea, or even to the immediate influence of Roman power on Jesus and his earliest followers. As the Jesus movement spread, its entanglements with

Roman rule grew more and more complex. The New Testament reflects a range of responses to Roman economic, military, political, and religious domination. For example, in Mark 12:14 (and its parallels Matt 22:17 and Luke 20:22), Jesus' opponents attempt to entrap him with the question, "Is it lawful to pay taxes to the emperor or not?" Jesus, aware that the motives prompting the question are less than sincere, makes a show of examining the coin used to pay the tax and then directs himself to his questioners: "'Whose head is this and whose title?' They answered, 'The emperor's.'" Then Jesus brings the encounter to a close with the saying, "Give to the emperor the things that are the emperor's, and to God the things that are God's." While these words are sometimes cited in the United States as a biblical warrant for the separation of church and state, in their immediate context they serve to provide Jesus with a clever means of escaping the trap by avoiding the appearance of seditious speech.

On the other hand, a postcolonial interpreter of this text might stress that these words of Jesus found their place in gospels that were put in writing only after Roman military forces crushed the Jewish revolt and destroyed the Temple in Jerusalem in 70 C.E. Against that background, one can hear Jesus insinuating a subtle resistance that puts Caesar in his place and gives God the upper hand, despite overwhelming evidence to the contrary in the inscription *Iudea capta* (Judea captured) that appeared on coins minted after 70 C.E.

Another response to the entanglement of early Christianity with the reality of Roman imperial power can be found in Paul's letter to the Romans, which was probably written in 57–58 C.E., before the destruction of the Temple in Jerusalem in 70 C.E. In Romans 13:1–7 Paul offers advice on how his audience is to relate to the authorities. He exhorts them, "Let every person be subject to the governing authorities; for there is no authority except from God, and those authorities that exist have been instituted by God. Therefore whoever resists authority resists what God has appointed, and those who resist will incur judgment" (13:1–2). Paul adds, "Pay to all what is due them—taxes to whom taxes are due, revenue to whom revenue is due, respect to whom respect is due, honor to whom honor is due" (13:7). This advice to the followers of Jesus in Rome, urging them to cooperate with the authorities, should be understood in the light of the predominantly Jewish origins of the Jesus movement in Rome. There had been a large Jewish community in Rome at least as early as the first century B.C.E., a community that some suggest may have included as many as fifty thousand people.

The impact of empire on the movements of populations, in forced and voluntary migrations toward (and away from) the metropolitan center, can be seen in the fact that the general Pompey (106–148 B.C.E.) had brought many Jews to Rome as slaves after his conquests in the east, particularly after overtaking Jerusalem in 63 B.C.E.[3] Thus, the memory of Roman imperial power lingered in the consciousness of Rome's Jewish population, which found itself at the heart of the empire as a consequence of the Roman exercise of military power.

Romans 13:1–7 should also be understood in the light of the Edict of Claudius (49 C.E.), in which, according to Acts 18:2, Claudius "ordered all Jews to leave Rome." The Roman historian Suetonius may shed some light on this when he writes: "Since the Jews constantly made disturbances at the instigation of Chrestus, he [Claudius] expelled them from Rome."[4] This reference to "Chrestus" or "Christos" suggests the likelihood that there were lively tensions within the first-century C.E. Jewish community of Rome over the identity and significance of Jesus. It also implies that the Romans viewed the "Christians" as indistinguishable from other members of Rome's large Jewish community. Paul's admonition in Romans 13:1–7 that Roman Christians are to conduct themselves as obedient subjects of the empire is, on one level, an indication of the apostle's counsel that they should not draw undue attention to themselves from the authorities. Understanding their precarious position at the heart of the empire even from a distance, Paul urges the Roman Christian addressees to go along with imperial authority. Such submission helped to assure their survival.[5] Yet one can also detect, just below the surface of Paul's urging of compliance, the likely undertones of a subtler resistance. To give "respect to whom respect is due, honor to whom honor is due" echoes the advice of Jesus, "Give to the emperor the things that are the emperor's, and to God the things that are God's," with all the ambiguity that those words imply!

Babylon Seated on Seven Mountains

Nowhere in the New Testament is the conflict between Christ and Caesar more vividly presented than in the book of Revelation, the Apocalypse of John. Written around 95 C.E., toward the end of the reign of the emperor Domitian (81–96 C.E.), Revelation is addressed to "the seven churches that are in Asia" (Rev 1:4), that is, to Christian communities located in seven cities of the Roman province of Asia. Some scholars have suggested that these seven cities connected by Roman roads—Ephesus, Smyrna,

Pergamum, Thyatira, Sardis, Philadelphia, and Laodicea—formed something of a circle that started from Ephesus. This region of western Anatolia, which forms part of present-day Turkey, came under Roman control in 133 B.C.E. and was constituted as the Roman province of Asia in 126 B.C.E. In the Apocalypse of John, Rome is symbolically identified as "Babylon the great, mother of whores and of earth's abominations" (Rev 17:5). It is seated on seven mountains (Rev 17:9), the seven hills of Rome, "the great city that rules over the kings of the earth" (Rev 17:18). "Babylon" is attested as a symbolic name for Rome in Jewish apocalyptic literature dated after 70 C.E. (e.g., 4 Ezra 3:1–2, 28–31). This name was an appropriate symbol for the imperial capital that captured Jerusalem and destroyed the Second Temple, more than five centuries after the Babylonian armies of King Nebuchadnezzar took Jerusalem and destroyed the first Temple in 587 B.C.E.

The perspective of the Apocalypse is emphatically urban. "Babylon" symbolically embodies all that is wrong with the present order of things, while the "New Jerusalem" (Rev 21) symbolizes all that is hoped for. Neither of these is a city where the book's addressees actually live, nor is either identified as the location from which the author writes. John writes from Patmos (Rev 1:9), an island vantage point that provided distance from both symbolic cities, as well as from the Asian cities whose economic, political, and religious entanglements with empire he confronts. Adela Yarbro Collins explains, "Perhaps the most significant change brought about by the Roman conquest was the definitive loss of autonomy by the individual cities."[6] This political loss of self-determination was marked in religious terms: "Roma" and "Caesar" (the city of Rome personified as a goddess and the emperor venerated as though he were divine) took the place of the traditional patron gods and goddesses of the cities.

While Roman power made itself felt in the province of Asia both economically (Rev 18:3: "The merchants of the earth have grown rich from the power of her luxury") and politically (Rev 17:18: "the great city that rules over the kings of the earth"), the Apocalypse opposed most aggressively the empire's embodiment in religious ritual and architecture. The emperor was *deus et dominus*, god and lord, present in the cities of the seven churches through the temples and rites associated with the religious veneration of the emperor and of the city of Rome, personified as the goddess Roma. For the Jewish communities of the province of Asia, this religious expression of imperial control proved especially troublesome. The statues of gods, goddesses, and heroes likely offended their sensibilities. But worse still, particularly for those whose memories of the destruction of the Jewish Temple in Jerusalem were still vivid, was the dedication of the imperial temple in Ephesus in 89/90 C.E. Revelation 21:22 ("I saw no temple in the city, for its temple is the Lord God the Almighty and the Lamb") can be understood as a response both to the massive and visible presence of the religious veneration of Rome and the emperor in the cities of the province of Asia, and to the destruction of the Temple in Jerusalem.

In the cities of the Apocalypse, Jews were situated on the border between insiders and outsiders, occupying intermediate status somewhere between citizen and resident alien. As the end of the first century approached, some Christians were nearly indistinguishable from Jews. Although they had their own gatherings, they would have participated in those of the local synagogue or synagogues as well, and thus would also have shared in the legal status of the local Jews.[7] However, those Jews "who became Christians and who separated voluntarily from the local Jewish community or were rejected by it were in a delicate position, beyond the margins of Roman legal recognition."[8] The Roman authorities were suspicious of Christian gatherings distinct from gatherings of the Jewish community.

This ancient rivalry in the Roman province of Asia, precipitated in large measure by the Roman perception of Jews outside of Judea, is reflected in the harsh words of John's Apocalypse in the message to the church in Smyrna against "those who say they are Jews and are not but are a synagogue of Satan" (Rev 2:9), and in the message to the church in Philadelphia against "those of the synagogue of Satan who say that they are Jews and are not, but are lying" (Rev 3:9).[9] Taking a closer look at this polemical language against the background of Roman imperial rule in the province of Asia can help us to understand the crisis over conflicting claims about ethnicity and identity.

"Those Who Say They Are Jews but Are Not"

In the message to the church at Smyrna, the Apocalypse's opposition to "those who say they are Jews and are not but are a synagogue of Satan" is precipitated by their alleged slander. Revelation 2:10 intimates that the alleged slander was about to lead to legal proceedings against the Christians by the Roman authorities at Smyrna: "Do not fear what you are about to suffer. Beware, the devil is about to throw some of you into prison so that you may be tested, and for ten days you will have affliction." While there is no evidence of large-scale activity on Rome's part to suppress the nascent

Christian movement, it is likely that local provincial and municipal authorities acted on a case-by-case basis to punish those who were judged threats to the public order. Revelation 2:9–10 suggests that at Smyrna, some Jewish Christians may have been reported to the authorities by their fellow Jews.

The expression in Revelation 2:9 "those who say they are Jews [*Ioudaioi*] and are not" suggests that John lays claim to the term *Ioudaioi* to designate the members of his own community. John seems to accuse his opponents at Smyrna of being inauthentic Jews. As Yarbro Collins points out, "It is anachronistic and misleading with regard to the book of Revelation . . . to assume that the author thought of the Church as a new religion and a new institution replacing Judaism." Revelation 2:9 "must not be seen as a rejection of religious and ethnic Judaism viewed from a distance but as a passionate polemic against a sibling or parent faith."[10] She further suggests that the inner-Jewish polemics of the Qumran community (site of the Dead Sea Scrolls) against other Jews parallels John's harsh designation of his opponents as a "synagogue of Satan." For example, one document refers to Jewish outsiders as "the congregation of traitors" and another portrays them in demonic terms as allies of the army of Belial.[11]

Language almost identical to that of Revelation 2:9 appears in Revelation 3:9, in the message to the church in Philadelphia. There John's addressees are told, "I will make those of the synagogue of Satan who say that they are Jews and are not, but are lying—I will make them come and bow down before your feet, and they will learn that I have loved you." Many commentators suggest that this is a reference to Isaiah 60:14: "The descendants of those who oppressed you shall come bending low to you, and all who despised you shall bow down at your feet." Some also see an ironic twist here: while in Isaiah 60:14 "the Gentiles are expected to grovel before Israel . . . in Rev 3:9 it is the Jews who are expected to grovel before the feet of this (largely Gentile) Christian community."[12] Following this trajectory of interpretation, some have seen Revelation 3:9 as a supersessionist affirmation of the triumph of Christianity and the submission of Judaism. Yet this conclusion is very much out of line with the evidence that Revelation 3:9 itself provides. The identification of John's opponents as "those of the synagogue of Satan who say that they are Jews and are not" makes it clear that this is not a struggle over status between Jews and non-Jews, but an inner-Jewish contest over the boundaries of legitimate Judaism, a war of words over which faction could claim authentic Jewish identity.

To the phrase found in Revelation 2:9, "those who say that they are Jews and are not," 3:9 adds a telling phrase: "who say that they are Jews and are not, *but are lying.*" The issue at stake in Smyrna *and* in Philadelphia was which faction could legitimately claim to be authentically Jewish and which faction fell short. By some estimates, there were between four and five million Jews in the territories of the Roman Empire during the first century C.E., so that Jews constituted about 7 percent of a total population of some sixty million. On the other hand, by the end of the first century, Christians may well have numbered no more than fifty thousand.[13]

While numbers do not tell the whole story, they indicate that the contest at Smyrna and Philadelphia over Jewish identity involved a struggle for recognition and even for survival. The relatively small Christian minority in western Asia found themselves on unstable ground: "While most religious associations could claim to be continuing as ancient tradition linked to a particular family, city, or ethnic group, and while such ancient traditions were respected, the only ancient traditions the Christians could claim were those of the Jews."[14] In the rigid either/or language characteristic of apocalyptic discourse, the book of Revelation maintains that its Christian addressees maintained authentic continuity with ancient Jewish tradition and that their opponents at Smyrna and Philadelphia, "who say that they are Jews and are not," constituted the synagogue of Satan, not the assembly of God.

As the difficult and gradual process of Christian self-definition continued into the second century, we find that the language used by first-century Christians to define themselves over against Jews was actually turned by some Christians against other Christians who opposed them. Yarbro Collins offers the example of Ignatius of Antioch's letter to the Smyrnaeans, in which he warns that "anyone who acts without knowledge of the bishop is serving the devil."[15]

They All Look the Same to Me:
Identity and the Gaze of Empire

Conflict can be described as "a struggle over values and claims to scarce status, power and resources in which the aims of the opponents are to neutralize, injure or eliminate their rivals."[16] On the basis of this description, Yarbro Collins concludes that the struggle between Christians and Jews in the Roman province of Asia was a struggle for survival, inasmuch as it was a contest over scarce status. She continues: "The conflict with Rome as interpreted by the book of Revelation was not merely a struggle for survival, but a struggle over power. The underlying issue may be articulated as a tension between autonomy and subservience."[17]

A postcolonial interpretation of these dynamics takes this a step further. It was the overwhelming and enduring reality of Roman imperial power, and of Jewish and Christian subjection to that power, that provided the spark for this conflict over identity in the first place. Autonomy meant authenticity and a degree of self-determination under the umbrella of the empire, while subservience meant assimilation and surrender.

Ania Loomba explains, "In any colonial context . . . specific ways of seeing and representing racial, cultural and social difference were essential to the setting up of colonial institutions of control." For example, in nineteenth- and twentieth-century British imperial strategies for social control of colonial possessions in Africa and India, "by attributing particular characteristics to specific tribes and groups, colonial authorities not only entrenched divisions between the native population, but also used particular 'races' to fill specific occupations such as agricultural workers, soldiers, miners, or domestic servants."[18] History teaches us that this colonial-imperial manipulation of identity is nothing new. After 70 C.E., the Temple tax that the Romans had allowed Jews to collect for the maintenance of the Temple in Jerusalem was transformed into the Jewish tax that the Roman authorities collected for the upkeep of the temple of the Capitoline Jupiter in Rome.[19] Emperor Domitian, under whose reign the Apocalypse of John was written, was especially exacting in his enforcement of this tax.[20]

The Roman authorities did not view Jews outside Judea as a national group but as an ethnic group, one of many such groups under imperial control. Thus, what it meant to be identified as a Jew and to identify oneself as a Jew in the province of Asia after the destruction of the Jerusalem Temple was a delicate matter: a negotiated identity that took shape in close relation to the ways in which one was perceived by one's fellow residents, by the local municipal authorities, and by the representatives of the Roman Empire. It was as true then as it is now that persons whom authorities categorized as "undocumented" and "unclassified" were persons whom they could not control and, therefore, who were dangerous in the eyes of the authorities. The conflict that plays itself out in the pages of the book of Revelation over who could lay claim to be "real" Jews was a contest for recognition that took place under the watchful gaze of the distant emperor's local representatives, the governor and the provincial administration. The Roman recognition of Jews as an ethnic group under the umbrella of the empire provided a degree of breathing room, a degree of self-determination and autonomy that was not available to those who were out of bounds.

Out from under the Shadow of Empire

For the first-century Christians of the seven churches of the Roman province of Asia, the addressees of John's Apocalypse, the contest over identity was nothing less than a struggle for survival. The story *in* the book has a happy ending: "Babylon" falls and heaven colonizes earth as a New Jerusalem descends from on high. Likewise, the story *of* the book of Revelation has a happy ending: Imperial Rome has fallen while John, his partisans, and their book have survived.

The first-century animosities that survive in its pages must not be allowed to colonize twenty-first-century consciences. Survival in the twenty-first century calls for solidarity and not for fratricidal struggle. Ancient rivalries—like the bitter rivalry between the addressees of the Apocalypse and their opponents—must not be allowed to define Jewish-Christian relations today. For twenty-first-century Jews and Christians, living under the shadow of new and ever more insidious threats to life and dignity, the lessons of our shared and troubled history summon us—in the words of "A Sacred Obligation"—to "strengthen our common efforts in the work of justice and peace to which both the prophets of Israel and Jesus summon us."

Notes

1. See R. S. Sugirtharajah, *The Bible and the Third World: Precolonial, Colonial, and Postcolonial Encounters* (Cambridge: Cambridge University Press, 2001), 251.

2. See Fernando F. Segovia, "Biblical Criticism and Postcolonial Studies: Toward a Postcolonial Optic," in R. S. Sugirtharajah, ed., *The Postcolonial Bible* (Sheffield, UK: Sheffield Academic Press, 1998), 57.

3. See Joseph A. Fitzmyer, *Romans: A New Translation with Introduction and Commentary*, Anchor Bible, 33 (New York: Doubleday, 1993), 27, 29.

4. Suetonius, "Claudius," in *Lives of the Caesars*, translated by J. C. Rolfe (Cambridge, MA: Loeb Classical Library, 1997–1998), § 25. On Rome and the Roman Christians, see Fitzmyer, *Romans*, 25–36.

5. Marcus Borg writes that at the time Paul's letter to the Romans was written, "Judaism was on the brink of catastrophe as a result of its longstanding resistance to Roman imperialism. An emerging Christianity, founded by a Jew whom the Romans had crucified—regarded still by Rome as a Jewish sect, and inextricably implicated, by history and culture, by ideology and associational patterns, in the Jewish world—was inevitably caught up in the crisis of Jewish-Roman relations" ("A New Context for Romans xiii," *New Testament Studies* 19 [1972–1973]: 218).

6. Adela Yarbro Collins, "Insiders and Outsiders in the Book of Revelation and Its Social Context," in Jacob Neusner and Ernest S. Frerichs, eds., *"To See Ourselves as Others See Us": Christians, Jews, "Others" in Late Antiquity,* Scholars Press Studies in the Humanities (Chico, CA: Scholars Press, 1985), 188.

7. Yarbro Collins, "Insiders and Outsiders," 196–97. Also see the treatment of "Anatolian Jewish Communities and Synagogues," and the useful bibliography provided by David E. Aune, *Revelation 1–5,* Word Biblical Commentary, 52 (Dallas: Word Books, 1997), 168–72.

8. Yarbro Collins, "Insiders and Outsiders," 198.

9. The word "synagogue" here refers to the assembly or community, and not to any specific building where the assembly gathered.

10. Yarbro Collins, "Insiders and Outsiders," 208.

11. Yarbro Collins, "Insiders and Outsiders," 208–9.

12. Aune, *Revelation 1–5,* 238.

13. See Aune, *Revelation 1–5,* 164.

14. Yarbro Collins, "Insiders and Outsiders," 198.

15. Yarbro Collins, "Insiders and Outsiders," 210.

16. Lewis A. Coser, *The Functions of Social Conflict* (New York: Free Press, 1956), 8; as cited in Yarbro Collins, "Insiders and Outsiders," 217.

17. Yarbro Collins, "Insiders and Outsiders," 218.

18. Ania Loomba, *Colonialism / Postcolonialism* (London: Routledge, 1998), 97.

19. Aune, *Revelation 1–5,* 171; Yarbro Collins, "Insiders and Outsiders," 196.

20. Suetonius, "Domitian," in *Lives of the Caesars,* § 12:2.

Further Reading

Friesen, Steven J. *Imperial Cults and the Apocalypse of John: Reading Revelation in the Ruins.* New York: Oxford University Press, 2001.

Gandhi, Leela. *Postcolonial Theory: A Critical Introduction.* New York: Columbia University Press, 1998.

Ruiz, Jean-Pierre. "Taking a Stand on the Sand of the Seashore: A Postcolonial Exploration of Revelation 13." In David L. Barr, ed., *Reading the Book of Revelation: A Resource for Students,* Resources for Biblical Study, 119–35. Atlanta: Society of Biblical Literature, 2003.

Segovia, Fernando F. *Decolonizing the Bible: A View from the Margins.* Maryknoll, NY: Orbis Books, 2000.

Sugirtharajah, R. S. *The Bible and the Third World: Precolonial, Colonial, and Postcolonial Encounters.* Cambridge: Cambridge University Press, 2001.

Wilken, Robert L. *The Christians as the Romans Saw Them.* 2nd edition. New Haven: Yale University Press, 2003.

7

CHAPTER

Christian Feminism and Anti-Judaism

Mary C. Boys

I N MANY RESPECTS, feminism within Christianity is an argument with the church: the way its tradition mutes, if not entirely erases, the voices of women; the way those with power to enforce their interpretation of those traditions often disdain other interpretations; and the way in which many male authorities ignore or trivialize the deep concerns articulated by women.[1]

Yet *how* this argument proceeds is crucial. Too often, a caricature of Judaism constitutes its warrant.

Consider the following example, taken from an electronic mail list to which I belong. The writer advocates taking an action about which others on the list have expressed concern, lest the strategy needlessly inflame church authorities and be counterproductive. Rejecting this concern, the writer aligns her position with Jesus: "Almost everything that Jesus did, from healing on the Sabbath to turning over the tables in the synagogue [*sic*] to processing into Jerusalem on a donkey with palms laid down on his path was seen as extremely political as well as an act of defiance because he was challenging the unjust status quo that was promoted by the religious hierarchy." Thus, she urges the group to defy religious authorities: "Jesus ended up crucified on a dump outside the city, not because he worked within the institutional Jewish hierarchy for change at their pace, but because he threatened the political, economic, social and religious power structures so much he was killed."

However well intentioned such an argument, it oversimplifies and distorts the ministry of Jesus, the Jew from Nazareth. It rests on an assumption often lurking in liberation thought: the binary opposition of oppressor (Judaism) and oppressed (Jesus). It repeats the longstanding tendency in Christianity to make Judaism the foil. It thereby illustrates the sage observation of Clark Williamson that Judaism is an "external fictive enemy" that becomes "the brush with which to tar real enemies who are internal to the church. Christ becomes the one who saves us from Judaism."[2]

Christian feminists, in attempting to reveal the liberating power of the Way of Jesus Christ for women in our time, may inadvertently continue the transmission of a theological "virus" that has tragically affected Jews and distorted the self-understanding of Christians: anti-Judaism. My principal concern in this chapter is to analyze ways in which the insidious virus that misrepresents Judaism has managed to attach itself to biblical interpretations directed toward justice for women in our church and world.

The question is this: How might Christians who advocate for greater justice for women also contribute to reconciliation with Jews? How can Christian feminists eliminate the virus of anti-Judaism?

Clarifying the Terms: Anti-Judaism and Feminism

It is important to distinguish anti-Judaism as a theological viewpoint and antisemitism as a sociocultural phenomenon. By "anti-Judaism" I mean attitudes, arguments, polemics, and actions that distort and disparage Judaism in order to support Christian claims of superiority. This is a complicated distinction, since understandings of Christianity resting on anti-Jewish perspectives tend all too readily to "slide over" into antisemitism, that is, into hatred of and hostility toward Jews.

Moreover, "anti-Judaism" is not a univocal term. It has taken on new layers over time, becoming ever more deadly. What began as an argument over differences between those who believed in Jesus (including Jewish disciples) and (other) Jews grew over the course of many centuries into a bitter dispute resulting in harsh treatment of Jews. The church consistently rationalized its actions by defaming Jews as a "deicide people" and "Christ-killers." At the heart of anti-Judaism is the charge echoed repeatedly that the Jews bear the burden of responsibility for the death of Jesus. Indeed, preaching and teaching about the passion and death of Jesus over the course of Christian history have rationalized hostility toward and violence against Jews as has no other single accusation. Its nearly constant accompaniment is the caricature of Judaism as legalistic, personified by the hypocritical Pharisees. Over the ages, anti-Judaism has fueled hostile attitudes toward Jews that in many cases have given rise to persecutions and even death.

As reprehensible as this legacy is, it is not identical with antisemitism; one can be an antisemite without any knowledge of Christianity's anti-Jewish theology. Nor is antisemitism alone the cause of the Holocaust; nineteenth-century "race science" and the romantic-idealism of the German *Volk* were crucial elements in the development of state-sanctioned genocide.[3] Nevertheless, the Holocaust (or, as many prefer to call it, the Shoah) demands examination.[4] For Christians, in particular, it requires confrontation with the lethal legacy of anti-Judaism—a confrontation that many Christian denominations are taking seriously in our time (see the chapter in this volume by Eva Fleischner).

Because anti-Judaism has replicated itself in many dimensions of Christian theological thinking for nearly two thousand years, it will be neither neatly nor quickly extricated. It is so pervasive that many Christians of great integrity are unaware of the distorted views of Judaism that they inherited. While this means that too many Christians base their self-identity on a distorted, defective understanding of Judaism, it does not make them antisemites.

Thus, in criticizing the theological perspectives of various feminist theologians, I am not accusing them of antisemitism. I am, however, questioning whether they have done justice to the complex relationship of Judaism to Christianity. Since my principal concern lies with those who use the rubric of "feminist" rather than "womanist" or *mujerista*, I will remain with this term, while recognizing the varying standpoints from which women address the problems patriarchy has wrought, as well as the lack of consensus about the most appropriate terminology.[5]

Among the various definitions of feminism, I find that of biblical scholar Sandra Schneiders especially astute. Feminism, she writes, is "a comprehensive ideology, rooted in women's experience of sexually-based oppression, that engages in a critique of patriarchy as an essentially dysfunctional system, embraces an alternative vision for humanity and the earth, and actively seeks to bring this vision to realization."[6] Schneiders grounds this alternative vision in the example of Jesus as he is presented in the gospel. She believes his example can contribute to the transformation of cultural feminism into a prophetic force that moves all creation toward a future in God's universal shalom.

But can the example of Jesus bear this much weight? Must the historical Jesus be an egalitarian in order for feminist visions to exercise their transforming power in our time? And must the historical Jesus be portrayed as one who overturned the tables of Jewish patriarchy in order for Christian women to do the same in their own tradition today?

Patriarchal Judaism, Liberating Jesus

Feminist theology has developed considerable depth and breadth in its brief history. Thus, one encounters significant variations in assumptions, methods, foci, conclusions, and degrees of sophistication. My concern is as much with popular versions as it is with scholarly perspectives, since the former tend to circulate more widely and thereby influence a greater number of people. Especially at the popular level, it is all too likely that the blatant anti-Judaism woven into argumentation will go unnoticed, particularly because the authors champion a good cause—one I, too, hold dear: justice for women in a church that too often squanders their gifts and dedication.

A prime case in point appears in the following:

> Palestinian Hebrew women were among the poorest in the world in Jesus' day. This was probably because they had no inheritance rights and could be divorced for the flimsiest of reasons. Hebrew men could divorce their wives for anything from burning the dinner (*Hillel*) to adultery (*Shammai*). Yet Hebrew women were not allowed to divorce their husbands. . . . A Hebrew woman had minimal to no property rights. . . . A child was held to be Jewish only if the mother was Jewish. Most Jewish girls were betrothed by their fathers at a young age. Jewish women were held to be unclean while menstruating. If she inadvertently touched a man while having her menses, he was obliged to undergo a weeklong purification ritual before worshipping at the Temple. . . . In early Judaism women did proclaim and prophesy, but in Jesus' day they weren't permitted to

proclaim Torah at synagogue because of their periodic "uncleanness." As a rule, only the Rabbis' wives were so educated. Women were not accepted as witnesses in Jewish law, nor could they teach the law. Women had no official religious or leadership roles in first-century Judaism. Jesus' behavior toward women, even viewed through the andocentric lens of the gospel texts, is remarkable.[7]

We have here a treasure trove of anti-Jewish themes, all revolving around the dominant motif: Judaism was hopelessly patriarchal. Its women were impoverished, subject to the whims of their husbands, forced into marriage at a vulnerable age, excluded because of menstruation, banned from giving witness or teaching, and barred from leadership. Not quite the Taliban—but close.

Portraying Judaism as utterly constricted by patriarchy then allows this writer (and many others) to remove Jesus from his Jewish matrix by asserting that Jesus' revolutionary attitudes toward women broke the grip of patriarchy. It is this Jesus who shows us what gender relations should be in the church today. Like Jesus, contemporary Christian women must prophetically resist the narrowness, misuse of power, and legalism of those religious authorities.

Other authors sound similar refrains. For example, we hear: "At the historical moment when Jesus was born into the world, the status of Jewish women had never been lower. . . . By the time of Jesus' birth, many decades of rabbinic commentary and custom had surrounded Old Testament literature. And these rabbinic traditions considerably lowered the status of women."[8] Or, "Jesus' relations with women seem to have been remarkably free, given the reserve that Jewish custom in his day required."[9] It is as if these feminist writers can only point to the liberating power of Jesus by placing him in stark relief against the alleged restrictions of Judaism.

I could multiply such examples, as they seem ubiquitous in feminist writing, particularly in the pastoral realm. The situation has begun to change in scholarly circles, although it persists among some feminist authors from the Third World and the East, who have less opportunity to learn of Judaism firsthand. We need in particular to pay attention to what those who write for popular publications are saying, given their wide dissemination.

Encounter with Judaism provides a critical lens on such claims, especially those related to the Second Temple period and Christian origins. In general, I think much of the anti-Judaism stems from insufficient knowledge of the complexities of this era, and from a general lack of awareness of developments in the dialogue between Jews and Christians.

Let me be clear: I am sympathetic to the desire to understand Jesus as one who liberated his followers—including (perhaps especially) women—from the oppressive structures of religious authorities. I, too, consider some religious authorities oppressive in our time, and wrestle mightily with the harmful consequences of their hubris and abuse of power. As a Catholic woman and a feminist, I am deeply angered and saddened by the way in which my own tradition trivializes and squanders the gifts of its women.

Nonetheless, I have come to agree with Mary Rose D'Angelo that portraying Jesus as the one "who saves women from Judaism" both oversimplifies and distorts the situation of Jewish women in first-century Palestine.[10] It does indeed seem, as Amy-Jill Levine writes, that in many feminist and liberationist circles "no plot is complete without a reference to the 'Jewish patriarchal system,' although very rare are comments on the similarly patriarchal pagan cultures of antiquity."[11] Sadly, I have come to see that many who do theology under the rubric of feminism have drunk all too deeply from the wells of anti-Judaism. In the quest to depict a Jesus who might liberate us from the evils of patriarchy, too many feminists have disfigured the Jewish Jesus.

The familiar anti-Jewish trope that the Pharisees are legalistic hypocrites receives new life from many feminist writers. Despite the abundant literature that presents a far more textured understanding of the Pharisees, most notably that of the late Anthony J. Saldarini, many Christian feminists continue to portray them as the symbol of precisely what is wrong with religious authorities.[12] For many years, biblical scholars have explained how the gospel writers mischaracterized Jesus' relationship with the Pharisees, collapsing whatever differences he might have had with them into the tensions the evangelists experienced with Jewish leadership in *their* day. Such explanations are widely available in both scholarly and pastoral works, yet many Christian feminists persist in heaping upon the Pharisees the sins of patriarchy. For example, one feminist scholar asserts that the Pharisees (and their colleagues, the scribes) "tried to keep control over people's access to God through control of the Law. Jesus denounced this pretension and returned to the people the true means of access to God: love and compassion."[13]

In many feminist writings, moreover, the laws of ritual purity, which the Pharisees are portrayed as championing, serve as the source of the clearest contrast between oppressive Judaism and liberating Jesus. We are instructed about the "dehumanizing situation in which the women of the time were enslaved." We learn how menstruating women were "discriminated against, degraded, and dehumanized."[14] Rather than explore the customs of the

Greco-Roman world and probe the mindset of ancient cultures, these authors implicitly blame patriarchy on Judaism. By wrenching first-century Judaism from its cultural context, too many Christian feminists betray their own ethnocentrism when writing about Jesus' Movement. Even less should feminists use Pharisees as symbols of clericalism, however useful that might seem to be to the cause. The Pharisees were not the equivalent of ordained ecclesiastical leaders—though I must confess the scathing critique of Matthew's Jesus against those who "make their phylacteries broad and their fringes long . . . [who] love to have the place of honor at banquets and the best seats in the synagogues, and to be greeted with respect in the market-places, and to have people call them rabbi" has more than once come to mind during certain Christian liturgical occasions.

In sum, many feminist writers contrast Jewish women of the Second Temple period with New Testament narratives to support their claims that "at its inception, pristine Christianity and Jesus himself were free of any misogyny or gender bias." Thereby, as Ross Kraemer notes, they implicitly, even inadvertently, buttress the argument of Christian superiority over Judaism.[15]

Liberating Christian Feminism from Anti-Jewish Readings

I propose two modest means of becoming more sensitive to anti-Jewish readings of Jesus and his Renewal Movement. First, feminists at both the popular and scholarly levels need to deepen their knowledge of the pervasiveness of anti-Judaism in Christian tradition and its tragic consequences. Students of the Bible, in particular, need to examine how the interpretation of texts has functioned in thwarting both the full flourishing of women's gifts *and adequate understandings of Judaism*.

Second, continued—and increased—collaboration between Jewish and Christian feminists at both scholarly and pastoral levels will immeasurably enhance our understandings of gospel feminism. We might learn about the purity laws from scholars such as Paula Fredriksen in *Jesus of Nazareth: A Jewish Life and the Emergence of Christianity*. From Rabbi Elyse Goldstein's *ReVisions: Seeing Torah through a Feminist Lens* we might discover how a Jewish feminist wrestles with the meaning of the purity rules for her own life. We might correct our tendency to engage in rabbinic proof-texting if we paid heed to Ross Kraemer's essay "Jewish Women and Christian Origins," in the important volume, *Women and Christian Origins*, she coedited with Mary Rose D'Angelo. We might hear new depths of interpretation of the

fourth gospel from Adele Reinhartz in her *Befriending the Beloved Disciple: A Jewish Reading of the Gospel of John.* By using Jewish commentaries—widely accessible through the Internet—we might come to more nuanced understandings of ways Jews also struggle with the meaning of problematic texts.

Christian feminists will refine but not diminish our argument with the church when we recognize that women's active participation and leadership in Jesus' Movement and in early Christian communities built upon Jewish hopes of a new and transformed world.[16] A recent work by Elizabeth A. Johnson, *Truly Our Sister: A Theology of Mary in the Communion of Saints,* offers a superb model of such a recognition. Johnson devotes nearly seventy pages to situating Mary, the mother of Jesus, in her context as a Galilean Jewish woman. In nuanced and graceful prose, Johnson draws widely from archaeological, exegetical, and historical works to reconstruct the world Mary lived in. In taking Mary seriously as a historical person, she offers a counterpoint to both the sentimentalized "meek and mild maiden" of much Christian piety and the victim of Jewish patriarchal strictures of some Christian feminism. Rather, Johnson places Mary in the religious life of a typical household of the Galilee:

> Gathered at home with family members carrying out their Sabbath rituals, and gathered in with other villagers in "synagogue" listening to scripture readings, participating in instruction, offering prayer, and probably joining in the singing of psalms, a Nazareth family entered into the centering peace of the Sabbath week after week. They would then return to the everyday grind, taught not only to bless God but also to deal lovingly with their neighbors. The Law commands them not to kill, steal, commit adultery, or lie. . . . The faithful Jew is commanded not to oppress others, not to hate, not to bear a grudge, to care for those in need, and to watch out especially for the most vulnerable in their midst, the widow and the orphan.[17]

The detailed portrait Johnson constructs of the social-cultural, political, and religious world of a first-century Jewish woman in the Galilee brings Mary alive by showing that her Jewish belief and practice should not be regarded as mere "background" but rather as constitutive to understanding her. As Johnson puts it, Mary "inhabited" the faith of her ancestors "foursquare." When we forget—as the church largely has—the "deeply Jewish roots of her own piety," we risk "multiple distortions."[18]

Just as Johnson's artful reconstruction of the Jewish Mary of Nazareth helps to redefine her, so, too, does confronting anti-Judaism force Christians

to redefine our self-understanding. At the heart of that redefinition is how we understand the way of Jesus Christ for our church and in our world today. We can understand the liberating, salvific power of his mission and ministry without the odious comparison/contrast with Judaism or Jewish authorities. Justice obliges to do this. It is time Christian feminists drew upon the scholarship of the Jewish-Christian dialogue in giving voice to our vision of the liberating power of the gospel.

I join other feminists in advocating for church authorities to remove the blindfold of power that prevents them from recognizing the depth and richness of contemporary Christian feminist theological writing and from stunting the desire—and calling—of women to exercise the full range of their gifts in the church. But I also join with our Christian Scholars Group in asking feminists to recognize the dimness of the Christian theological vision that wrongly paired the figure of the sightless Synagoga, blind to the revelation of Christ, with the all-seeing Ecclesia. If feminism is to offer a reorienting vision to the church, it must do so in ways that recognize the distinctive visions of both Judaism and Christianity.

Many in the Christian tradition have finally acknowledged the tragic consequences of Christianity's distorted image of Judaism. It is vital we correct the feminist vision accordingly.

Notes

1. This chapter is an abbreviated and revised adaptation of my essay "Patriarchal Judaism, Liberating Jesus: A Feminist Misrepresentation," *Union Seminary Quarterly Review* 56, nos. 3–4 (2002): 48–61.

2. Clark M. Williamson, *Way of Blessing, Way of Life* (St. Louis: Chalice, 1999), 214.

3. See Gregory Paul Wegner, *Anti-Semitism and Schooling under the Third Reich* (New York: Routledge Falmer, 2002).

4. In biblical terms, a "holocaust" is a "whole burnt offering." As one of the sacrifices commanded by God, a holocaust is a good thing. The Hebrew word "Shoah" (catastrophe, or whirlwind of destruction) better denotes the unspeakable brutality of the Nazi genocide.

5. See Delores S. Williams, *Sisters in the Wilderness: The Challenge of Womanist God Talk* (Maryknoll, NY: Orbis Books, 1995); Maria Pilar Aqino, Daisy L. Machado, and Jeannette Rodriquez, *A Reader in Latina Feminist Theology: Religion and Justice* (Austin: University of Texas Press, 2002); Kwok Pui-lan, *Introducing Asian Feminist Theology* (Cleveland: Pilgrim, 2000). See also Letty M. Russell and

J. Shannon Clarkson, *Dictionary of Feminist Theology* (Louisville, KY: Westminster / John Knox, 1996).

6. Sandra M. Schneiders, *With Oil in Their Lamps: Faith, Feminism and the Future* (New York and Mahwah, NJ: Paulist, 2000), 4.

7. Christine Schenk, C.S.J., "Celebrating the Inclusive Jesus," *Celebration: An Ecumenical Worship Resource* (February 2000): 81–82.

8. Cited in Judith Plaskow, "Feminist Anti-Judaism and the Christian God," *Journal of Feminist Studies in Religion* 7, no. 2 (fall 1991): 104–7, reprinted in Helen P. Fry, ed., *Christian-Jewish Dialogue: A Reader* (Exeter, UK: University of Exeter Press, 1996), 233.

9. Monique Alexandre, "Early Christian Women," in Pauline Schmitt Pantel, ed., *A History of Women in the West, Vol. 1: From Ancient Goddesses to Christian Saints* (Cambridge, MA: Belknap Press of Harvard University Press, 1992), 420.

10. Mary Rose D'Angelo, "Gender in the Origins of Christianity: Jewish Hopes and Imperial Exigencies," in Joseph Martos and Pierre Hegy, eds., *Equal at the Creation: Sexism, Society and Christian Thought* (Toronto: University of Toronto Press, 1998), 25.

11. Amy-Jill Levine, "Lilies of the Field and Wandering Jews: Biblical Scholarship, Women's Roles, and Social Location," in Ingrid Rosa Kitzberger, ed., *Transformative Encounters: Jesus and Women Re-Viewed* (Leiden, Netherlands: Brill, 1999), 332.

12. See Anthony J. Saldarini, *Pharisees, Scribes and Sadducees in Palestinian Society* (Wilmington, DE: Michael Glazier, 1988).

13. Tereza Cavalcanti, "Jesus, the Penitent Woman, and the Pharisee," *Journal of Hispanic/Latino Theology* 2, no. 1 (1994): 40.

14. H. Kinukawa, *Women and Jesus in Mark: A Japanese Feminist Perspective* (Maryknoll, NY: Orbis Books, 1994), 12, 27.

15. See Ross S. Kraemer, "Jewish Women and Christian Women: Some Caveats," in Kraemer and Mary Rose D'Angelo, eds., *Women and Christian Origins* (Oxford: Oxford University Press, 1999), 36.

16. D'Angelo, "Gender," 25.

17. Elizabeth A. Johnson, *Truly Our Sister: A Theology of Mary in the Communion of Saints* (New York: Continuum, 2003), 170.

18. Johnson, *Truly Our Sister*, 171.

Further Reading

Johnson, Elizabeth A. *Truly Our Sister: A Theology of Mary in the Communion of Saints*. New York: Continuum, 2003, esp. 137–206.

Kraemer, Ross, and Mary Rose D'Angelo, eds. *Women and Christian Origins*. New York: Oxford University Press, 1999.

8

CHAPTER

Jewish Feminist Scholars: Vibrant Voices in New Testament Study

Deirdre Good

Y EARS AGO, when I first came to New York City and was introduced to the world of opera, it was love at first sight. I went to the Metropolitan and to City Opera as often as I could afford it and began a compact disc collection of operas. My head was full of Italian arias and lyrics, of Norse sagas and tragic deaths. I loved the emotional interpretation opera gave to triumph and tragedy, life and death. I became aware, however, that while there were good singers to be heard at these venues, I had missed Birgit Nilsson, Elizabeth Schwarzkopf, Joan Sutherland, and Marilyn Horne in their prime. And before them, of course, the great Maria Callas. I went to a concert given by Dame Joan Sutherland and her husband Richard

Bonynge, but it was not opera. I did manage to catch Marilyn Horne in *Semiramide* once. But during the first few years of my grand passion, I felt as though I hd arrived too late.

Yet in a few years, new singers appeared—Cecilia Bartoli, Renee Fleming, Dorothea Roschmann, Jane Eaglen, and Bryn Terfel—offering rich interpretations and new discoveries of their own. My thoughts nowadays do not turn backward to those whom I have not heard but to dreams of works I could commission now that there are such splendid singers.

It is much the same in the field of feminist scholarship on the topic of anti-Judaism and the New Testament. When I began teaching, fresh from graduate school, over twenty years ago, the words of Krister Stendahl and Rosemary Ruether were almost the only ones to be heard on this topic. They were more than enough for a while. And they reminded us that women and men could be (and still are) jointly engaged in articulating God's eternal covenant alongside the human pursuit of justice. Since then, thanks be to God, we have learned that we cannot maintain the distinctiveness of Jesus at the expense of his Jewish environment. We know the perils of supersessionism present in lectionary selections proclaimed every week in Christian churches.

In particular, Jewish women scholars have contributed rich resources: lives of Jesus; studies of anti-Judaism within New Testament scholarship itself; and critical feminist scholarship on central areas of New Testament study, including older feminist scholarship. Their work is the focus of this chapter. Given the degree of anti-Judaism that many Christian feminists have folded into their work (see the chapter in this volume by Mary Boys), the perspectives of Jewish feminist scholars are of enormous value in correcting the distortions and oversimplifications of such work.

Because the body of their work is so extensive, I have chosen to provide an overview of the contributions of seven Jewish feminist scholars, and then to focus in somewhat greater detail on several. The brevity of this chapter precludes a detailed analysis of any one scholar, let alone all of them. My goal is to offer readers a sampling of their voices as a way of illuminating the contributions Jewish women have made to the conversation with Christian feminist theology.

And, just as new singers appeared on the opera stage, so too are new Jewish scholars of Christian origins emerging. So even by the time this book is published, the chorus of Jewish voices will have increased, much to the benefit of Christian as well as Jewish audiences.

Of the seven Jewish scholars whose work is considered in this chapter—
Paula Fredriksen, Susannah Heschel, Ross Kraemer, Amy-Jill Levine, Judith
Plaskow, Adele Reinhartz, and Claudia Setzer—two teach at a Catholic
college and one at a Protestant theological school.[1] Plaskow specializes in
contemporary religious thought, with an emphasis on feminism; Kraemer
in women's religious history; and Heschel in modern Jewish thought, with
a focus on Christian theological work that contributed to and sustained
Nazi ideology. Fredriksen, Levine, Reinhartz, and Setzer are scholars of the
New Testament.

A Trio of Scholars of Religious Studies

Judith Plaskow, who teaches at a Catholic college (Manhattan College), was
among the first Jewish feminists to explore patriarchal bias in Christian
texts—in her case, the texts of leading Protestant theologians Reinhold
Niebuhr and Paul Tillich. Beginning with her dissertation at Yale in the
early 1970s, and continuing with the publication in 1980 of *Sex, Sin and
Grace*, Plaskow analyzed the way in which Niebuhr and Tillich's understanding of sin rested upon gender bias.[2] Most notably, she revealed the way
in which their assumption that pride was the overriding sin ignored women's
experience. Plaskow then turned her considerable analytic powers to the
assumptions of Christian feminists, exposing the way in which some had
held Judaism responsible for patriarchy.[3] She further developed this critique
in a 1991 article suggesting that feminist struggles with "patriarchal
Christologies" generate a "dilemma that leads back into the trap of anti-
Judaism." If, she asks, "claims about Jesus' distinctiveness are intrinsic to
Christianity," then "is there any way to make these claims that does not end
up rejecting or disparaging Judaism as their left hand?"[4] Plaskow's question
remains as a challenge.

Bearing broad similarities with the work of Plaskow, Susannah
Heschel's work on anti-Judaism draws upon her original research in (East)
German archives. Her scholarship traces the depths of theological bias
against Judaism that established and sustained the ground for Nazi ideology. I have heard her speak with passion and authority on this topic, and
consider her work of the utmost importance.

Of particular note is her searing critique of the Institute for the Study
and Eradication of Jewish Influence on German Church Life, founded in
1939. The Institute created a "niche for itself within a Nazi regime that had
little use for theologians." As a way of inflating their own importance, the

Institute's theologians highlighted their alleged expertise as scholars of Judaism. Yet, as Heschel shows, the Institute became a "vehicle to disseminate propaganda in support of persecution of Jews." Moreover, their servitude to the interests of the Third Reich had roots deep in Protestant New Testament scholarship in which "Judaism was fetishized as a degenerate, legalistic religion to distract from the failure of Christian theology to maintain a coherent claim to originality and uniqueness."[5] Heschel expands this critique of New Testament scholarship in her 1999 book, written with Robert Ericksen, *Betrayal: German Churches and the Holocaust.*[6]

No one can doubt the influence of this tradition on New Testament scholarship in the twentieth century, particularly through the work of Walter Grundmann and Gerhard Kittel in the multivolume series *Theological Dictionary of the New Testament*. It is ironical, given the ideological distortions of this resource, that a team is still translating the companion volume, *Theological Dictionary of the Old Testament*, into English! Some at least have pointed out the shortcomings of the theological aspects of this multivolume work.[7] Others have raised the possibility that the political situation in Nazi Germany caused changes in the work of individual authors (e.g., Rudolf Bultmann's second edition of *The Theology of the New Testament* downplays connections to and the influence of Hebrew scriptures). Only Heschel, however, has had the tenacity to identify the connections between its authors, the German Protestant Church, and the Institute for the Study and Eradication of Jewish Influence on German Religious Life.

At the same time, her study of the work and influence of nineteenth-century Jewish scholar Abraham Geiger reveals a body of scholarship that Protestant (and Catholic) New Testament scholars should take seriously. Historian Geiger situates Jesus within Jewish life of his day, portraying him as a Pharisee.[8] Yet Christian scholars, limited by their ideological blinders, have rejected Geiger's portrayal of a Jewish Jesus because it seems to undermine Christian claims of Jesus' uniqueness. The moral imperative of Heschel's work is a warning to us all: de-Judaizing Christianity by portraying an Aryan Jesus or the Cynic, non-Jewish Jesus of the Jesus Seminar and several modern lives of Jesus is a form of anti-Judaism.

Like Heschel's work, Ross Kraemer's historical analysis has exposed anti-Judaism. Kraemer's work, however, deals with antiquity and offers readers a more complex understanding of the status of Jewish women in the Second Temple period. In contrast to some Christian scholars who emphasize the subjugated status of Jewish women in order to highlight the liberating possibilities of Jesus' Movement and Christianity, Kraemer painstakingly details the status of women in Greco-Roman culture. She widens the context; what is often attributed to *Jewish* constructions of gender must be regarded as the gender constructions of antiquity. Ancient understandings of gender pressured all women, not just Jewish women, to conform. Thus, in analyzing why women might have become disciples of Jesus, Kraemer argues it is necessary to identify issues of importance to Jews of both genders in the first century: the oppression of Roman rule, the corruption of the Herodian rulers, the efficacy of the Temple. Sources do not support gender differentiation within Judaism as a motivation for women to follow Jesus.

In situating the lives of Jewish women in the wider world of Greco-Roman culture, Kraemer shows that *gender imposed restrictions on all women*, whether in constraining their participation in public life or in regulating their dress and access to education. Nevertheless, variables such as social class, free birth or enslavement, demographics, and diet also affected women. The constraints on women took on particular forms, so Jewish women thus had limited participation in the temple cult, and less access to learning and legal status. Yet in some communities, Jewish women played leading roles in communal life, donating financially and serving as officers of the synagogues. A major conclusion one might draw from Kraemer's work is that discussion of first-century Jewish women must always be situated in the larger context of women in the Greco-Roman world.[9]

A Quartet of New Testament Scholars

Just as Kraemer has broadened the picture of Jewish women, so Claudia Setzer has illumined the complexities of the interaction between Jews and Christians in the first two centuries. Setzer focuses on the varied ways in which Jews responded to Christians, showing the range from tolerance to physical threats to verbal attacks. In discussing Jewish "persecution" of Christians (e.g., the stoning of Stephen, Acts 7:57-60), she suggests that the term covered a great deal of territory—from harassment to judicial flogging to mob violence. "Persecution" is imprecise in another way: although implying sympathy with the victims and judgment on the responsible party, it gives no clue about what motivated the "persecutors" or how they understood their actions. For example, once Paul becomes a believer in the Way of Jesus, he says in retrospect that he *persecuted* the early church. At the time of his actions, however, did he not understand himself as *safeguarding* Judaism?

Setzer concludes that Jews who did not share belief in Jesus and Christians (both Jewish and Gentile) differed about when they became separate entities, with Jews not seeing Christians as separate until the mid-second century. Christians, however, were conscious much earlier of being distinct from other Jews. She suggests that the social sciences help to interpret this phenomenon. On the one hand, as long as the parent group does not categorize those who deviate as outsiders, it can hope for their return. On the other, those disaffected from the larger parent group typically claim that they alone truly represent the values and goals of the parent group.[10]

Setzer's latest book, *Resurrection of the Body in Early Judaism and Early Christianity: Doctrine, Community, and Self-Definition*, looks at a number of early communities where belief in resurrection seemed to be a boundary marker for who was in and out of the community. In trying to answer the question of why such an abstract idea became so crucial that people were "written off" for not accepting it, Setzer draws upon language and categories from the social sciences and rhetorical studies. She concludes that the resurrection of the body is a useful symbol in the construction of community because it carries multiple ideas in tow, including the power and providence of God, the unity of body and soul, ultimate justice, proof from scripture, and the legitimacy of those who preach it. Resurrection becomes shorthand for these ideas. She also traces the burgeoning of an articulate resurrection apologetic in early Christian thinkers from Justin onward. Resurrection seems to carry many of the same ideas that appear in Jewish sources (and is implicit in the Hebrew Bible), but it gets a new lease on life in many Christian circles.[11]

In their recent book, *Jesus, Judaism and Christian Anti-Judaism: Reading the New Testament after the Holocaust*, five Jewish and Christian scholars analyze ways in which the New Testament itself is a source of Christian anti-Judaism.[12] I will concentrate on the three women (Fredriksen, Levine, and Reinhartz), using the essay of each as an opening to their larger work that holds particular significance for Christians.

Historian Paula Fredriksen's essay "The Birth of Christianity and the Origins of Anti-Judaism" argues that as the identity and theology of certain types of Gentile Christianities developed in the second century, so too the use of demeaning views of Judaism grew to express that theology. Apologists for Gentile Christianity argued with Jews (whether explicitly or implicitly) about which community more truly read the scriptures. The theologies of these apologists served to clarify self-identity over and against "Jews," that is, they provided a Christian antitype.

Fredriksen's *Jesus of Nazareth, King of the Jews: A Jewish Life and the Emergence of Christianity* is the first book on Jesus by a woman scholar who is neither a priest, nor a rabbi, nor, by her own admission, a theologian.[13] And yet her book is also traditional, as is another book written from a Jewish perspective.[14] Indeed, what serious scholar writing on Jesus today would cavil at the book's premise that Jesus was a first-century Jew who tried to communicate with other Jews? Fredriksen analyzes the complexities of Jewish life in first-century, Roman-ruled Palestine that led to his death.

Fredriksen acknowledges that "the single most solid fact about Jesus' life is his death." She examines the relative responsibility of Jews and of Romans for the crucifixion of Jesus, and, in a nuanced manner, assigns responsibility for Jesus' death to Pilate and Jewish religious leaders. Noting that "though Jesus was executed as a political insurrectionist, his followers were not," it follows, she argues, that many modern interpretations of him have failed to note the political nature of the charge against him (see Joseph Tyson's "The Death of Jesus" in this volume). In a carefully wrought discussion of the several historical "contexts," Fredriksen probes the differences between Judea and the Galilee, and examines the role of the followers of John the Baptist, illumining the light these forces shed on the gospel account.

A long chapter in Fredriksen's *Jesus of Nazareth*, "Trajectories: Paul, the Gospels, and Jesus," traces links backward from evidence for the mission to Gentiles in the diaspora to traditions in the gospels similar to or supportive of themes in Paul's letters. By tracing trajectories, Fredriksen obtains a glimpse into the earlier stages of Jesus' Movement. If data match information about early Judaism from independent sources such as Josephus' histories or the Dead Sea Scrolls, Fredriksen argues, they can help identify aspects of earliest Christianity that may go back to the lifetime and mission of Jesus himself. For example, Paul's apocalyptic statements in his letters about the nearness of the end are corroborated by the message of God's imminent kingdom reported as Jesus' first words in Mark's gospel ("The Kingdom of God is at hand.") Like Paul, Mark goes on (in chapter 13) to identify travails, social as well as celestial, as marking the onset of the end. Changes to Mark in Matthew and particularly Luke soften Mark's urgency. Following this trajectory backward into "the documentary void that surrounds the historical Jesus" (89), Fredriksen notes the prominence of apocalyptic language from Isaiah in early gospels, like Mark's, confirming, among other things, the announcement of God's reign and the centrality of Jerusalem "at the heart of this ancient redemptive myth" (96). Belief in an imminent end burgeons into ethical teachings (refusal to judge, passive resistance to evil, sexual continence) that were valid only in the short term.

Another trajectory Fredriksen traces back to both Paul and Mark probably goes back to Jesus himself, perhaps at his final Passover in Jerusalem: the practice of a communal meal anticipating the coming kingdom. Likewise, the Essenes observed a common meal in anticipation of the end-time messianic banquet. Similarly, the claim of the gospels that Jesus was Messiah, the anointed one of God, is also found in Paul: that Jesus was the son of David "according to the flesh," that is, by physical descent. While early writers clearly redefine "Messiah" to bring their understanding into line with their religious convictions about Jesus (the Messiah is one who suffers, dies, and rises after three days), the concept nonetheless coheres with Jesus' crucifixion and the inscription over the cross, "The King of the Jews." This discussion is very important. For those who are in search of the historical Jesus, the discussion speaks to the question of messianic self-consciousness. Yet Fredriksen avoids this morass—into which many New Testament scholars fall—preferring to dwell on the meaning of the crucifixion as a historical event enacted by the Romans, who intended it to deter the followers of Jesus. I think, however, the issue requires more discussion. Matthew, for example, elaborates the motif through use of the prophet Zechariah (see Matt 21:5, drawing upon Zech 9:9). He thus opens a window both onto the Hellenistic ideal of a meek king and onto the person of Jesus, born "King of the Jews," as the Magi first call him (Matt 2:2). Matthew does this without differentiating between who Jesus was and his own, later description of Jesus.[15]

By situating Jesus in the complexities of first-century, Roman-ruled Palestine, Fredriksen offers understandings that counter the anti-Jewish interpretations so typical among people who adopt the ahistorical, literalist reading of scripture that Philip Cunningham addresses in his chapter in this volume.

Amy-Jill Levine, in her essay in *Jesus, Judaism and Christian Anti-Judaism*, "Matthew, Mark and Luke: Good News or Bad?" argues that historical-critical readings of biblical texts must acknowledge the complexity of perspectives, since the same texts may give rise to anti-Jewish, neutral, or even pro-Jewish readings. In her "cautionary conclusion," Levine identifies links between interpretations of anti-Jewish texts and the tragic consequences such readings have had for Jews. When Jews and Christians study anti-Jewish passages together, they make more adequate interpretations possible. Moreover, interpretation is part of a developing tradition. Most Christians, for example, no longer (if they ever did) read New Testament texts in a literalistic fashion, such as the insistence in 1 Timothy 2:15 that women will be "saved through childbearing" or the vision of Revelation 14:1–4 that the saved are 144,000 "who have not defiled themselves with women, for they are virgins . . . [who] follow the Lamb wherever he goes." Rather, over time, realization of the toxic consequences of interpretation as well as new insights about texts have revealed new layers of meaning:

> Through history, through what some would call the actions of the Holy Spirit, texts that negate the fullness of human life, texts that appear to enjoin evil, slavery, or war, are given new interpretations. The time is surely here for the anti-Jewish texts, or, perhaps to put it better, the texts that can be and have been seen as anti-Jewish, to undergo the same critical, merciful treatment.

The tools of modern biblical study that situate texts in their contexts are, Levine argues, necessary but insufficient. Theology must be part of the process; theology must accompany history in order for anti-Jewish readings to be eradicated. It was theology, she notes, that provided the basis for the church to decide—centuries too late—that slavery was contrary to love of God and neighbor. This changed theological outlook resulted in new interpretations of texts. Now theology must respond to the charge that arose with special fervor in the wake of the Enlightenment: that we can understand the significance of Jesus when we contrast his loving message with the legalism of ossified Judaism.

Part of the theological task involves correcting assumptions, such as the equation of impurity with sin or that Jews regarded the "Law" as burdensome. Liberation theology, in particular, is implicated in such falsifications, as Levine details at length in a brilliant essay, "Lilies of the Field and Wandering Jews," in which she cites numerous examples from feminist-liberationist works that reflect the "weeds of anti-Judaism."[16] Many of the instances she documents reflect an assumption of binary opposition in which the significance of Jesus is heightened by contrasting him to a patriarchal, legalistic, and monolithic Judaism. Levine's examples reveal how much anti-Judaism continues to plague Christian commentators. The following is a sampling from among the many "weeds" she finds in the fields of commentaries:

- Jesus was not like the Jews, who "excluded foreigners from [their] ethnic borders in order to retain their purity of blood."

- Women, because they were not circumcised, "could not be part of God's covenant."
- "Women in India have not come very far from Judaic times," when women were "powerless, nameless, voiceless."
- The account of the hemorrhaging woman (Luke 8:40–56; Mark 5:33–34; Matt) centers on a woman who felt herself "degraded"; Jesus saw "her as a person dehumanized by the laws that have been used only to satisfy the honor of men with power."
- "Jesus died as a result of the clash between his God [uppercase] and the god [lowercase] of Pharisaic Judaism. . . . Jesus' crucifixion marked the temporal triumph of the patriarchal god of Judaism."

In speculating on what might eliminate these weeds of anti-Judaism, Levine again argues for the importance of personal contact, both with Jewish sources of the Second Temple period (e.g., Dead Sea Scrolls, Josephus, Philo, Apocrypha, and Pseudepigrapha) and with Jews. She notes that another generation of feminist scholars may perpetuate their predecessors' distorted views of Judaism. "Worse," she writes, "as women scholars begin to write for their own communities in Asia, Africa, Latin America, Eastern Europe, etc., the weed of anti-Judaism threatens to overrun the new plantings." Levine believes that "Jesus can remain the liberationist Christian feminists want without being removed from his Jewish context."

The final essay in *Jesus, Judaism and Christian Anti-Judaism*, by Adele Reinhartz—"The Gospel of John: How the Jews Became Part of the Plot"—analyzes how the fourth gospel weaves together three interrelated levels or stories in which "the Jews" function in positive and negative ways: a narrative about the historical Jesus; a story about the Johannine community, for which this gospel was a central document; and a story about the universe that also explains God's relationship to humankind. In the primary narrative the hero is Jesus and his opponents are the Jews and their authorities, who believe that he poses a threat to their community in light of its delicate relations with Rome. They are responsible for his death despite the fact that Pilate orders Jesus' crucifixion. In the second level we discern the Johannine community as it struggled to define itself in relation to the surrounding world. For many scholars the gospel articulates the Johannine community's experience of expulsion from a larger Jewish community. But this interpretation simply places responsibility for anti-Judaism on the shoulders of the Jews themselves. In fact, there is no evidence that such a persecution took place. In the third level, the hero is the Word becoming flesh and the villain "the ruler of the world" (14:30). The hero descends to the world and in his mission defeats "the ruler of the world" and returns to the Father. Behind the Word Christology lie texts like Proverbs 8 and Sirach 24. Contrasting metaphors describe dichotomous states of being (light/darkness; above/below) and activities (believing/disbelieving; love/hate), the positive being associated with Jesus and the negative with opponents, particularly Jewish characters in the narrative. In the end it is impossible to deny that the Johannine Jesus is described as having superseded the Jewish covenant and taken over its major institutions and symbols. Yet it is also possible to say that John's descriptions of relationships between Jews and Jewish Christ-confessors are actually more nuanced than the sweeping denunciations of the narrator or an expulsion theory. For example, in John 11, when Jesus arrives in Bethany in response to a request from Mary and Martha to heal their (dead) brother Lazarus, he finds them in mourning surrounded and comforted by many Jews (11:19). Likewise 12:10–11 indicates that Jewish leaders are upset about Jews who begin to believe in Jesus on account of Lazarus. They do not expel Jewish believers in Christ from the Jewish community.[17]

Conclusion: "Dead Man Walking"

The modern opera *Dead Man Walking,* by American composer Jake Heggie and playwright Terrence McNally, building on the book of the same name by Sr. Helen Prejean, offers a model for where we are going. At the end of the opera, Joseph de Rocher's salvation is still in the balance. The violence of what he has done is as graphically portrayed as his execution by lethal injection. But it is through his relationship with Sr. Helen Prejean that he approaches redemption and salvation.

With the help of feminist scholarship from Jewish women, we must acknowledge the complicity of the gospel narratives and some interpreters in the crime of anti-Judaism (albeit in different ways) and their use to justify anti-Jewish sentiments and actions. After their trial and sentencing, what of them can we rehabilitate? With Sr. Helen Prejean we must keep focused on the possibility of redemption even for the worst criminal and sing: "He will gather us together." We are engaged in a spiritual journey wherein *together* we must answer this question in wider communities: within Christian communities and with our Jewish brothers and sisters.

Notes

1. Both Setzer and Plaskow teach at Manhattan College in Riverdale, New York, and Levine at the Divinity School of Vanderbilt University in Nashville, Tennessee. The four New Testament scholars are typically more interested in the historical than the theological dimension of the world of the texts. Although space does not allow for description of their work, I take note also of New Testament scholars Pamela Eisenbaum and Sara Tanzer, both of whom teach at Protestant seminaries (Eisenbaum at the Iliff School of Theology [United Methodist] in Denver, and Tanzer at McCormick Seminary [Presbyterian Church U.S.A.] in Chicago).

2. Judith Plaskow, *Sex, Sin, and Grace: Women's Experience and the Theologies of Reinhold Niebuhr and Paul Tillich* (Washington, DC: University Press of America, 1980).

3. Judith Plaskow, "Blaming Jews for Inventing Patriarchy," in Evelyn T. Beck, ed., *Nice Jewish Girls* (Trumansburg, NY: Crossing, 1982); originally published in *Lilith* 7 (1979): 9–11, 14–17.

4. In Helen P. Fry, ed., *Christian-Jewish Dialogue: A Reader* (Exeter: University of Exeter Press, 1996), 235; Plaskow's essay originally appeared as "Feminist Anti-Judaism and the Christian God," *Journal of Feminist Studies in Religion* 7, no. 2 (fall 1991): 104–7.

5. Susannah Heschel, "Post-Holocaust Jewish Reflections on German Theology," in Carol Rittner and John Roth, eds., *From the Unthinkable to the Unavoidable* (London: Greenwood, 1997), 55–66. See also her "Nazifying Christian Theology: Walter Grundmann and the Institute for the Study and Eradication of Jewish Influence on German Church Life," *Church History* 63 (1994): 587–605; and "New Testament Scholarship on the 'Aryan Jesus' during the Third Reich," in Benjamin G. Wright, ed., *A Multiform Heritage: Studies on Early Judaism and Christianity* (Atlanta: Scholars, 1999), 67–92.

6. Susannah Heschel and Robert Ericksen, *Betrayal: German Churches and the Holocaust* (Philadelphia: Fortress, 1999).

7. See James Barr, *The Semantics of Biblical Language* (Oxford: Oxford University Press, 1961).

8. Susannah Heschel's *Abraham Geiger and the Jewish Jesus* (Chicago: University of Chicago Press, 1998) was awarded a National Jewish Book Award that year.

9. See Ross Kraemer, "Jewish Women and Christian Women: Some Caveats," and "Jewish Women and Women's Judaism(s) at the Beginning of Christianity," in Kraemer and Mary Rose D'Angelo, eds., *Women and Christian Origins* (New York: Oxford University Press, 1999), 35–49 and 50–79, respectively.

10. Claudia Setzer, *Jewish Responses to Early Christians: History and Polemics, 30–150 C.E.* (Minneapolis: Fortress, 1994), 165–90.

11. Claudia J. Setzer, *Resurrection of the Body in Early Judaism and Early Christianity: Doctrine, Community, and Self-Definition* (Leiden, Netherlands: Brill, 2004).

12. Paula Fredriksen and Adele Reinhartz, eds., *Jesus, Judaism and Christian Anti-Judaism: Reading the New Testament after the Holocaust* (Louisville, KY: Westminster / John Knox, 2002).

13. Paula Fredriksen, *Jesus of Nazareth, King of the Jews: A Jewish Life and the Emergence of Christianity* (New York: Knopf, 1999).

14. See Geza Vermes, *Jesus the Jew: A Historian's Reading of the Gospels* (Minneapolis: Fortress, 2003).

15. I have argued this in Deirdre Good, *Jesus the Meek King* (Philadelphia: Trinity Press International, 1999).

16. Amy-Jill Levine, "Lilies of the Field and Wandering Jews: Biblical Scholarship, Women's Roles, and Social Location," in Ingrid Rosa Kitzberger, ed., *Transformative Encounters: Jesus and Women Re-Viewed* (Leiden, Netherlands: Brill, 1999), 330–52.

17. Reinhartz develops this three-tiered reading of the Gospel of John in her book *Befriending the Beloved Disciple* (New York: Crossroad, 2002).

Further Reading

Heschel, Susannah. *Abraham Geiger and the Jewish Jesus*. Chicago: University of Chicago Press, 1998.

Kitzberger, Ingrid Rosa, ed., *Transformative Encounters: Jesus and Women Re-Viewed*. Leiden, Netherlands: Brill, 1999.

Kraemer, Ross Shepard, and Mary Rose D'Angelo, eds. *Women and Christian Origins*. New York: Oxford University Press, 1999.

PART

Judaism Is a Living Faith, Enriched by Many Centuries of Development

9
CHAPTER

"In Every Generation": Judaism as a Living Faith

Peter A. Pettit and John Townsend

RECENTLY, in a Sunday morning adult forum that one of us was teaching in a local Christian congregation, a man described the trajectory of God's people through history. "The Jews before Jesus were on the track, but when God presented a major leap forward through the teaching of Jesus, they didn't leap with it and were simply left behind." Acknowledging that they certainly had continued on historically as a community, he asserted that the Jews nevertheless had been dropped from covenantal life with God. They remained "stuck" while the people of God—those who followed and ultimately those who worshiped Jesus—carried it forward. No one in the forum challenged his view.

This picture of Jews as anachronistic remnants of a time and religion long surpassed unfortunately retains its currency. Yet Judaism is not simply the religion of what Christians call the "Old Testament." Just as we Christians have built our religion upon the basis of this collection of books, so have our Jewish neighbors. Just as Christians have developed a religion from this root that stresses love, so have Jews. The daily prayers for every Jew stress that the primary command is to "love the Lord your God with all your heart, and with all your soul, and with all your might." Indeed, the Gospel of Mark (12:28–29) has Jesus, when asked which commandment is most important, cite this prayer.[1]

Because Judaism and Christianity today both claim the heritage of biblical Israel, many mistakenly assume that they compete for that heritage.[2] They work from the logic of "zero-sum": only one can be legitimate and the other must be a pretender, whether deluded and mistaken or deliberately and perversely misleading. In such a view, the true faith (whichever it is) has nothing to learn from the other, except perhaps by the negative example of mistakes to be avoided. In fact, this has been the prevailing view of Judaism for a majority of the Christian church since the age of Augustine (ca. 400 C.E.), who portrayed the Jews as "stranded in useless antiquity."[3]

Paul, a Jewish apostle of Jesus in the first century C.E., wrestled with the coexistence of unbelievers and believers—Jews who rejected any messianic or divine claims about Jesus, on the one hand, and those, on the other hand, both Jew and Gentile, who accepted them. In his letter to the Romans, he made it clear that he thought everyone should see in Jesus what he saw: the power of God's righteousness bringing redemption and salvation to the whole world.

Many of his fellow Jews did not see it this way, however, and Paul wondered, "Has God rejected God's own people?" "Most assuredly not" (or, "No way!"), came the reply just as quickly, "for the gifts and the calling of God are irrevocable." This response goes against what has long been the conventional understanding: Paul affirmed that God has chosen both those who believe in Jesus and those who do not. He calls it a mystery, but confesses that "all Israel will be saved," that God will "be merciful to all" (see Rom 11 for all these quotations).

Until that day, God continues to work in both communities with the powers of creation, redemption, and sanctification, to use the classical Christian language of the Trinity. Of course, the Jews of the last two thousand years have not associated these terms with three persons in the God whom they daily acclaim as One. But Jews affirm these same powers of God in the liturgy of the synagogue and whenever they study scripture and its interpretation.

Other aspects of God have become important, too, because of the Jews' distinctive experience, both within and apart from Christendom. If Paul is right—and we believe he is—God has been at work in these developments in Judaism as much as in the growth of the church. So Christians ignore the life and insight of Judaism over these two millennia at the risk of missing something true and meaningful about God. More directly, we do so at the risk of misunderstanding those who, Paul said, are beloved of God.

Learning more about both the record and how Jews have experienced it offers Christians new insights into God's ways among us. Here we will offer a broad overview of Jewish history, highlighting five periods and reflecting on what Christians might learn from it.

Crisis and Canon

Whenever the people of God underwent a major crisis in ancient times, they sorted through their inherited traditions (scriptures), examined their lives and their world, and began to tell the story of God's work among them in new ways that made sense of the crisis. In the sixth century B.C.E., the Jerusalem Temple that Solomon had built was destroyed and the people were sent into exile in Babylon for two generations.

The Torah story that emerged from that crisis begins with God's ordering of the whole creation and ends (in Deuteronomy) with the people of Israel still outside the promised land. In the exilic context of its writing, the Torah affirms that the whole earth and all creation are God's, and that Israel could live and thrive without the promised land and without the Temple. Surely both land and Temple remained hopes and dreams for Israel—the land was still the focus of the people's journeying, and the plans for the Temple were described in great detail in God's word from Mt. Sinai. But the powerful Torah message is that Jews could be Jews even when sovereignty and Temple are only hopes.[4]

Later in the sixth century B.C.E., a new ruler, King Cyrus, sent the Jews back to Jerusalem from Babylonia, and in the century that followed they were permitted to rebuild the Jerusalem Temple. For the period that followed, up until 70 C.E., Jews lived in a world of both Torah and Temple. As Joseph Tyson's chapter "Jesus—A Faithful Jew" shows, by the first century C.E. there were many ways in which different Jewish groups taught their followers to orbit around those two poles of their religious identity. In suppressing the revolt of Jewish Zealots, Roman forces destroyed the Temple and burned Jerusalem in 70 C.E, triggering another crisis.

Once again the tradition proved resilient, and Judaism emerged from the catastrophe of 70 C.E with a newly reshaped focus. Synagogues had begun to proliferate as community gathering centers even while the Temple still stood, and their prayer services were scheduled at the times of the daily Temple sacrifices. Often these included the same prayers that the priests recited in Jerusalem.

For a time, it seems that some priests did continue to offer sacrifices in the midst of the Temple ruins. But the adjustment to a religion without Temple sacrifice became particularly necessary after a second revolt—the Bar Cochba rebellion of 132–135 C.E. After the Romans crushed this revolt, the emperor barred Jews from living in Jerusalem and prohibited worship at the Temple site. During this period two major Jewish groups came to the fore. The first was the Christian church, which became less Jewish as more Gentiles became Christians.

The second included the Pharisees, who formed the basis of what later became Rabbinic Judaism (the titles "rabban" and "rabbi" were most likely introduced only after the fall of the Temple and were limited to those in the land of Israel). It is necessary to keep in mind, however, that Rabbinic Judaism did not become normative within Judaism for some time. Most Jews were far too acculturated to Greco-Roman culture, as the remains of their synagogues and other artifacts indicate.[5] Rabbinic Judaism achieved its full eminence only after the empire became Christian in the fourth century.

The Mishnah is the first compilation of rabbinic teaching; the name reflects both its character as "second Torah" and the imperative that it be "repeated" from generation to generation. Edited around the year 200 C.E. by Rabbi Judah from materials attributed to teachers from the previous two centuries, the Mishnah consists primarily of legislation on how Jews ought to live. Divided by subjects into tractates, this legislation could even supersede what we might regard as the literal meaning of the Hebrew Bible. For example, the Mishnah interprets "eye for eye, tooth for tooth" (Exod 21:24; Lev 24:20; Deut 19:21) to mean that one should pay compensation for injury rather than undergo matching bodily harm.[6] The Mishnah also includes considerable legislation about running the Jerusalem Temple, an indication of a continuing hope that the Temple would be rebuilt.

During the centuries that followed, commentators expanded the Mishnah to meet changing needs. These expansions are called *gemara,* or "completion," and developed separately in the main centers of Judaism, Israel and Babylonia. The Mishnah with its respective *gemaras* became the Babylonian and the Jerusalem talmuds. The Jerusalem Talmud was redacted rather abruptly, probably about 375 C.E. The Babylonian Talmud (the *Bavli*), however, continued to grow into the early sixth century, with a few additions coming later.[7] The Babylonian Talmud remains the central religious and legal authority in Rabbinic Judaism.

Like the Pharisees who were their forerunners during Temple times, the authorities of the Mishnah (known as *Tannas*) emphasized the practice of a life pattern (*halakhah*) that would mark God's people as distinctively as the Temple had marked the horizon of the Judean hills. According to Shimon the Righteous, this pattern would sustain not only Jewish life after the Temple's destruction, but the whole world: "On three things does the world rest: on Torah, on worship, and on acts of mercy."[8]

This formulation shifted the focus from the Temple to daily life, and the rabbinic tradition that would gradually achieve dominance over the next five centuries emphasized the importance of Jewish perseverance, whether God seemed near or far, ready to act or mysteriously distracted. Such an emphasis made good sense for a people who watched the power of imperial Rome destroy their Temple and sack their capital city, and who witnessed a nascent imperial Christianity relegate them to second-class citizenship and legislate against the practice of their religion. If God was not taking the initiative to stop such indignities, could it be God who would best decide how Jews were to respond?

In Deuteronomy 30:12, the Torah states that God's commandment is "not in heaven." The rabbis of the talmudic period (known as *Amoras*) understood this to mean that interpretation of scripture would come through human scrutiny of the Torah text and debate about its application to life. They tell the story of a rabbi who was debating others; one day, when asked for proof of his position, he invoked God's own voice from heaven. Immediately, all in the room heard that divine endorsement, yet the other rabbis still rejected his position, saying, "It is not in heaven." The story goes on to say that at that same moment in heaven God chuckled approvingly at the skillfulness and insight of the rabbis.[9]

In another mishnaic passage, Ben Zoma asks his students several questions. "Who is wise? Who is strong? Who is wealthy? Who is honored?" In each case, the conventional answer focuses on the recognition and deference of others. But Ben Zoma turns the answers around and grounds these virtues in individual, even internal, qualities. He says that one is wise who learns from all people; that one is strong who masters the inclination to do evil; that one is wealthy who is satisfied with whatever is available; that one is honored who honors all things in creation.[10] As Western Jews learned to live under the power of the Christian church and Christian rulers in the years leading up to the establishment of the Holy Roman Empire, their canon led them into wisdom that afforded personal dignity and human virtue from sources that were unassailable by any external social or political power.

The Christian church can learn from this era in Jewish life. The shameful treatment that a Christian state and church doled out to the Jewish people proffers a sobering lesson. The insight that God was at work among those Jews offers a positive lesson as well. Jews showed that even in circumstances that promise little comfort and few advantages for our lives, we can live the life of God's people faithfully. Even when it is difficult to see that God is present and acting on our behalf, we can grab hold of the scriptures that are God's Word and find in them, for ourselves and by ourselves, the way to respond as God's people in this world. Rather than despair at the loss of the Temple and power, and even the respect of those in power, Rabbinic Judaism drew a new kind of strength from the confidence that what God had once given would be sufficient for all times, and that what is most important in life cannot be taken away by anyone from the outside.

Maximizing Life on the Margins

Father Edward Flannery has described Jewish life in Christian lands during the Middle Ages as "the vale of tears."[11] There were devastating chapters, to be sure, beginning with the First Crusade in 1096 and extending throughout the world of Jewish life. The long and terrible—and sinful—history of Christian denigration of Jews, which in too many eras resulted in persecution and death, must never be ignored. In the political realm, social relations, economic development, and religious teaching, the Jews were made to serve the purposes of Christian society in terms dictated by both lords and bishops. In the Christian view, Judaism was a "necessary other," the negative through which Christianity shone its positive light. This view was largely a projection of Christian ignorance; there was much more to Jewish life and experience than the "wandering Jew" and the moneylender. Still, too few Christians know of the richness of postbiblical Judaism.

Eleventh-century France was the setting in which Judaism gained its most widely acclaimed Torah and Talmud commentaries. Rabbi Shlomo ben Yitzchak of Troyes (1040–1105), best known by the acronym "Rashi," wrote the standard commentary on the Babylonian Talmud, which had already become "the" Talmud. In fact, Rashi's commentary is essential for understanding the Talmud and is printed in every edition beside the text on the inside margins—the inner margins so that wear and tear on the edges of the books will not jeopardize his insights. Rashi also wrote works explaining the plain meaning (*peshat*) of biblical texts. A key element of his method was to interpret unfamiliar Hebrew and Aramaic terms by referring to the everyday French equivalents that his community would know. His biblical explanations can be found in the works of subsequent Christian Bible commentators, including Martin Luther, who also is well known for translating the Bible into the language of the day (in his case, German).

Even under the best of circumstances, Jews were rarely safe under Christian rulers. Jews generally tried to avoid open confrontation, but at times they were forced into debate. A notable case was that of the Spanish philosopher and exegete Nachmanides (also called "Ramban," an acronym for "Rabbi Moses ben Nahman"; 1194–1270). With the support of the Dominicans and the Franciscans, a Jewish convert to Christianity, Pablo Christiani, proposed to King James I of Aragon that a public debate take place with Nachmanides. With a promise of immunity from punishment, Nachmanides accepted the offer. The debate took place in July of 1263 with a clear victory on the part of Nachmanides.[12] At first the king kept his word and even paid Nachmanides 300 solidos, but, succumbing to pressure from the Dominicans, Pope Clement IV forced the king to abandon his promise. Nachmanides was put on trial in 1265, condemned, and forced to leave Spain. Another result of Nahmanides' victory was that Jews were forced to attend sermons by Dominican friars.

The greatest Jewish philosopher of all time, Rabbi Moses ben Maimon ("Rambam," or "Maimonides"; 1135–1204) also came from Spain. A physician by profession, the Rambam fled Muslim Spain in a period of anti-Jewish persecution and settled in Egypt, where his medical skills were recognized and employed by the famous Muslim ruler Saladin. His two greatest works are testimony to Jewish achievements of the Middle Ages.

The *Guide of the Perplexed* sets forth the Jewish religion in philosophical terms drawn from Aristotle. Though Judaism was well known as ancient and distinctive, this presentation made clear that it was neither esoteric nor accessible only by an intellectual elite. With Maimonides' *Guide*, Judaism could be grasped in the framework of a widely accepted classical philosophical system. In Latin translation, the *Guide* influenced Christian medieval thinkers, including Thomas Aquinas.

Maimonides' second great work, the *Mishneh Torah*, organized the Jewish life pattern (*halakhah*) into a clear topical arrangement from the more freely associative sequences of the Talmud. As literacy and learning spread throughout succeeding centuries, a person could locate all the pertinent Jewish law on a given topic much more easily in the *Mishneh Torah* than in the *Bavli*.

While Maimonides may have been the best-known Jewish medieval scholar, for later Jewish orthodoxy the most influential sage was Joseph ben Ephraim Caro (1488–1575). Caro built upon an earlier compilation of public and private law by Jacob ben Asher (ca. 1270–1340), and developed a commentary into a code entitled *Shulhan Arukh* (Prepared Table). For the most part, this code is the basis for Jewish law. While Jewish life has its roots in the Babylonian Talmud, it is the *Shulhan Arukh*, along with post-sixteenth-century additions, that has become the standard for Jewish jurisprudence.

The ordering of Jewish life into a defined and delimited *halakhic* system carried a particular significance in the late Middle Ages. Whether on the margins of medieval Christian society or in the second-class *dhimmi* status afforded by Islam, Judaism found a place in its host cultures for only a fragmentary expression of its self-understanding. Lacking the dignity of full respect from its political patrons, it took a measure of fulfillment from the thoroughness with which the Torah addressed and shaped Jewish life.

The *halakhic* system identified 613 commandments (*mitzvoth*) in the text of the biblical Torah. Of these, 365 are positive commands and 248 are prohibitions. They encompass symbolically all one's time and all one's being, as the commandments equal the number of days in a year and the prohibitions equal the number of organs in the body (by the medieval count). Moreover, on one day each week, the wholeness of the creation could be celebrated and indulged in the distinctive Jewish observance of the Sabbath (Shabbat).

The twenty-five hours of Shabbat that begin on Friday sundown became a sanctuary in time for a people with little security in the surrounding culture. The two central themes of Shabbat are creation and freedom. Shabbat itself is modeled on God's rest at the completion of creation, while the Jewish observance of Shabbat depends on the freedom that came with the Exodus and the end of slavery. Like God at the end of creation, on Shabbat the Jew is entitled to step back from the hard work of industry and creating that press on people throughout the week. Only the rescue of human life in imminent danger can take precedence over this weekly *imitatio Dei*. So food is prepared in advance, lights are not kindled, no burden is carried outside the home, no writing is undertaken—all to honor creation and recall that humans finally are fully dependent on God's provision for every moment of life.

The church has much to learn from such a practice of reflection and celebration. Shabbat is not a restricted time, hedged in by a host of prohibitions and beset with burdensome requirements. To the contrary, it is a dedicated time, pushing aside lesser concerns, nourishing the body and soul of those who observe it. Despite the fragmentation and uncertainty of life on the margins of a culture defined by others, Shabbat held a precious balance of creation's original integrity. Just as Christians speak of Eucharist as the "foretaste of the feast to come," so do Jews in celebrating Shabbat anticipate the fullness of life that awaits us in the fulfillment of new creation.

A Calling to Restore Wholeness

Hope and anticipation often drive a passion for action, and the idealism of Shabbat provided the lens through which one particular Jewish tradition focused that passion. Many of the Shabbat customs that are most symbolic and endearing were initiated among mystics in the hill town of Tsefat (Safed) in the northern Galilee during the sixteenth century. Wearing the white of wedding celebrations to greet the "Shabbat bride," the mystics would sing Shabbat's entrance with hymns that echo the Song of Solomon, "Come, my beloved" (*Leka dodi*) and "Come, oh bride" (*Bo'i kalla*). They, too, initiated the practice of studying Torah through the whole night as the festival of *Shavuot* (Weeks) begins.

Why Tsefat? And why the sixteenth century? And what does mysticism have to do with a passion for action? The sixteenth century brought turmoil to Europe in the Protestant Reformation and the drive of nationalisms against the centralized Roman Empire. It also found Jews displaced from Spain and Portugal after their expulsion in 1492. Tsefat was a preferred destination for the exiles, who brought with them the memory and habits of Jewish life in what has been called "the Golden Age," though many had been forced to continue the practices under cover after having been forcibly converted to Christianity by the Inquisition. In Tsefat, with the charismatic leadership of several rabbis, they reconstituted their joyous community.

Rabbi Isaac Luria (1534–1572) was the greatest of the Tsefat figures, although he lived there for only the last three of his brief thirty-eight years. Born in Jerusalem and raised in Cairo after his father's death, he became first a talmudic expert and then a student and teacher of Jewish mysticism, which came to be known as *Qabbala* (received [wisdom]). Its roots can be found in the Bible, then elaborated during the last days of the Jerusalem Temple and the beginnings of Rabbinic Judaism as commentary on the "throne vision" of Ezekiel (1:4–28; 10:1–22). Its essential text is the thirteenth-century *Zohar* (Splendor), complied by the Castillian Moses de Leone (1240–1305), and it flourished in Tsefat as in few other places.

An essential image of Luria's *Qabbala* portrays the shattering of creation in its first moments—a "big bang" image very different from the one that twentieth-century science offers. From the oneness of God's being, ten "emanations" (*sefirot*) went forth to constitute the creation, each one more distant from the essence of God, and therefore less spiritual and refined. When God sent the pure light of the divine presence through the emanations to fill creation, the most distant *sefirot* were unable to contain it, and shattered. Bits of the light were trapped in the shattered pieces of the created order, without an open pathway to their source in the Eternal. Only when all the sparks of light are freed from the broken vessels of creation where they are trapped will God's will for creation finally be realized.

The process of freeing the sparks and bringing creation closer to its spiritual ideal is called *tikkun olam* ("repair of the universe"), and it requires the participation of God's people. Every good deed that fulfills a commandment, every righteous moment spent in Shabbat joy or Torah study, every compassionate touch and generous gift, not only has its immediate effect in the world, but it frees a divine spark and contributes to *tikkun olam.*

This is where the junction of action and mysticism, of *halakhic* codes and esoteric speculation about divine emanations, finds its meaning. In spite of all the chaos that surrounded them, in spite of their exile from Europe, in spite of the upheaval of society, in spite of their relative impotence to affect the grand social equations of their time, the Lurianic Qabbalists poured their passion for action into faithful living and joyous ritual. They did so believing that these are inherently vital to the ultimate redemption of a broken world.

In the rational approach of the modern world, *Qabbala* and other forms of mysticism may seem out of touch and marginal to our mainstream religious communities. Indeed, it was quite a surprise when Gershom Scholem, the twentieth century's greatest scholar of Jewish mysticism, demonstrated how widespread was the acceptance and practice of *Qabbala* in the centuries after Luria. Most communities adopted at least some of its Shabbat practices and many Jews read the *Zohar* and studied Luria's teachings.

Yet it makes sense. We also live in a time when there seems to be little we can do to steer the course of history or to influence the larger realities of our world, like countries and multinational corporations and the forces behind the "culture wars." However, if we understand these to result from the world's fundamental inability to receive God's fullness and shine with it, then every bit of repair that we can do, whether in our daily walk or in our regular worship, has its impact, however unnoticed.

Identity and Allegiance

As the modern world dawned, the marginalized life of Jews that had given such impetus to *halakhic* codification and mystical motivation was transformed. The "self-evident truths" of American humanism and the anticlerical populism of the French Revolution are symbols of a new social order. In the modern world, Jews can participate freely as individuals, claiming national citizenship side-by-side with Christians and all others, and exercising their God-given freedom of religion as they choose. But the path out of the ghetto (emancipation) was not always smooth and straight. In France, Jewish citizenship was alternately granted and revoked throughout the nineteenth century. But the opportunities of social equality were never far away, and the Jewish community was challenged to respond to them.

"We will grant nothing to the Jews as a nation, but everything to the Jew as an individual." With this principle, Comte Stanislaus de Clermont-Tonnerre in 1789 signaled the tension that enlivened the question of Jewish identity in the modern era. Is being Jewish a religious category that merely fills in one line on a person's demographic inventory? What of its ethnic aspects, its cultural dimensions, and even the national character of the religious identity? Becoming a Jew through the covenant of circumcision means identifying with a people, a nation; can such a religious identity ever become strictly private? ("To be a citizen on the street and a Jew at home" was another of the nineteenth-century solutions suggested for sustaining Jewish identity.) Ironically, just as Jews were being welcomed more fully into the dominant culture, they were being asked to divorce their Judaism from their public identity as they entered it.

The movement of modernity known as Reform Judaism, especially in its classical German expression in the mid-nineteenth century, embraced the opportunities of emancipation and shaped Jewish life around the Western religious model. More important than its adoption of Christian architectural styles and liturgical music was its identification of "ethical monotheism" as the essence of the Jewish religion. Reform Judaism holds very few absolutes about lifestyle and none in ritual that attach to this essence out of necessity; true to its name, the movement allows Judaism to be reformed in every generation to express its essential genius.

In contrast and response, the Orthodox movement has asserted the priority of *halakhic* practice and communal participation as the hallmarks of Jewish life. Though varied and nuanced in their respective communities, the many branches of Orthodoxy concur in rejecting the blandishments of modernity and the possibility of assimilating to non-Jewish culture.

The Conservative movement, an American development that consolidated around the turn of the twentieth century, centers its Jewish identity in the historical expression of Jewish communities through the ages. It is grounded more concretely than Reform in the practices and expressions of the past, refusing to abstract the essence of Judaism into a principle or concept as does Reform. At the same time, it recognizes the reality of historical change and development in a way that Orthodoxy does not.

The Reconstructionist movement reflects the internationalism of its early twentieth-century origins by emphasizing the distinctiveness, but not the uniqueness, of Jewish culture. Respecting the cultural creativity and integrity of every human clan, this movement sees in the particularity of Jewish election a universal notion of vocation that each people and nation can discover for itself. Jews are elected—to be Jews—just as other peoples are elected to be what they are, most distinctively.

Each of these movements is modern in the sense that it responds to the contemporary challenge of balancing religious identity with humanistic individualism and political citizenship. One of the greatest tests that modern Judaism faces is in shaping the State of Israel simultaneously as a Jewish national homeland and a modern democratic nation. The course of nation-states in the modern world has been primarily to renounce any meaningful religious identification and allow their citizens to express their religious beliefs freely in the private sector. Fascinating contrasts have thereby developed, as in the comparatively intense religiosity of the United States, with its official "wall of separation" between church and state, and the deeply secular character of European society, even in countries that have an official state religion. How Israel will fare in its efforts to hold together the twin sources of national identity will remain for the twenty-first century to see.

The challenges of modernity came home to Jews more directly than to Christians, perhaps, because in the modern era Western culture largely remained de facto Christian in its character. It is in the more recent "postmodern" era that the church has begun to confront its real divorce from the dominant culture. Prayer, Christian religious symbols, and traditional "Judeo-Christian moral standards" are no longer taken for granted as foundational to Western society; as in a radical social contract theory, society seems able to take on any shape at all, as long as those who participate agree to the terms.

Does the individual then simply take religious convictions into the privacy of the home? Can there be a place in the public arena for arguments grounded in religious belief? Should each religious community, and ethnic group, and nationalist movement be granted its own equal place based on its distinctive contribution to human diversity? We recognize the urgency of these questions in our own time, and we can look to the last two hundred years of Jewish history to learn important lessons as we seek to work out our own answers.

Blessing Born of Silence

None of the Jewish responses to modernity prepared the Jewish people—or the world—to confront the atrocities of National Socialism in Germany during 1933–1945. Working systematically under an ideology that combined racial profiling, belief in evolutionary progress, and romantic German nationalism, the Nazis dehumanized the Jews categorically and undertook to annihilate them. Neither the modernist Reform Jews who had assimilated thoroughly into German and European society for more than two generations, nor the antimodernist Orthodox in the comparative isolation of their Eastern European villages (*shtetls*), escaped the poison that the Nazis spewed across Europe. Two-thirds of European Jews—one-third of worldwide Jewry—was slaughtered in less than half a decade.

For any religious person, the overriding question that must be faced after such a horror is, "Where was God?" It is a question that has fundamentally reshaped both Jewish and Christian self-understanding. Some have argued that the more pertinent—perhaps the only pertinent—question is "Where were good and decent people?" Extensive research and theory have been devoted to the attempt to understand the human participants, whether they be the Nazi perpetrators, the many European collaborators, the bystanders around the globe, the victims, the rescuers, the leaders, or the common crowd. One of the clearest benefits of this exploration has been a profound understanding of the role that centuries of Christian anti-Judaism played in cultivating the cultural soil where Nazi ideology could take root and thrive, as Eva Fleischner discusses in her chapter in this volume. We have yet to plumb the depth of the implications of that understanding.

Still, it is the question of God and such monstrous, outright evil that confronts us most insistently. In the works of Jewish thinkers over the past two generations, that question has begun to yield some insights, albeit without any consensus. One of the earliest responses asserted that the Jewish people had been wrong about God all along. It wasn't so much that "God is dead," as that God had never been there. Judaism was a cultural artifact with a long and venerable history worthy of continuing, but not because of any divine election or covenant, since no recognizable God in any understanding of Judaism could have allowed the destruction of so many of the covenant people.

Others argued that this made it too easy. It let God off the hook, so to speak, by allowing God to slip out the back door. Rather, these thinkers asked, should we not hold this silent God accountable and learn how to live with a God who will not always rescue, who will not always respond? Still others disagreed that God was silent, or absent, or unresponsive. Some even went as far as to say that God was complicit in the carnage, since the Jewish people of the early twentieth century had strayed far from traditional practice and needed to fulfill their obligations as God's people. Without suggesting that they could answer why God would choose the Nazi scourge as the means, they argued that the purpose of this tragedy is clear: to renew Jewish identity, faithfulness, and practice.

Still others rendered God irrelevant to the question. What is important then is not where God was or how to relate to God now, but only to take the new terms of Jewish existence and build on them. If a Jew in the Nazi era was a person destined by evil for annihilation, then the holy Jewish calling in this new epoch is to live and to bring new Jewish life into the world. Procreation, promulgation of Judaism, and perpetuation of Jewish identity become the new pillars on which perhaps even the whole world is sustained.

This broad range of responses has emerged in writings as diverse as poetry, drama, theology, philosophy, historical analysis, fiction, political theory, and more. It has helped to shape the debate about what the State of Israel is and means, and has informed the development of international standards of human rights and antiracism. It has also provided a broad foundation on which Christian ethicists and theologians have again confronted the question of God and evil in their own terms.

What seems inherent in the search for meaning after God's profound silence in Nazi times is a conviction that some blessing can be wrestled from that silence. Surely there are those who simply despaired—even some who first wrote of their experiences in a search for meaning ended with despair, including suicide. Yet for those who continue to search, even if they find an absent God, a chimerical God, a perverse God, or an irrelevant God, there is a common conviction that something constructive can be drawn from even so bleak and devastating an experience.

Can Christians not learn from this something of what the first disciples must have experienced in the days after Jesus' death? Is not the question of God and evil also the first question of Good Friday, before anyone knew it was good? Even if any direct connection to the formative days of Christian faith seems strained, there is much to gain by attending to our Jewish brothers and sisters in their wrestling with God. It has been a long time in the "Christian West" since any evil touched the Christian community with the ferocity of the Nazi attack on God's people. Surely their responses to it can sharpen our own meditations and reanimate our responses when God seems silent.

Why It All Matters

In the five eras we have highlighted here, the Jewish people have responded to their experience in the faith that God is at work among them. Their experience and the meaning they have drawn from it are of more than passing interest to the Christian community.

First, the people who bear this witness to their experience are our neighbors. In the global village of the twenty-first century, they are more our neighbors today than ever, even if we have no Jews living on our street or in our town. Just as the spread of Islam has brought us to realize that Muslims everywhere are our neighbors in more important ways than we previously imagined, so with our Jewish neighbors, wherever they may be. Their experience and their understanding of it make a difference.

With a lessening of the cultural dominance that white, Christian, Western European norms once exerted, all our neighbors from other cultural traditions become more real in their differences, and we benefit from understanding those differences. This is especially true for those others who are closely related to us. Cardinal Walter Kasper has suggested that the Jewish people may be considered "a sacrament of otherness" for the church, both embodying and symbolizing God's blessing as it comes to us in everything that is not as we are.[13]

Second, the church has learned to affirm that God is faithful to the covenant with Israel throughout its generations. We no longer restrict that faithfulness to the fulfillment of biblical promise that Christians know in Jesus Christ, though that is also a part of God's faithfulness. What good would it be, however, to affirm God's faithfulness to Gentiles in Jesus Christ if God were shown to be capricious in regard to the Jews? So if God is faithful to the Jews even to the present day, then God's handiwork and covenantal love must be evident in the experience of the Jewish community even to the present day.

Third, the awakening of the church to its anti-Jewish heritage and habits is a cautionary note that demands greater awareness of our Jewish brothers and sisters and a more truthful accounting of their experience. Our ancestors' willingness to replace the real Jews of their communities with a projected image of "the Jew" who served as a foil for Christian truth and virtue brought tragic effects time and again. We dare not risk similar tragedy by averting our eyes or dismissing what we hear from those who yet have, as Paul says, "the adoption, the glory, the covenants, the giving of the law, the worship, and the promises" (Rom 9:4).

Finally, our identity as God's people is dependent on the relationships we have with all of God's creation, and not least with those who also know themselves to be God's people. Theologian Catherine Keller has described contemporary life as one that is lived "from a broken web."[14] We are not autonomous individuals in the model of the classic hero, but relational selves who draw strength and learn selfhood and accept limits from all those others who live with us, whose lives and experience interpenetrate our own. Like spiders on a web, we are affected by every touch, every tremor, every action that takes place anywhere in the web of our relationships.

Christians have long misunderstood and misjudged the place of Jews in our web of existence. Christian theologians who have assessed the role of anti-Judaism in the success of Nazi antisemitism note that Christianity was undermined, even deformed, by its special animus toward Jews. A clearer, more appreciative understanding of Jews and their experience as the people of God is essential to understanding Christian identity more fully. The record of God's work in and among the Jews since Christianity came on the scene is a neglected resource in our theological quest. We continue to neglect it only at the peril of our own continuing handicap.

A Final Image and an Invitation

In a particularly memorable conversation, an observant Orthodox Jew said, "I have come to God through Torah and you through Jesus Christ, but we both seem to have arrived at the same place." Some might argue whether it is we who are on the journey toward God, or God who reaches out to us.

Yet in either case there is room for both Jews and Christians to acknowledge that the differences between our experiences can embody the strength of diversity rather than the weakness of division.

Whether our Jewish neighbors choose to join us in the exploration or not, Christians—by the logic of affirming the Jewish covenant—have opened a new chapter in the story of God's work in the world. With a good deal of homework on which to catch up, the excitement lies ahead—living and learning the ways of God in that new openness to what God is doing in and with and through God's people, the Jews.

Notes

1. Similarly, Matt 22:35–40; Luke 10:15–28.

2. See Donald Harman Akerson, *Surpassing Wonder: The Invention of the Bible and the Talmuds* (Chicago: University of Chicago Press, 2001). He argues that "neither [the Jesus-faith nor Rabbinic Judaism] can legitimately share a single label with its ancient [biblical] predecessor" (404).

3. Augustine, *Against the Jews* 6:8.

4. See James A. Sanders, *Torah and Canon* (Philadelphia: Fortress, 1972).

5. See, especially, E. R. Goodenough, *Jewish Symbols in the Greco-Roman Period*, vols. 1–13 (New York: Parthenon, 1953–).

6. Misnah Tractate *Baba Qamma* 8:1. Cf. also Matt 5:38–39.

7. For this dating, see Yaakov Elman, "Marriage and Marital Property in Rabbinic and Sasanian Law," in Catherine Heyzer, ed., *Rabbinic Law in Its Roman and Near Eastern Context* (Tübingen: Mohr-Siebeck, 2003), 227–76.

8. Mishnah Tractate *Avot* (*Pirke Avot*) 1:2.

9. Babylonian Talmud Tractate *Baba Metzia* 59b.

10. Mishnah Tractate *Avot* (*Pirke Avot*) 4:1.

11. Edward Flannery, *The Anguish of the Jews* (New York: Paulist, 1985), 90.

12. Nachmanides wrote a summary of the arguments in the still extant *Sefer Vikkuah*, that is, *Book of Debate*.

13. Cardinal Kasper used this phrase in an address on the thirty-seventh anniversary of *Nostra Aetate*, at www.jcrelations.net/en/?id=2189.

14. Catherine Keller, *From a Broken Web: Separation, Sexism, and Self* (Boston: Beacon, 1986).

Further Reading

Encyclopedia Judaica. 18 vols. Philadelphia: Coronet Books (reprint), 1994. An edition is also available in CD-ROM. See http://www.jewishsoftware.com/products/Encyclopedia_Judaica_66.asp.

Roth, Cecil. *A History of the Jews*. New York: Schocken, 1961.

Shanks, Hershel, ed. *Christianity and Rabbinic Judaism: A Parallel History of Their Origins and Early Development*. London: SPCK, 2002.

Strack, H. R., and Günter Stemberger. *Introduction to the Talmud and Midrash*. Translated and edited by Marcus Bockmuehl. Minneapolis: Fortress, 1992.

Telushkin, Joseph. *Jewish Literacy: The Most Important Things to Know about the Jewish Religion, Its People, and Its History*. New York: William Morrow, 1991.

Wylen, Stephen M. *Settings of Silver: An Introduction to Judaism*. 2nd edition. New York: Paulist, 2002.

PART

VI

The Bible Both
Connects and Separates
Jews and Christians

10

CHAPTER

Contemporary Christians and Israel's Ancient Scriptures

Walter Harrelson

THE BIBLE both connects and separates Jews and Christians." This heading from "A Sacred Obligation" offers an innocent-appearing way of describing the history of Jewish-Christian relations through the centuries. Christians have claimed the Jewish scriptures as their own, but they have organized and interpreted them in ways that have underscored the differences between the two communities. In recent years, the study of the Jewish and Christian scriptures by both communities has done much to disclose what the two communities have and hold in common and what separates them. Some Jewish scholars have made the study of the Christian Bible their specialty, and some Christian scholars have made the study of the Jewish Bible (not the "Old Testament") their specialty. And more and more biblical scholars, both Jewish and Christian, read and study the Bible together, seeking to understand how it is that it both connects and separates Jews and Christians.

115

The differences, however, that separate Jewish and Christian interpretations of the Bible must not be exaggerated. Thus, in this chapter I focus in particular on correcting Christian misunderstandings of the Hebrew Bible.

The Term "Old Testament"

In recent years, an increasing number of Christians have come to realize that the term "Old Testament" may connote "outdated" or "irrelevant." While scholars have not reached consensus on the most suitable substitute, two of the most frequently used alternatives are "First Testament" and "Shared Testament." Other terms frequently employed are "Hebrew Bible," "Hebrew Scriptures," and "Jewish Bible." Rejection of the term "Old Testament" is part of the contemporary commitment to avoid pejorative references to the sacred writings of the Jewish people. The designations "Old" and "New" have often suggested that the Christian New Testament not only ranks higher in value than the Old Testament but in fact takes the place of the "Old" revelation.

At the same time, of course, Christians find in the events and teachings of the New Testament a key to the understanding of the "Old." The task is to identify that key to understanding in a way that does not claim that the Christian reading is the only possible or valid reading. Similarly, Jewish scholars who specialize in the study and interpretation of the Christian Bible may rightly claim that their key to its proper and valid understanding differs from that of their Christian colleagues. The Bible both connects and separates the two communities.

Prophetic Denunciations of the Community of Israel

An all-too-common misreading of the Jewish scriptures by Christians is the identification of God's judgment upon the covenant community as fully and richly deserved, thereby preparing the way for Israel to be rejected by God in favor of the Christian community. If Israel were in fact as faithless and disobedient as the prophets testify (see for example Amos 2:6–5:27; Isa 1:2–20; Ezek 16 and 23), then surely Christians have reason to believe that Israel had its chance to continue as God's faithful people but forfeited that chance by its faithlessness. Such an interpretation, of course, fails (1) to take account of the rigorous demands that prophets laid upon the people of the covenant; (2) to acknowledge the hyperbole of prophetic speech; and—most importantly of all—(3) to account for the piety, the moral insights, and the overall religious Israelite heritage found in the "Old" Testament as a whole.

Differences in interpretation of biblical texts can readily bear out this distinction. Two prayers of Moses in Exodus 32, for example, might be read as pointing to different tendencies in a "Jewish" and a "Christian" reading of the Hebrew Scriptures. That is, both Jews and Christians interpret Exodus in light of the characteristic emphases of their respective traditions. For the "Jewish" community, the initial prayer of Moses in Exodus 32:11–14 (see the parallel text in Deut 9:25–29)—which has Moses appealing to God's promise to the ancestors and God's own standing among the nations as the ground for God to forgive a rebellious people—resonates with the centrality of peoplehood. It also typifies the boldness of Israel's speech before God. Such an emphasis is characteristic of biblical prayers in the Hebrew Scriptures. See, for example, Psalm 44:

> Rouse yourself! Why do you sleep, O LORD?
> Awake, do not cast us off forever!
> Why do you hide your face?
> Why do you forget our affliction and oppression?
> For we sink down to the dust; our bodies cling to the ground.
> Rise up, come to our help.
> Redeem us for the sake of your steadfast love. (vs. 23–26)

Isaiah 63:7–64:12 offers another example. The prophet interrogates God:

> Look down from heaven and see,
> from your holy and glorious habitation.
> Where are your zeal and your might?
> The yearning of your heart and your compassion?
> They are withheld from me. (63:15)

Then, in a poignant voice, the prophet reminds God:

> For you are our father,
> though Abraham does not know us;
> you, O LORD, are our father;
> our Redeemer from of old is your name. (63:16)

God's own name, God's honor and standing among the nations of earth, is at stake in the fate of Israel.

What one might identify as resonating with the "Christian" tradition is Exodus 32:30–34 (with no parallel in Deut 9). Here the text shows Moses placing his own life on the line on behalf of the sinful people, thereby offering a resonance with Christian understandings of salvation through Jesus. This prayer minimally insists that if the people cannot be forgiven and permitted to continue their journey, Moses does not wish to live: "So Moses returned to the Lord and said, 'Alas, this people has sinned a great sin; they have made for themselves gods of gold. But now, if you will only forgive their sin—but if not, blot me out of the book that you have written'" (vs. 32–33). A "Christian" layer of interpretation might read the prayer as showing Moses ready to die on behalf of the people. Such a reading can hardly fail to remind Christians of Jesus in the garden of Gethsemane.

Thus, when Jews and Christians read the Hebrew Scriptures, they may discern different layers and resonances because they bring with them the symbols, beliefs, and practices of their living traditions.[1]

The Picture of Israel's God

Christians through the centuries have deplored the pictures of Israel's God in the Hebrew Scriptures: a tribal deity favoring Israel and calling for the extermination of other peoples (see already Exod 23:23), one who demands the sacrifice of a first-born child (Gen 22), who calls on Israel never to make peace with certain peoples (Deut 25:17–19), and who punishes children for the sins of their father (2 Sam 12). Such biblical pictures would seem to require critical assessment of the Jewish and the Christian scriptures. Interpreters of the Bible are also drawn to particular biblical texts and teachings that are clearly presented as definitive texts. Exodus 34:6–7 is such a text, presented as Moses' most awesome and specific audition on the sacred mountain. God speaks directly, not only giving the divine name (YHWH) but defining the character of deity as "a God merciful and gracious, slow to anger, and abounding in steadfast love and faithfulness, keeping steadfast love for the thousandth generation, forgiving iniquity and transgression and sin." All such texts that stand out as definitional and characteristic of deity need to be given their proper weight.

Torah as Law

Another misreading of the Hebrew Bible by Christians is the understanding of Torah (God's instruction, teaching, law) in the Jewish Bible by reference to the contrast "Law and Gospel" in the New Testament. Such an understanding fails to account for the variety of meanings of Torah in the

Hebrew Bible, in particular those meanings revealed in such texts as Psalms 19:7–14 and 119. The difference is also implicit in the way Jews and Christians begin and number the Ten Commandments found in Exodus 20 and Deuteronomy 5. The first commandment in Jewish usage is Exodus 20:2, "I the LORD am your God who brought you out of the land of Egypt, out of the house of slavery" (also Deut 5:6). That is, the Jewish numbering of the Ten Commandments begins with an identification of God as the LORD, the very one who brought Israel from slavery in Egypt to freedom at the sacred mountain. Torah is a gift of love and grace.

The Christian community identifies the first commandment as "You shall have no other gods besides me" (Exod 20:3). God's love and grace are implied in this way of numbering the commandments, but not as explicitly as in the Jewish identification of the first commandment as "I the LORD am your God who brought you out of Egypt. . . ." Unfortunately, the polemical use of the contrasting terms "law" and "grace" in the New Testament has often obscured for Christians the full meaning of Torah as both law and grace.

Promise and Fulfillment

The early Christian community found the meaning of the Christian revelation by reference to Israel's scriptures, in particular those texts that portray the divine promises that awaited consummation in times to come. Other Jewish communities also used these promise-texts to account for the deity's actions in their own day. The discovery among the Dead Sea Scrolls of a document called the Florilegium (that is, a collection of literary pieces or fragments), which consists of a string of biblical texts drawn from different places in the Hebrew Bible, illustrates this practice. In Christian circles, the major texts were Genesis 3:15 (God's judgment on the serpent in the garden of Eden), Genesis 49:9–10 (Jacob's blessing on Judah), Numbers 24:17 (Baalam's promise of a star), 2 Samuel 7 (Nathan's promise to David, which also figures prominently in the Florilegium), and the many promises of a new ruler, a new Zion, and a new Israel that are scattered throughout the prophetic literature.

These "messianic" prophecies, as they came to be called, became the proofs for the early Christian community that it had replaced, in God's purposes, the community of the "old" covenant. See how the author of the Epistle to the Hebrews uses even Psalm 8, a text about the place of the human person in the purposes of God, to refer to Jesus the Christ, the Son of Man of gospel references (Heb 2:5–9).

At the same time, these very promises of Israel's sages and prophets may bring the two communities together when they are read in a different perspective. While, over the centuries, Christian claims that the promises of God to Israel found their fulfillment in the Christian revelation, today Jews and Christians are equally challenged by these promises of what God purposes to bring to pass on a transformed earth. Jews and Christians, working together on these special biblical texts, may discover that the very texts that once were divisive actually provide ground for a hope held in common. A brief examination of these promises may suggest ways in which such an outcome might be indicated.

God's Promises: Judgment, Hope, and Lure

The prophets of Israel characteristically presented their promises of God's coming transformation of the life of Israel against the background of Israel's failures to live up to the demands of covenant faith. Isaiah 2:1–5, with its picture of the nations' march to Zion, where they would learn God's Torah and lay aside their weapons of warfare, is preceded by a devastating picture of "harlot Zion" (Isa 1:21), sick to death and ripe for destruction. The parallel passage in Micah 4:1–4 is also preceded by a portrait of Zion as utterly corrupt and soon to be "plowed like a field" (Mic 3:12). These arrangements of the text suggest that what God has in store for Israel on the coming blessed day of promise should and must be a powerful motivating force to spur the community on to help realize that which God has promised.

Texts that speak of Israel's coming just ruler (for example, Isa 9:1–7, 11:1–9, Mic 5:1–5, Zech 9:1–9) have the same force: earthly rulers are judged not only in light of God, the one just and merciful ruler. They are judged also in light of the promised earthly ruler whom the community awaits.

These promises of Israel's prophets also offer firm confidence in God: what God has promised will, despite all evidence to the contrary, find fulfillment. Earthly rulers may be parodies of what rulers should be, but they will in time be succeeded by God's true ruler, one who knows the divine will and will align the society with that will. Small wonder that so many of Israel's promises from the time of the prophets have their origin in the period just prior to or during the Babylonian exile!

The promises also appear to have acted upon the community of Israel as motivation for action, for arousal from lethargy, as a call to get in step with the divine undertakings. The logic and rhetoric of Isaiah 40:1–55:13 bear out this surmise. This prophet from the Babylonian exile develops a new and fresh mode of address to help the community recognize just how near, how certain, and how glorious is the "new creation" that is awaiting Israel. The beauty of these texts is timeless:

> Thus says the Lord,
> who makes a way in the sea,
> a path in the mighty waters,
> who brings out chariot and horse, army and warrior
> they lie down, they cannot rise,
> they are extinguished, quenched like a wick:
> Do not remember the former things,
> or consider the things of old.
> I am about to do a new thing;
> Now it springs forth, do you not perceive it?
> I will make a way in the wilderness
> and rivers in the desert. (Isa 43:16–19)

Christian Participation in Israel's Promises

One way to affirm Jesus' teaching concerning the "kingdom of God" (or, in the circumlocution of the Gospel of Matthew, "kingdom of heaven") is to associate Jesus' understanding of the fulfillment of the divine purpose in his day as just this prophetic fulfillment. What the prophets had promised was finding its fulfillment in Jesus' day—not in apocalyptic, otherworldly terms but precisely in the life of the community of Israel. The Gospel of Luke makes this point powerfully, with its presentation of Jesus' sermon at Nazareth (Luke 4:16–30) and its question from John the Baptist (Luke 7:18–23): "Are you the one who is to come or are we to wait for another?" For the evangelists, the kingdom of God was made present in the ministry of Jesus.

A Broad Definition of Messianism

None of the "promise" texts from the Hebrew Bible referred to above (e.g., Isa 2:1–5; Mic 4:1–4; Isa 9:1–7; Zech 9:1–9; Isa 40:1–55:13) is in fact a messianic text, since none of them is clearly referring to a royal figure from the last days who would bring God's cosmic purposes to fulfillment. By the time of the beginnings of Christianity, however, various Jewish groups (for example, the community that produced the Dead Sea Scrolls) were developing such a broader picture of messianism, one that involved the fulfillment of the divine purposes on a transformed earth, not only the restoration of the kingdom of David in the land of Israel. This broadened perspective on the diverse notions of messianism is underscored in the 2001 document of the Pontifical Biblical Commission, *The Jewish People and Their Sacred Scriptures in the Christian Bible*.[2] The document makes creative use of the promise/fulfillment theme and insists on the continuing vitality and validity of Jewish biblical exegesis. It asserts at one point that the messiah whose coming is anticipated within the Jewish community "will have the same traits of that Jesus who has already come and is already present and active among us" (21:5). That is, Jewish exegesis of the Shared Testament has its own integrity and validity apart from its meaning within the Christian community. Moreover, Jewish messianic hope also has its integrity, although the Christian may claim in faith that the *traits* of the Christian Messiah will be borne by the Messiah who is yet to come according to Jewish belief.

God's Salvation

While it is true that the Christian community has given large place to heaven and the hope of salvation beyond physical death, authentic Christianity has also held, with the Jewish Bible, that salvation has to do with life on earth. God's creation, though damaged in all its parts by human failings and deliberate acts, is still God's good creation, yet to fulfill its intended purpose. Otherworldly texts abounded in the world within which Christianity developed, but many of the Christian communities resisted their influence and, like the Jewish communities, kept them at some distance. The greatest aid to the church in that connection was its firm hold on the Jewish Bible, the Christian "Old Testament." While the Christian community would continue to emphasize those parts of the Hebrew Bible that supported its promise/fulfillment scheme, it still held on to the practical guidance for daily life found in the traditions of Israelite wisdom. It also held on to the piety and candor of the life of prayer illustrated in the psalms and in the other praises and prayers of the scriptures. Moreover, the life of cultic worship assured the regular uses of the Hebrew Bible in ways not directly tied to Christian messianism, thus offering a way to maintain the legal, moral, and aesthetic heritage of Israel's Bible.

Similarly, in Jewish commentary on its scriptures, the richness of Prophets and Sacred Writings, along with Torah, were plumbed and made part of the liturgical, moral, aesthetic, and practical daily guidance of the scriptural heritage. Today, as Jews and Christians study the Bible together, in their respective ways and with their respective emphases, the entire heritage of each is available to the other. Fresh perspectives and approaches are available to interpreters, along with the classical ones. Available too is the Spirit who can, and often does, make all things new.

Notes

1. For a lively sense of how early Jewish interpreters read texts, see James L. Kugel, *Traditions of the Bible: A Guide to the Bible as It Was at the Start of the Common Era* (Cambridge: Harvard University Press, 1998).

2. In addition to the print edition listed below, this document may be found at www.vatican.va/roman_curia/congregations/cfaith/pcb_documents/rc_con_cfaith_doc_20020212_popolo-ebraico_en.html.

Further Reading

Pontifical Biblical Commission. *The Jewish People and Their Sacred Scriptures in the Christian Bible.* Vatican City: Liberia Editrice Vaticana, 2002.

VII
PART

Affirming God's
Enduring Covenant
with the Jewish People
Has Consequences for
Christian Understandings
of Salvation

CHAPTER

11

Jesus as the Universal Savior in the Light of God's Eternal Covenant with the Jewish People: A Roman Catholic Perspective

Peter C. Phan

I N RECENT YEARS a number of Christian theologians, recalling Paul's teaching that God's covenant with Israel remains eternal (Rom 11:29), have affirmed that God's redemptive power is still at work in and through Judaism.[1] This recognition that Judaism continues to function as a way of salvation, at least for Jews, poses serious challenges to Roman Catholics. It seems, at first sight, to contradict their church's longstanding double teaching that Jesus is the unique, universal, and absolute savior, and that outside the church there is no salvation. So the affirmation of the continuing validity of God's covenant with Israel calls for a reexamination of these two traditional teachings, especially the former. This brief chapter seeks to outline, from the Roman Catholic perspective, a theology of religions and of the role of Christ as savior that remains both harmonious with the Christian faith in Jesus as the savior of the whole of humankind and receptive to the acknowledgment of Judaism as a still valid way of salvation.

The Second Vatican Council (1962–1965)

Any reinterpretation of the doctrine of the universality and uniqueness of Jesus as savior within Roman Catholic theology must take into account the teaching of the Second Vatican Council on the possibility of salvation for non-Christians and on the existence of "elements of truth and grace" within non-Christian religions. With regard to the salvation of non-Christians, Vatican II, reversing the church's centuries-old condemnation of non-Christians to hell,[2] affirms that "those who have not yet received the Gospel are related to the People of God in various ways."[3] Among these people the council explicitly mentions five groups: Jews, Moslems, those seeking the unknown God in shadows and images through their religions, those who do not practice any specific religion but sincerely seek God, and those who, without any fault on their part, have not yet arrived at an explicit knowledge of God (e.g., atheists). All these people, the council says, "may achieve eternal salvation," though of course not without the grace of Christ.[4]

With regard to non-Christian religions, Vatican II acknowledges that the "rites and customs of peoples," including their religions, should be "saved from destruction" and "purified and raised up, and perfected for the glory of God."[5] In its Decree on the Church's Missionary Activity (*Ad Gentes*), the council affirms that these religious elements "may lead one to the true God and be a preparation for the gospel."[6] These "elements of truth and grace" are the "secret presence of God"[7] and "the seeds of the Word."[8] In its Declaration on the Relation of the Church to Non-Christian Religions (*Nostra Aetate*), Vatican II uses the categories primitive religions, Hinduism, Buddhism, Islam, and Judaism. Of these religions the council affirms: "The Catholic Church rejects nothing of what is true and holy in these religions. It has a high regard for the manner of life and conduct, the precepts and doctrines which, although differing in many ways from its own teaching, nevertheless often reflect a ray of that truth which enlightens all men and women."[9]

With regard to Judaism in particular, the council acknowledges the "spiritual ties which link the people of the new covenant to the stock of Abraham" and says that "the church of Christ acknowledges that in God's plan of salvation the beginnings of its faith and election are to be found in the patriarchs, Moses and the prophets."[10] It recalls Paul's teaching that "the Jews remain very dear to God, for the sake of the patriarchs, since God does not take back the gifts he bestowed or the choice he made." It is of great importance to note that even though in *Nostra Aetate*, Vatican II treats Judaism alongside other religions, the Catholic Church repeatedly affirms the unique and privileged position of Israel in God's plan of salvation and its special relationship to Christianity. Indeed, the Catholic Church does not regard Judaism as just one of the non-Christian religions with which it enters into interreligious dialogue, as Eugene Fisher explains in his chapter in this volume. Rather, it affirms explicitly and unambiguously the reality of divine revelation and grace—and not merely "elements of truth and grace" or "secret presence of God" or "seeds of the Word"—in Judaism as well as the continuing validity of God's covenant with Israel.

A Christian Theology of Religious Pluralism

In spite of its positive evaluation of non-Christian religions in general, and of Judaism in particular, Vatican II self-consciously refrains from affirming that these religions as such function as "ways of salvation" in a manner analogous, let alone parallel, to Christianity. The last three decades, however, have witnessed extensive reflection on the relationship between Christianity and non-Christian religions, especially Judaism. A new theology of religions has reassessed the role of Christ as the unique and universal savior and the function of non-Christian religions themselves within God's plan of salvation.

In a recent work, Catholic theologian Paul F. Knitter, who has written extensively on religious pluralism, helpfully categorizes contemporary theologies of religions into four basic types, which he terms "replacement," "fulfillment," "mutuality," and "acceptance" models.[11] The first model affirms that Christianity is the only one true religion and that it will replace, totally or partially, all other religions that are considered as humanity's sinful attempts at self-salvation. The second, while affirming Christianity as the one true religion, acknowledges the presence of elements of truth and grace in other religions and advocates a mutual, though not equal, complementarity between Christianity and other religions through dialogue. The third holds that there are many true religions, none necessarily superior to the others, which are all called to dialogue and collaborate with each other, especially in projects of liberation, in order to realize their true nature. The fourth model stresses the diversity of religions from one another and refuses to seek a common ground among them; rather it urges each religion to foster its own aims and practices.

Jesus as the "Universal," "Unique," and "Absolute" Savior

Needless to say, each of these four theologies of religions views the role of Christ as savior and the three adjectives characterizing it (i.e., "universal," "unique," and "absolute") very differently. The first model takes literally the New Testament affirmations that Jesus is the only and exclusive revealer, mediator, and savior of humankind (John 14:6; Acts 4:12; 1 Cor 3:11; 1 Tim 2:5; 1 John 5:12). It also regards explicit faith in Jesus as absolutely necessary for salvation (John 3:36). The fourth model likewise professes that Jesus is the unique, universal, and absolute savior, as traditionally confessed by the Christian faith. It leaves, however, the possibility of other "saving figures" and "ways of salvation" neither affirmed nor denied; about the latter it simply pleads ignorance. The third model takes the New Testament passages cited above and the three adjectives describing Jesus the savior as poetry affirming Jesus' special character but not his exclusivity. In other words, Jesus is *totus Deus*—wholly God, insofar as he fully responded to God's love in the Spirit—but not *totum Dei*— the whole of God or divine, understood in the metaphysical sense.

Before attempting a theology of Jesus as savior that is both consonant with the Roman Catholic tradition and cognizant of the redemptive power of God at work in the Jewish tradition, it is necessary to recall, though briefly, the teaching of the declaration *Dominus Iesus* of the Congregation for the Doctrine of the Faith (August 6, 2000) on Jesus as savior.[12] Of interest to our theme are the declaration's statements on Jesus as the unique and universal savior and on the relation between Christianity and other religions.

With regard to Jesus as revealer, *Dominus Iesus* affirms that "in the mystery of Jesus Christ, the Incarnate Son of God . . . the full revelation of divine truth is given" (no. 5) and rejects the "theory of the limited, incomplete, or imperfect character of the revelation of Jesus Christ, which would be complementary to that found in other religions" (no. 6). Concerning Jesus as savior, *Dominus Iesus* states that "Jesus Christ has a significance and value for the human race and its history, which are unique and singular, proper to him alone, exclusive, universal, and absolute" (no. 15). As to the relationship between Christianity and other religions, *Dominus Iesus* condemns the view that the church is "*one way* of salvation alongside those constituted by the other religions, seen as complementary to the Church or substantially equivalent to her, even if these are said to be converting with the Church toward the eschatological kingdom of God" (no. 21). Hence, it says that even though "the followers of other religions can receive divine grace, it is also certain that *objectively speaking* they are in a gravely deficient situation in comparison with those who, in the Church, have the fullness of the means of salvation" (no. 22). These claims stirred up a storm of protest.

Christ and Christianity in View of the Continuing Validity of the Jewish Covenant

In the wake of the protest against *Dominus Iesus* by many Christian as well as non-Christian theologians, some Vatican officials pointed out that Judaism was not targeted by the declaration's negative judgment on non-Christian religions. Nevertheless the declaration did not explicitly exempt Judaism. While it is true that the Catholic Church has always recognized the special status of Judaism and its historical and theological connections with Christianity, nevertheless, the claim we make in "A Sacred Obligation" that "Jews, who do not share our faith in Christ, are in a saving covenant with God" intensifies the problems religious pluralists pose. Our claim is that at least one non-Christian religion, namely Judaism, is a way of salvation ("a saving covenant with God") apart, at least on first sight, from Christ and Christianity.

The challenge for Roman Catholic theologians, then, is to articulate a coherent and credible Christology and soteriology (theology of salvation) that both honors the Christian belief in Jesus as the savior of all humankind and includes the affirmation that Judaism is and remains eternally a "saving covenant with God." In other words, our challenge is to develop a non- or post-supersessionist Christology, or more generally, an inclusivist-pluralist Christology: understandings of Jesus Christ that do not depend on disparaging Judaism or other religions. The intent of this kind of Christology is not so much to elaborate a Christian theology of Judaism as such (which may or may not be interested in having its faith validated by Christians) as to reflect on how Christians should understand *themselves* in reference to Judaism and, by extension, to other religions.

A Post-Supersessionist Christology: Ten Elements

1. The most fundamental element of a post-supersessionist Christology is an unambiguous and explicit rejection of the idea that Christ abrogates Judaism. Over the centuries many have believed that Christ is the "fulfill-ment," "fullness," and "definitiveness" of divine revelation, and that, there-fore, God's self-gift to and covenant with Israel have been abolished, either because of Israel's guilt in rejecting and killing Jesus (as implied in the charge of faithlessness and deicide against the Jews) or because of the intrinsic supe-riority of Jesus' ministry and of Christianity (the "new" covenant supplant-ing the "old" covenant). Rather, we must premise our theology on the idea that God allows the two covenanted peoples, Israel and the church, to exist side by side in order to instruct and encourage each other "to do justly, and to love mercy, and to walk humbly" with their common God (Mic 6: 8).

2. Next, we must retrieve the ancient notion of multiple covenants. As Saint Irenaeus, the second-century bishop of Lyons, put it, God made sev-eral covenants: under Adam, under Noah, under the law, and under the gospel.[13] Hence, God is covenanted not only with Israel (under the law) and Christians (under the gospel) but also with humanity as a whole (under Adam), and even with the entire universe (under Noah). The first three covenants (including God's covenant with Israel) have not been abolished or invalidated, nor have they been absorbed or dissolved into the fourth. Even though the first three have been, to use Irenaeus' expression, "recapit-ulated" in the fourth (brought under Christ as their head), they have not lost their proper identity and integrity. On the contrary, precisely because they have been "recapitulated" in Christ, they have achieved and maintain their full identity and integrity, even today. Therefore, when we talk about God's "new" covenant in Jesus, we must keep in mind the continuing sig-nificance and validity of these other covenants.

3. The most challenging task of a post-supersessionist Christology con-sists in providing an explanation for how it is theologically possible to both recognize the continuing validity of God's covenant with Israel and main-tain faith in Jesus as the person in whom God has acted to save humanity.

There are two dimensions in this explanation, one concerning the activ-ities of the Logos (Word) of God in Jesus (christological), and the other concerning the activities of the Holy Spirit (pneumatological). According to the Christian faith, the divine Logos, the Son of God the Father, took flesh (or is incarnated) as a Jew, that is, in Jesus of Nazareth, and is there-fore personally identified with him.[14] However, the Logos was not, and could not be, exhaustively embodied in Jesus of Nazareth, since Jesus was spatially and temporally limited. Thus, Jesus could not exhaustively express the divine, infinite saving power in his human words and deeds. This is part of what is meant by saying that the Logos "emptied himself" (see Phil 2:7) in the man Jesus and was subjected to human limitations (though not to sin). There is, therefore, a "distinction-in-identity" or "identity-in-distinction" between the eternal, "un-incarnate" Logos and the Jew Jesus in whom the Logos became flesh in time and with whom he is personally identified. Hence, the activities of the Logos, though inseparable from those of Jesus, are also distinct from and go beyond Jesus' activities, before, during, and after the Incarnation.

4. In addition, the Holy Spirit, though intimately united with the Logos, is distinct from him and operates in a saving manner outside and beyond him, before, during, and after Jesus' ministry. The Holy Spirit "blows where he wills" (John 3: 8). To use Irenaeus' colorful metaphor, the Logos and the Holy Spirit are the two "hands" of God the Father with which God acts in the world. Of course these two "hands" of God do not act independently of—much less in opposition to—each other. Nonetheless, they operate distinctly and diversely from each other, though always in conjunction with each other. Thus, God's saving presence through Word and Spirit is not limited to the Christian covenant: the divine, saving presence was active and continues to be so in the history of Israel. We might add that God is capable of extending this presence to the whole of human history, especially in the sacred books, rituals, moral teachings, and spiritual practices of all religions.

In this way, what the Holy Spirit says and does is truly different from, though not contradictory to, what the Logos says and does. What the Logos and the Spirit do and say in Israel and in non-Christian religions may be truly different from, though not contradictory to, what Jesus and the Spirit do in Christianity. Needless to say, these activities of the Logos and the Spirit do not mean that the human responses that constitute part of Judaism and other non-Christian religions as religious institutions are always free from sin and error. Of course, the same thing must be said of Christians as well!

5. Religious plurality, then, is not just a matter of fact but also a matter of principle. That is, Judaism and other non-Christian religions should be seen as part of the plan of divine providence and endowed with a particular role in the history of salvation. They are not merely a "preparation" for, "stepping stones" toward, or "seeds" of Christianity and thus destined to be "fulfilled" by it. Rather, they have their own autonomy and their proper role as ways of salvation, at least for their adherents.

6. In light of what has been said above, one may question the usefulness of words such as "unique," "absolute," and even "universal" to describe the role of Jesus as savior today. They might once have served the purpose of affirming the reality of God's definitive offer of salvation in Jesus for the whole of humanity. But words are unavoidably embedded in sociopolitical and cultural contexts. Colonialist imperialism, economic exploitation, political domination, and religious marginalization often tainted the contexts in which these words were used in many parts of the world. No matter how they are theologically qualified (and they may die the death of a thousand qualifications!), words such as "uniqueness," "absoluteness," and "universality" connote in the ears of non-Christians, especially those who have been victims of violence and exploitation at the hands of Christians, arrogance, exclusiveness, and self-absorption. More importantly, they are not the most effective means to convey Christ's message of humble service and compassionate love, especially to victims of political, economic, and religious persecution. In particular, in the post-Holocaust era, these expressions have outlived their usefulness. They should be jettisoned and replaced by other, theologically more adequate equivalents.

Christ's "uniqueness," "absoluteness," and "universality" are not exclusive, eliminative, and abrogative but, to use Jacques Dupuis's expressions, "constitutive" and "relational."[15] That is, because the Christ event, according to the Christian faith, belongs to and is the definitive realization of God's plan of salvation, Christ is "constitutive" of salvation in a very special manner. In him God has brought about salvation for all humanity in a most effective and powerful manner.

Moreover, because non-Christian religions and in particular Judaism are themselves part of God's plan of salvation, of which the Christ event is the definitive point, Christ is related to these religions, especially Judaism, and vice versa. So there a reciprocal relationship between Jesus and non-Christian religions, in particular Judaism. Hence, the Christ event is not only constitutive but also "relational." Autonomy and relatedness are not mutually contradictory, but grow in direct proportion to each other. Furthermore, because non-Christian religions possess an autonomous function in the history of salvation, different from that of Christianity, they cannot be reduced to Christianity in terms of "preparation" and "fulfillment."

7. There is then a reciprocal relationship between Christianity and Judaism and the other religions. Not only does Christianity complement the non-Christian religions, but also the other religions complement Christianity. In other words, the process of complementarity, enrichment, and even cor-

rection is two-way, or reciprocal. This reciprocity in no way endangers the Christian confession that the church has received from Christ the fullness of revelation, since it is one thing to receive the definitive gift of God's self-revelation in Jesus, and quite another to *understand* it fully and to *live* it completely. Indeed, it is only in a sincere and humble dialogue with other religions that Christianity can come to a fuller realization of its own identity and mission and a better understanding of the constitutive revelation that it has received from Christ. By the same token, Judaism and other religions can achieve their full potential only in dialogue with each other and with Christianity.

8. Furthermore, though Jesus Christ is confessed by Christians to be the fullness of revelation and the definitive savior, there is also a reciprocal relationship between him and other "saving figures." Jesus' "uniqueness"— or more appropriately, his "definitiveness"—is not absolute but relational. In this sense, Jesus' revelation and salvation are also "complemented" by God's self-revelation and redemption manifested in other "saving figures." In this context it is useful to recall that Jesus did not and could not reveal everything to his disciples. It is the Holy Spirit who will lead them to "the complete truth" (John 16:12–13). It is quite possible that the Holy Spirit will lead the church to the complete truth by means of a dialogue with other religions in which he is actively present.

9. One of the fundamental beliefs of the Christian faith is the so-called Second Coming of Christ. Christians are still waiting in hope for the coming of Christ as the glorious Messiah and Lord to judge the living and the dead. The Pontifical Biblical Commission's important document *The Jewish People and Their Sacred Scriptures in the Christian Bible* asserts that when the Jewish Messiah appears, he will have some of the traits of Christ, and that Christians will recognize the traits of Jesus in him.[16] If this is the case, then we might recognize at least two ways of understanding the saving action of God in human history. One is through the christological symbols of the Jesus of the Christian faith, the other through the religious symbols of Judaism, among which is the Jewish Messiah. These two ways are distinct from each other, but do not contradict or eliminate each other. On the other hand, there will be, at least at the end of time, some significant overlap between the Christian Jesus and the Jewish Messiah. How they will ultimately converge at the end of time is a matter of faith and hope. Meanwhile, Christians and Jews must join their actions and hearts, in mutual forgiveness and love, so that the ultimate unity they hope and pray for may be realized as much as possible even here and now.

10. This brings us to the last but not least aspect of Christian-Jewish relations. Dialogue between Christianity and Judaism (as well as with other religions) cannot be carried out simply as an exchange of theological views, though this academic conversation has its own importance. Rather this theological dialogue must be complemented by three other forms of dialogue, as the Pontifical Council for Interreligious Dialogue and the Congregation for the Evangelization of Peoples has identified:

a. The *dialogue of life*, where people strive to live in an open and neighborly spirit, sharing their joys and sorrows, their human problems and preoccupations. b. The *dialogue of action*, in which Christians and others collaborate for the integral development and liberation of people. c. The *dialogue of theological exchange*, where specialists seek to deepen their understanding of their respective religious heritages, and to appreciate each other's spiritual values. d. The *dialogue of religious experience*, where persons, rooted in their own religious traditions, share their spiritual riches, for instance, with regard to prayer and contemplation, faith and ways of searching for God or the Absolute.[17]

It is only out of this humble and loving practice of the fourfold dialogue that an adequate theology of Jesus Christ as God's constitutive and relational saving action in human history and of God's eternal covenant with the Jewish people can be elaborated.

Notes

1. See, for instance, the following representative works: Norbert Lohfink, *The Covenant Never Revoked: Biblical Reflections on Christian-Jewish Dialogue* (New York: Paulist, 1991); and John T. Pawlikowski, *Jesus and the Theology of Israel* (Wilmington, DE: Michael Glazier, 1989). Also, Vatican Commission for Religious Relations with Jews, *Notes on the Correct Way to Present the Jews and Judaism in Preaching and Catechesis in the Roman Catholic Church, no. 3;* cf. the *Catechism of the Catholic Church* (1992), no. 839, and the Pontifical Biblical Commission, *The Jewish People and Their Sacred Scriptures in the Christian Bible* (Vatican City: Editrice Vaticana, 2001), part II, § 46.

2. See, for instance, the Council of Florence's decree to the Jacobites (1442): "[The Holy Roman Church] . . . firmly believes, professes and preaches that 'no one remaining outside the Catholic Church, not only pagans,' but also Jews, heretics and schismatics, can become partakers of eternal life; but they will go to the 'eternal fire prepared for the devil and his angels' (Matthew 25: 41), unless before the end of their life they are joined to it." English translation in Joseph Neuner and Jacques Dupuis, eds., *The Christian Faith in the Doctrinal Documents of the Catholic*

Church (New York: Alba House, 2001). See Francis A. Sullivan, *Salvation outside the Church? Tracing the History of the Catholic Response* (New York: Paulist, 1992).

3. See Vatican II's "Dogmatic Constitution on the Church" (*Lumen Gentium*), no. 16. Translation in Austin Flannery, ed. *Vatican Council II: The Conciliar and Post Conciliar Decrees* (Collegeville: Liturgical Press, 1984), 367.

4. *Lumen Gentium*, no. 16. Translation in Flannery, 367.

5. *Lumen Gentium*, no. 17. Translation in Flannery, 368–369.

6. *Ad Gentes*, no. 3. "Decree on the Church's Missionary Activity." Translation in Flannery, 814.

7. *Ad Gentes*, no. 9. Translation in Flannery, 823.

8. *Ad Gentes*, no. 11. Translation in Flannery, 825.

9. *Nostra Aetate*, "Declaration on the Relation of the Church to Non-Christian Religions," no. 2. Translation in Flannery, 739.

10. *Nostra Aetate*, no. 4. Translation in Flannery, 740.

11. See Paul Knitter, *Introducing Theologies of Religions* (Maryknoll, NY: Orbis Books, 2002).

12. The English text is available in Stephen J. Pope and Charles Hefling, eds., *Sic et Non: Encountering Dominus Iesus* (Maryknoll, NY: Orbis Books, 2002).

13. See Irenaeus, *Against Heresies*, III, 11, 8.

14. In technical language, the "person" of Jesus (the Greek term is *hypostasis* or *prosopon*), as the Council of Chalcedon (451) affirms, is the Logos himself, whereas his "natures" (in Greek, *ousia* or *physis*) are both divinity and humanity. In other words, *who* Jesus is, is the Logos; and *what* Jesus is, is human and divine.

15. See Jacques Dupuis, *Toward a Christian Theology of Religious Pluralism* (Maryknoll, NY: Orbis Books, 1998), 283.

16. See Pontifical Biblical Commission, *Jewish People*, part I, § 21.

17. The Pontifical Council for Interreligious Dialogue and the Congregation for the Evangelization of Peoples, *Dialogue and Proclamation*, 42 (May 19, 1991); in English in William Burrows, ed., *Redemption and Dialogue: Reading Redemptoris Missio and Dialogue and Proclamation* (Maryknoll, NY: Orbis Books, 1993), 3–55.

Further Reading

Dupuis, Jacques. *Toward a Christian Theology of Religious Pluralism.* Maryknoll, NY: Orbis Books, 1998.

Knitter, Paul. *Introducing Theologies of Religions.* Maryknoll, NY: Orbis Books, 2002.

Phan, Peter. *In Our Tongues: Perspectives from Asia on Mission and Inculturation.* Maryknoll, NY: Orbis Books, 2003.

Pontifical Biblical Commission. *The Jewish People and Their Sacred Scriptures in the Christian Bible.* Vatican City: Editrice Vaticana, 2001.

Sullivan, Francis. *Salvation outside the Church? Tracing the History of the Catholic Response.* New York: Paulist, 1992.

12

CHAPTER

The Universal
Significance of Christ

Clark M. Williamson

"A SACRED OBLIGATION" states that although Christians taught for centuries that salvation is available only through Jesus Christ, "Christians can now recognize in the Jewish tradition the redemptive power of God at work." We speak of Jews as being in a "saving covenant with God," and acknowledge that we Christians need new ways of "understanding the universal significance of Christ." This chapter explores one new way of understanding salvation from a Christian perspective.

Are Only Christians Saved?

Let us begin with the question of whether people who do not believe in Jesus Christ can be or are nevertheless saved by God, or whether they are everlastingly condemned to a "hell . . . where the fire is never quenched"

(Mark 9:47–48). Most Christians are readily familiar with such comments and the two New Testament verses which claim that salvation is possible only through Jesus. Speaking of the crucified Christ, Acts says: "There is salvation in no one else, for there is no other name under heaven given among mortals by which we must be saved" (Acts 4:12). And Jesus, responding to Thomas' troubled question, "How can we know the way?" says: "I am the way, and the truth, and the life. No one comes to the Father except through me" (John 14:6). On the face of it, these two statements would seem to settle the matter: there is no salvation apart from believing in Jesus Christ.

Things are seldom so simple, however, and such a quick conclusion avoids two responsibilities. First, it does not look at depth into the meaning of these apparently exclusivistic passages, about which more will be said later, and, second, it does not look at other New Testament passages that say that God's free and sovereign grace is for all people, for all the world. We are responsible for bringing both the exclusive and the all-inclusive passages into the conversation if we do, indeed, respect the authority of scripture—and do not simply plumb it for nuggets that support a position that we already hold. We must be willing to let it draw us into a conversation about the meaning of salvation.

Inclusive Salvation: Texts

These other passages include 1 Timothy 2:4, which says that God our Savior "desires *everyone* to be saved and to come to knowledge of the truth." 2 Peter 3:9 proclaims, "The Lord is not slow about his promise, as some think of slowness, but is patient with you, not wanting any to perish, but *all* to come to repentance." John 3:17 declares, "God did not send the Son into the world to condemn the world, but in order that the *world* might be saved through him." John adds: Jesus is the "Lamb of God who takes away the sin of the world" (John 1:29). Paul remarks, "As one man's trespass led to condemnation for all, so one man's act of righteousness leads to justification and life for *all*" (Rom 5:18). He repeats the point in Romans 11:32: "For God has imprisoned all in disobedience so that he may be merciful to *all*." Colossians 1:19–20 puts it: "For in him all the fullness of God was pleased to dwell, and through him God was pleased to reconcile to himself *all* things, whether on earth or in heaven." We emphasized "all" and "world" to make the point clear. No Christian approach to salvation that neglects these inclusive, universalist passages can claim to be genuinely biblical.

Recalling Mark's comment in 9:47–48 about being condemned to "hell . . . where the fire is never quenched," we should note that there is also, in the book of Revelation, the counterclaim that death and hell are subject to the Lordship of God and that in the final judgment they will be destroyed: "Death and Hades gave up their dead that were in them" before the "great throne" of God and when the "book of life" was opened, death and Hades themselves "were thrown into the lake of fire" (Rev 20:14) and extinguished. Earlier, "Michael and his angels" defeated and evicted Satan and his angels and prevented them from holding any place at all in the kingdom of God (Rev 12:7–12). It is important to keep in mind that the genre of the book of Revelation means that its images and concepts are all oriented to the future. This means that its author did not expect God's victory over death and Hades to be visible within human history, but only as time approaches the last judgment.

To put it simply: the hell that would damn those made in God's image is subject to the powerful grace and love of God made known in Jesus Christ. Death and hell cannot prevail against this unfathomably gracious love. Jesus had said to Peter, "You are Peter, and on this rock I will build my church, and the gates of Hades *will not prevail* against it" (Matt 16: 18). Hell is emptied by God's grace and thrown into the lake of fire.

God Is the Savior

Let us return to the two passages cited initially, Acts 4:12 and John 14:6. Both involve the "name" of God. Acts mentions it explicitly ("there is no other name") and John has Jesus use it: "I am [the name of God as given in Exodus 3:14–15, "I Am Who I Am"] the way." This name in Hebrew, *Ehyeh asher ehyeh*, would be better translated as "I will be what I will be," because Hebrew has no simple present tense and because this name deepens the mystery of God. In scripture it is usually presented as "the Lord," because Jews did not pronounce the name but instead presented it as "YHWH" and when reading scripture pronounced the word *Adonai*, "the Lord." In the gospels, Jesus never pronounces the name of God but, instead, teaches us in the Lord's Prayer to pray that the Lord's name be hallowed.

Jesus' own name in Aramaic was *Yeshua*, a name meaning "YHWH saves." Two places in the New Testament make this clear to those who know the Exodus story of God's giving God's name to Moses. Matthew 1:21, in telling the story of Jesus' birth, tells of an angel saying to Joseph of Mary's child, "you are to name him Jesus [YHWH saves], for he will save his people from their sins." And Philippians 2:9 speaks of God as having given Jesus "the name that is above every name, so that at the name of Jesus every knee should bend . . . and every tongue confess that Jesus Christ is Lord, to the glory of God the Father." The name that is above every name is not the title "Christ," but the name of Jesus, that is, "YHWH saves."

Hence, the verses in Acts and John that initially seem to be exclusivist with regard to salvation are now more complicated for us. They are theocentric, not Jesus-centric. John's gospel is both theocentric and deeply concerned to make clear that Jesus' mission was to make God's name known: "I have come in my Father's name" (5:43); the works that he does are done in "my Father's name" (10:25); he is celebrated as "the one who comes in the name of the Lord" (12:13); his suffering is to glorify the name of his Father (12:28); and he summarizes his mission as the Sent One of God by praying, "I have made your name known to those whom you gave me from the world" (17:6). All of this calls to mind God's command to Moses: "But this is why I have let you live: to show you my power, and to make my name resound through all the earth" (Exod 9:16).

The promise of God to Abraham and Sarah, "in you all the families of the earth shall be blessed" (Gen 12:3), is given by God to Moses as a vocation, reiterated by Jesus and used by Paul to describe the gospel: "All this is from God, who reconciled us to himself through Christ, and has given us this ministry of reconciliation; that is, in Christ God was reconciling the world to himself" (2 Cor 5:18–19). YHWH is the subject of all the salvation verbs of the Torah-Christ story, including those in Acts 4:12 and John 14:6.[1] No countervailing power, even Satan or Hades, can prevail against God's accomplishing of God's purposes; there is no other power over which God is not Lord.

Human beings are saved *from* sin and its effects by God as Father, Son, and Holy Spirit, one God, Mother of us all. We are saved *to* a life of saying yes to God's grace as made known to us in Jesus Christ, and *to* a life of everlasting blessedness, inclusive well-being, in God's own life when *God* will be all in all. All are saved through God's reconciliation in Jesus Christ, *as Paul rightly said*; some are saved (in the sense of understanding that they are saved and living new and transformed lives) by the Holy Spirit in the course of history; and all will be saved in the consummating end of things in ultimate redemption.

Do Human Beings Face a Dual Destiny?

The alternative position usually goes under the name of "dual destiny," that is, it claims that human beings face a dual destiny in that some are damned and some are saved. But when we ask the question why some are damned and others not, we receive two mutually incompatible answers. One answer is that some are saved because they did the right thing, held the right belief, underwent baptism (or the right form of baptism), or had the right attitudes. If this is the answer, then people save themselves by meeting the requirements, however they may be defined, of salvation. This answer attaches conditions to the proclamation of God's singular free and gracious gift of salvation. To claim that we must do something to earn this gift, whatever that something might be, is to turn the *free* gift of God's unconditional love into a condition apart from which God is not free to love. This is the proper definition of "works-righteousness." This answer overlooks the fact that the most committed believers in God's love and the betrayers and deniers of God's love are not two different groups of human beings but one and the same group of human beings: "all have sinned and fall short of the glory of God" (Rom 3:23). This answer denies that we are saved by God's grace, a denial that is itself denied by the claim that all are saved in Jesus Christ.

The other answer typically is that some are saved and some are damned by God's impenetrable decision to save some and condemn others. Those who are saved through no merit of their own are saved by the grace of God. But when God's loving grace is merged with the assumption, whether implicit or explicit, that God is raw, absolute power, God and God's grace become utterly inscrutable. This is not the God we know in Jesus Christ or the history of the Israel of God with the God of Israel. Instead, it is an unknown "god" secreted behind the God whom we know in Jesus Christ, in whom God's will for the reconciliation of all with all is not enigmatic. This position affirms God's grace but denies that the grace of God is decisively disclosed in Jesus Christ, a denial that is itself denied by the affirmation that God is the God of Israel and the God of Jesus Christ.

What is additionally at stake, underneath the mutually incompatible and individually incoherent defenses of dual destiny, is another claim: that outside the church there is no salvation. This position holds that salvation is exclusively available through the church—that God's grace is, as it were, channeled, and that there is only one channel, the church. That there are numerous churches of a wide variety of kinds opens up the possibility that any one of them can claim, as many have, to be the "only true" church and, hence, the only reliable channel of salvation. But whether the claim is made in a highly sectarian way or whether it is the "soft" claim that any and all churches are reliable channels of God's grace, in either case the church is the broker of salvation. It has absolute power over all our lives to grant or withhold the exclusive means of grace and the hope of salvation. The claim that there is no salvation outside the church grants idolatrous power to the church and its clergy and denies, as it is denied by, the claim of the gospel that all people are the objects of God's all-embracing love. God is, as Charles Wesley put it in the hymn "Love Divine, All Loves Excelling," "pure unbounded love." We may not erect boundaries of our own around God's love.

Salvation Is from the Jews

In the Gospel of John 4:1–27, Jesus is engaged in a conversation with a Samaritan woman in a city named Sychar, where Joseph's well was. The conversation turns on the subject of "living water," the water that Jesus gives and that will "become in them [those who receive it] a spring of water gushing up into eternal life" (v. 14). The Samaritan woman comments on the difference between Samaritans and Jews: "Our ancestors worshiped on this mountain, but you ["the Jews" in some ancient manuscripts] say that the place where people must worship is in Jerusalem" (v. 20). Jesus' response includes the remark: "You worship what you do not know; we worship what we know, for salvation is from the Jews" (v. 22).

Jesus is not saying that salvation is the exclusive property of the people Israel; after all, he has offered the Samaritan woman the water that gives life. But he is saying that salvation is "from" the people Israel. Commenting on this passage, the Christian theologian John Howard Yoder notes that it challenges the assumption that Christians all too readily make that Jews are "outside the salvation story." This assumption then means that we have to ask ourselves how to bring the gospel of salvation to them. "But," he notes, "if . . . 'salvation is from the Jews,' that might be the wrong question."[2]

Our earliest writer of the New Testament, the apostle Paul, thought that it was, indeed, the wrong question, that it got things backwards. In his letter to Rome, Paul asks: "Is God the God of Jews only? Is he not the God of Gentiles also? Yes, of Gentiles also, since God is one" (Rom 3:29). Notice that little word "also." We Gentiles are also included in God's love, as indeed the self-disclosure of God to Israel had long ago affirmed to Abraham and Sarah—in your descendants the Gentiles will be blessed.

The letter to the Ephesians reminded its readers

that at one time you Gentiles by birth, called "the uncircumcision" by those who are called "the circumcision" . . . remember that you were at that time without Christ, being aliens from the commonwealth of Israel, strangers to the covenants of promise, having no hope and without God in the world. But now in Christ Jesus you who once were far off have been brought near by the blood of Christ. For he is our peace; in his flesh he has made both groups into one and has broken down the dividing wall, that is, the hostility between us. (Eph 2:11–14)

For Paul the question is not how Jews can be saved. They have the covenants of promise. The question was, rather, how we Gentiles can be saved. For it is we who were strangers to those very promises, "having no hope and without God in the world." The ministry of Jesus Christ, particularly his crucifixion (his blood), brought us "near" the commonwealth of Israel. "So then you are no longer strangers and aliens, but you are citizens with the saints [the people Israel] and also members of the household of God" (Eph 2:19).

Notice, again, that little word "also." Twice we have seen it occur in Paul's writing about us Gentile followers of Jesus—we are those who are also saved.

Jesus Re-presents Salvation

YHWH/Adonai did not initiate salvation during the ministry of Jesus. YHWH had long been involved not only in creating but in re-creating, redeeming, the people Israel. God's freely given, salvific love indeed made Israel the people of YHWH. Of his fellow Jews, his "kindred according to the flesh," Paul says: "They are Israelites, and to them belong the adoption, the glory, the covenants, the giving of the law [Torah, way], the worship, and the promises." (Rom 9:4).

They are Israelites. Paul does not say that they "were" the Israel of God or that they "will be"; they simply are what they have always been: the people of God, *bene Yisrael.* They are the people of God by God's electing grace, by God's decision, by God's naming of them (Gen 32:28). The people Israel belong to God.

To them belongs the adoption; Israel is the son, the daughter, of God. "When Israel was a child, I loved him, and out of Egypt I called my son" (Hos 11:1). "Adoption" means being chosen, selected, handpicked. God's gracious election of Israel is the ground of Israel's hope and the final reason why "all Israel will be saved" (Rom 11:26). The good news of God's gracious election of Gentiles is coherent only if God graciously elected Israel; our adoption by God's reconciling love present in Jesus Christ confirms God's reconciling adoption of Israel.

To them belongs the glory, the *doxa*, the manifest presence of God. Indeed, God dwells "among" the people Israel (Gen 25:8), in the nomadic sanctuary, in the wilderness wandering, in the temple, in exile, in suffering; God is Immanuel, God with us, transcendence dwelling within community. God is present, the later rabbis say, when Jews read the Torah: "If two sit together and words of the Torah are spoken between them, the Divine Presence rests between them" (Mishnah, *Aboth* 3:2).

To them belong the giving of the covenants and the Torah, the way of God that is a way of life, blessing, and peace. Consider these words from Deuteronomy 10:12–15.

> So now, O Israel, what does the Lord your God require of you? Only to fear the Lord your God, to walk in all his ways, to love him, to serve the Lord your God with all your heart and with all your soul, and to keep the commandments of the Lord your God and his decrees that I am commanding you today, for your own well-being. Although heaven and the heaven of heavens belong to the Lord your God, the earth with all that is in it, yet the Lord set his heart in love on your ancestors alone and chose you, their descendants, out of all the peoples, as it is today.

At the heart of the covenants and the Torah we find YHWH's unfathomable love for the people Israel and the very fathomable love of Israel for YHWH; Israel lives out her love for YHWH in adhering to the commandments, the *mitzvoth*, because they are the commandments of love, of Torah as born in love and of love expressed in Torah, commandments.

Hence, the graciously given love of God enacted in the ministry of Jesus Christ is presented anew, more recently, to us Gentiles in a manner akin to the way in which Paul speaks of himself as having been granted an appearance of the risen Christ—"last of all, as to one untimely born" (1 Cor 15:8). The possibility of salvation itself is constituted by God's unconditional and gracious love of us. Salvation becomes manifest again in Jesus Christ, clearly, for the reconciliation of all the world. His significance is not that in him and only in him salvation becomes possible. It is that the salvation that had long been offered by God to Israel as also for the blessing of the Gentiles has now become clearly manifest, evident. To claim that Christ makes salvation possible implies that it is God who needs to be reconciled, a reconciliation that Christ accomplishes by some work. But it is we who need to be reconciled, not YHWH, who was actively present in Christ reconciling us to God, to Israel, to one another, and to all the world.

Incarnation

The Jewish theologian Michael Wyschogrod, recalling the many instances in Scripture where YHWH is said to dwell among the people Israel, says that God "entered [the] . . . world through a people whom he chose as his habitation. There thus came about a visible presence of God in the universe, first in the person of Abraham and later his descendants, as the people of Israel."[3] If there are no sacraments among Jews, says Wyschogrod, "it is because the people of Israel in whose flesh the presence of God makes itself felt becomes the sacrament."[4] The people Israel are a carnal election; God elects Abraham and Sarah and their "seed," their descendants. This is why YHWH's election of Israel is a purely gracious election. Had God chosen a people because of its high level of moral attainment, its worldly glory, the purity of its religious ardor, that people's election would depend on their retaining whatever quality it was on which the choice of them was based. But God made a physical covenant with Abraham and gave no justification, no reasons, for having done so. "Salvation is of the Jews," Wyschogrod concludes, "because the flesh of Israel is the abode of the divine presence in the world. It is the carnal anchor that God has sunk into the soil of creation."[5]

Wyschogrod's description of how God is depicted in the scriptures of Israel enables us better to understand similar claims made in relation to Jesus Christ in the New Testament, as when John's gospel says of Jesus that in him the Word of God "became flesh and lived among us, . . . full of grace and truth" (1:14). Older translations that say he "tabernacled among us" or "pitched his tent" better express the Hebraic ways of describing God's presence among the people Israel. Such statements were made by Jews who were using the language of the scriptures of Israel. If God in God's freedom could choose to dwell in the people Israel, God in God's freedom could choose to dwell in one particular member of the people Israel, Jesus of Nazareth.

An ancient trinitarian tradition, in a lovely metaphor, regarded the Word and the Holy Spirit as the "two hands" of God—the Word being God's free giving of God's self-disclosure to human beings and the Spirit so working upon the hearts of human beings as to enable the Word to be wholeheartedly accepted by those to whom God offered Godself. In the gospel story of Jesus, the Spirit was graciously active in Jesus' life at his conception, baptism, temptation, first sermon, his healings, transfiguration, resurrection, and the giving of the great commission.

In Jesus Christ the creative and redeeming purpose of YHWH is clearly disclosed to humanity—what God the Word freely gives, God the Spirit empowers Jesus freely to receive. Jesus is immeasurably blessed by the Holy Spirit of YHWH and is the gift to the world of the God of Israel and the Israel of God that it may know of its redemption.

Notes

1. See James A. Sanders, *Canon and Community* (Philadelphia: Fortress, 1984), 59.

2. John Howard Yoder, in Michael G. Cartwright and Peter Ochs, eds., *The Jewish-Christian Schism Revisited* (Grand Rapids, MI: Eerdmans, 2003), 245.

3. Michael Wyschogrod, *The Body of Faith* (Northvale, NJ: Jason Aronson, 1996), 10.

4. Wyschogrod, *Body of Faith*, 25.

5. Wyschogrod, *Body of Faith*, 256.

Further Reading

Jones, Joe R. *A Grammar of Christian Faith*. Vol. 2. Lanham, MD: Rowman & Littlefield, 2002.

Guthrie, Shirley C. *Christian Doctrine: Revised Edition*. Louisville, KY: Westminster / John Knox Press, 1994.

Migliore, Daniel L. *Faith Seeking Understanding*. Grand Rapids, MI: Eerdmans, 1991.

Morse, Christopher. *Not Every Spirit: A Dogmatics of Christian Disbelief*. Valley Forge, PA: Trinity Press International, 1994.

Suchocki, Marjorie H. *The End of Evil: Process Eschatology in Historical Context*. Albany: State University of New York Press, 1988.

Williamson, Clark. *Way of Blessing, Way of Life: A Christian Theology*. St. Louis: Chalice Press, 1999.

VIII
P A R T

Christians Should
Not Target Jews
for Conversion

13

CHAPTER

Covenant and Conversion

Philip A. Cunningham

F
OR WELL over a thousand years, Christians have been fascinated with the prospect of converting Jews to Christianity. In various times and places, Christians have engaged in coerced baptisms of Jews, in secretly baptizing Jewish children and then forcibly removing them from their families, in destroying Jewish books and prohibiting instruction in the Jewish tradition, in requiring Jews to listen to hours of threatening preaching, and in demanding that Jewish leaders debate church doctrines publicly with their Christian counterparts. Jews who refused these conversionary tactics sometimes were exiled or killed. Jews who accepted baptism were spied upon for evidence of backsliding into Jewish customs, such as lighting candles for the Sabbath. Such practices occurred periodically into the twentieth century.

These egregious violations of religious freedom were largely unknown in North America, although social pressures encouraged immigrants from all backgrounds to assimilate into the majority culture. Nonetheless, even today various Christian groups specifically seek out Jews for baptism. Sometimes

151

deceptive practices are employed, including using Jewish symbols and practices to make overtures to Jewish youngsters without parental consent.

In the decades after the Shoah, some Christians have begun to have reservations about the special place that Jews have held in Christian missionary efforts over the centuries. In article 7 of "A Sacred Obligation" the Christian Scholars Group states that Christians should not target Jews for conversion. The authors came to this conclusion primarily because of their "conviction that Jews are in an eternal covenant with God." "A Sacred Obligation" has not been alone in grappling with the implications of covenant and conversion. A 2002 dialogue statement of delegates of the U.S. Catholic Bishops' Committee on Ecumenical and Interreligious Affairs, *Reflections on Covenant and Mission*, indicates that "the Church must bear witness in the world to the good news of Christ so as to prepare the world for the fullness of the kingdom of God. However, this evangelizing task no longer includes the wish to absorb the Jewish faith into Christianity and so end the distinctive witness of Jews to God in human history."[1] Similarly, a study curriculum of the United Church of Canada "argues that the failure of Christians to convert Jews *en masse* to Christianity could have been anticipated (because of God's continued covenantal relationship with Judaism)." It recommends "that the United Church state as a matter of policy that it 'rejects and repudiates . . . all mission and proselytism seeking to convert Jews to Christianity.'"[2]

The recognition of Israel's never-ending covenant leads to the consideration of such topics as Christian efforts to convert Jews, the meaning of revelation and salvation, and New Testament texts such as Matthew 28:19. I will briefly consider these matters, but first it is necessary to explain the understanding of biblical interpretation that guided the authors of "A Sacred Obligation."

Four Understandings of the Bible

I suggest that four overarching approaches account for the variety of Christian perspectives on the Bible. Some Christians so stress the divine inspiration behind God's scriptural word that they adopt an ahistorical stance toward the Bible. Favoring what they may call a "plain sense" reading of the text, they show little interest in the circumstances in which a biblical book was written, the perspectives prevalent at the time, or the text's literary styles and purposes. Such Christians see the reading of the Bible as essentially a personal interaction between the text and the believer under the guidance of the Holy Spirit. They tend to come from churches that emphasize the singular and final authority of the Bible. We might call this perspective the "Bible as divine word" approach.

Other Christians emphasize that the Bible is God's word expressed in human speech. They highlight the role played by humans in composing the text while not denying divine inspiration. Thus they believe it is essential to read the Bible in its literary and historical contexts in order to avoid misunderstanding it or projecting modern prejudices onto the text. As one recent Christian document has put it, "Holy Scripture, inasmuch as it is the 'word of God in human language,' has been composed by human authors in all its various parts and in all the sources that lie behind them. Because of this, its proper understanding not only admits the use of [a contextual] method but actually requires it."[3] Such Christians tend to come from churches that see the Bible as the preeminent, but not exclusive, authority that must dialogue with the faith experiences and histories of today's faith communities. They also understand that the Bible must be "actualized" or brought to life in today's social and cultural conditions, which are very different from the scripture's originating circumstances. I call this perspective the "incarnational" approach, since it holds God's word to be incarnated in human language and history.

Still another group regards the Bible as a profound instance of human literary genius. They see little or no need to posit a divine influence in its origins or composition. Such persons may or may not consider themselves to be people of faith, and the Bible exerts little or no special authority for them. This perspective might be called the "Bible as human artifact" approach.

Finally, some Christians, particularly those of the Eastern Orthodox traditions, encounter the Bible primarily through worship. They read the Bible through the lens of the liturgy, including hymns, prayers, ritual actions, and sacraments. While not denying the human aspects of the Bible, these Christians accentuate the divinely inspired character of the Bible as shaping worship. This perspective could be called the "liturgical" approach to the Bible.

Of these four overarching viewpoints—the Bible as divine word, as incarnated word, as historical artifact, as liturgically enacted—it is the incarnational perspective that is most influential among the authors of "A Sacred Obligation." Thus our group situates biblical texts on covenant in their historical and literary contexts, and "actualizes" them in the historical reality of today's churches that repent of the evils that Christians have inflicted upon Jews for centuries.

Nonincarnational perspectives that either exclusively emphasize or totally deny the divine character of the Bible will prove insufficient to this task. Regarding the "Bible as divine word" leads to ahistorical readings that may mask avoidance mechanisms by which Christians seek to escape responsibility for the tragic relationship of Christians and Jews. The agnosticism of the "Bible as human artifact" approach is of limited help to faith communities striving to do God's will in an increasingly complex world. Only an incarnational approach is adequate to the task.

Covenant

Although the Bible speaks of God entering into or promising a number of "covenants" (e.g., with Noah, with Abraham, with Israel at Mount Sinai, with David, announced through Jeremiah, etc.), it is possible to abstract from these specific moments and consider the concept of "covenant" as a theological reality (see the chapter by Mary Boys on "The Enduring Covenant" in this volume). In this sense, a community in covenant walks through life with God in a relationship of mutual responsibilities. Covenant is a sharing in life with God. Theologically, it is not so much a legal contract of alliance as a dynamic interaction. It might therefore be best expressed as a continuing action verb, as "covenanting." Since God is one of the participants in the relationship, covenanting with God is by its very nature everlasting and will endure until the full establishing of God's reign at the end of history. Covenant with God goes on even when the human partners sin and suffer the consequences for not meeting their covenantal obligations fully. As Christians we have experienced all these aspects of covenant because of our relationship with God in Christ.

Over the ages, Jews have understood their duties to their divine covenant partner in different ways. For Jews today it is through the study of God's gift of the Torah that they discern the divine will for the Jewish people. A key aspect of Jewish covenanting is the obligation to follow God's commands. In doing so, Jews give witness to God before all peoples and so ready the world for the peace and justice of the kingdom of God. If Jewish covenanting with God must by its nature live on until the end of days, then this obligation and this distinctive witness are intended by God to endure throughout history as we know it.

Although the chapters in this book by Clark Williamson and Peter Phan focus on the topic of salvation ("A Sacred Obligation," article 6), it might here be said that such an intimate and everlasting relationship as covenanting with the Holy One must in itself be "saving" because it is a participation in God's will. As Walter Cardinal Kasper has put it, "This does not mean that Jews in order to be saved have to become Christians; if they follow their own conscience and believe in God's promises as they understand them in their religious tradition they are in line with God's plan, which for [Christians] comes to its historical completion in Jesus Christ."[4]

Christians understand that their covenanting in Christ is in continuity with Israel's covenanting. Paul expresses this in Romans 11:13–24 with his famous metaphor of the olive tree in which the wild Gentile branches are grafted onto the holy Jewish root.

A renewed appreciation for Israel's covenanting does not thereby reduce Christianity to "Judaism for the Gentiles." Christians believe that the incarnation of the Logos (God's inviting Word) in Jesus of Nazareth through the power of the Spirit achieves the most intense union of the human and the divine imaginable. Christians, therefore, might understand the Incarnation as the most profound instance of divine-human covenanting, although the full consequences of the life, death, and resurrection of the incarnated Logos will not unfold until the end of time.

Christians are also convinced that the "Christ event"—the life, death, and resurrection of the Jew Jesus—is essential to the final establishment of the new creation in its fullness. By uniting mortal humanity and transcendent divinity, the incarnate Logos has caused the saving power of God to permeate deeply human life and death. The church is bound to give witness to this before the entire world. Moreover, if the Jew Jesus incarnates *Israel's* covenanting with God, embodying what life in covenant was and is all about, then *Israel's* covenanting life with God must be permanent and vital in order for the church's covenanting with God through Christ also to be permanent and vital.

Some Christians, while accepting that Jews abide in covenant with God, nevertheless conceive of this totally in terms of preparing for the birth of Christianity. Such Christians care little about the richness of rabbinic and later Jewish traditions, and thereby trivialize what covenanting with God means. On the contrary, in Christian terms, life in covenant with God for Jews as well as for Christians by definition involves relationship with the divine Word and sanctifying Spirit. The ongoing Jewish tradition is therefore a fruit of the Holy Spirit and worthy of study by Christians, as several Christian churches have stated in recent decades (see "A Sacred Obligation," article 4). It also demands to be respected and cherished by Christians as the outgrowth of a profound, even if not Christ-centered, partnership with God.

The recent Christian acknowledgment of the permanence of Israel's covenanting means that we Christians also understand that Jewish covenanting is a distinctive, if related, witness to God before the world. Respecting Israel's enduring covenant requires concluding that God does not want a world without the distinctively Jewish way of covenanting.

However, the argument that Christians should not seek to baptize Jews conflicts with two conscious or unconscious Christian assertions: (1) Jews should have recognized Jesus as their own savior (and so subsequent Rabbinic Judaism is essentially the result of an error); and (2) God intends all humanity to be baptized (and so Jews should not be excluded from this goal). A Christian with such beliefs would likely find it unimaginable that a "real" Christian would not seek to convert Jews. Nonetheless, both notions are difficult to sustain when examined with an "incarnational" approach to the biblical witness and in terms of Christian theologies of revelation and of the mission of the church. I will explore each of these two topics in turn.

Jews and Christian Faith

The belief that Jews should have recognized Jesus as Lord and Christ has roots in the New Testament. Paul, for example, was distressed at his failure to convince his "kin according to the flesh" (Rom 9:1–5ff). Although the Gospel of John states that "salvation is from the Jews" (4:22), it also declares that "whoever does not believe has already been condemned, because he has not believed in the name of the only Son of God" (3:18). However, as mentioned above, an incarnational understanding of the scriptures demands that these texts be understood in their own historical and social contexts.

Most, if not all, New Testament writers believed that they were living in the final stages of human history. A pervasive New Testament conviction is that the resurrection of Jesus demonstrated that the present age was giving way to the glorious age to come. All three synoptic gospels, for instance, present Jesus saying, "This generation will not pass away before all these things take place" (Matt 24:34; Mark 13:30; Luke 21:32). The looming end of history gave the perspectives of the writers of the New Testament a certain finality and urgency. Thus, someone like Paul could assert that "all Israel will be saved" because "the gifts and the call of God [to Israel] are irrevocable" (Rom 11:26, 29). Yet at the same time he was "in great sorrow and constant anguish" over his Jewish kinfolk (9:2), partially because of his sense that "time is running out" (1 Cor 7:29). The New Testament writers could not have imagined that people would be reading their words two thousand years later. Nor would they have seen any need to ponder the ongoing role of Judaism in a human history that they saw as reaching its climax.

Contemporary Christians, however, know that history did not end. We also have experiences of the enduring fidelity of the Jewish people to God, often despite Christian oppression, that first-century churches could not have foreseen. Since today's Christians cannot help but recognize Judaism's long-term vitality after two millennia, the shorter-range vision of the New Testament authors is inadequate as the sole basis of Christian theological approaches to Judaism. New Testament words cannot be simply "downloaded" out of their context and "installed" in our own.

One's theology of revelation is also relevant here. Christian faith is resurrection faith. The recognition of Jesus as divine Son or Word of God or Savior is a consequence of the experience of the Crucified One as raised to Lordship. As Paul wrote, "If Christ has not been raised, then empty is our preaching; empty, too, your faith. . . . We are the most pitiable people of all" (1 Cor 15:14, 19). Since it discloses the activity of God, the resurrection of Jesus is a revelatory event. But revelation is an interactive process that requires both God's self-disclosure *and* human perception and affirmation of it. Faith begins when humans respond to a God who reveals, who invites a response, and who enables recognition of the invitation. Faith is the gift of God's grace.

Specifically Christian faith arose when "God was pleased to reveal his Son" (Gal 1:16) to certain Jews who were thus enabled to perceive the exaltation of the Crucified One. The proclamation of the resurrection experience made the revelation transformative to some and not to others—"terror and amazement seized them" (Mark 16:8); "but some doubted" (Matt 28:17); "they did not believe them" (Luke 24:11); and "I will not believe" (John 20:25)—but always "by the grace of God" (1 Cor 15:10).

Therefore, human beings are not really competent to blame others for failing to "believe" the proclamation of the good news of Christ crucified and raised. Not only might the human proclamation of the gospel be poorly or incomprehensibly given, but, more importantly, no human being can know the mysterious workings of God's purposes and grace in the heart of another. Certainly, medieval Jews who refused forced baptism out of fidelity to their covenant with God and so were slain by fanatical Christians cannot be faulted for rejecting the gospel.

Christians cannot presume that the Jewish "no" to Jesus, even in the centuries before the church became powerful, was the result of Jewish blindness. Perhaps Divine Providence always intended for the two covenanting communities of Rabbinic Judaism and Christianity to be born in the late Second Temple period, and so bestowed the grace of faith in the crucified and raised One selectively on some and not on others. Paul seems to have thought along these lines when he wrote about God "foreknowing" those who would have faith in Christ (Rom 8:29; cf. 11:25–27).

Conceivably, at the end of days Jews will come to appreciate why Christians revere Christ Jesus, while Christians will come to value Jewish love for the Torah. Both may profoundly recognize the presence of their divine covenant partner in the other and so will exclaim with Paul, "Oh, the depth of the riches and wisdom and knowledge of God! How inscrutable are his judgments and how unsearchable his ways!" (Rom 11:33).

This eschatological vision is partially inspired by the Pontifical Biblical Commission's recent study, *The Jewish People and Their Sacred Scriptures in the Christian Bible.*[5] After noting that "Jewish messianic expectation is not in vain," the commission went on to observe, "The difference is that for us [Christians] the One who is to come will have the traits of the Jesus who has already come and is already present and active among us" (§ 21). For Christians, these "traits" must refer to the crucified and raised Word who brings the Church into covenant with God. But if "Jewish messianic hopes are not in vain," then they will also recognize the eschatological Messiah, logically on the basis of "traits" mediated through the Jewish tradition.

But until that day, we Christians should trust that God will bring about the new creation as God wills and that Jews are part of the divine plan for this. We should work for the kingdom's coming along with those whom we now affirm as covenantal partners with God.

Must the Whole World Be Baptized before God's Kingdom Comes?

A second conviction among many Christians is that God intends the whole world to be baptized as a prelude to the age to come. The most pertinent New Testament basis for this perspective is the scene unique to Matthew 28:19–20a, in which the resurrected Jesus instructs his disciples, "Go, therefore, and make disciples of *panta ta ethnē* [the original Greek is important here, as will be seen], baptizing them in the name of the Father, and of the Son, and of the Holy Spirit, teaching them to observe everything I have commanded you." The trinitarian baptismal formula, found nowhere else in the New Testament, indicates that Matthew is presenting the customs of his own local church community. Moreover, since none of the other gospels is aware of the explicit command to make disciples of *panta ta ethnē*, the directive seems to be Matthew's way of legitimating the bringing of the good news of Christ to the Gentiles.

The mission to the Gentiles was a major debate in the early churches. If Gentiles were permitted to join what were originally exclusively Jewish church communities, what norms of Jewish life should these newcomers observe? The fact that such topics were fiercely disputed in the New Testament churches strongly suggests that Jesus left no authoritative word on the subject. On such a central topic as kosher food regulations, for example, Mark indicates that such standards no longer exist (Mark 7:19). Luke thinks that Gentiles should observe some minimal dietary regulations (Acts 15:20, 29). The Matthean Jesus, in contrast, declares that "whoever breaks one of the least of these commandments [of the Torah] and teaches others to do so will be called least in the kingdom of heaven" (Matt 5:19).

Matthew's community apparently observed Jewish religious customs quite extensively. Those who just cry "Lord, Lord!" will not enter the Father's kingdom, but only those who *do* the Father's will (7:21; see also 25:31ff). The Matthean church is to put the Torah definitively interpreted by Jesus into practice. It is most fitting, then, that Matthew concludes his gospel with the instruction to teach *panta ta ethnē* to "observe all that I have commanded you."

Given Matthew's Jewish orientation, it seems clear that this Greek phrase is best translated as "all the Gentiles." The typical rendering as "all the nations" fails to convey to modern readers that for first-century Jews, including Jews in Christ, "the nations" were the *goyim*, the Gentiles, the non-Jews. The Matthean Jesus directs his disciples to go out to the Gentile nations and teach them the Torah that Jesus has commanded his followers to observe.

Again, one cannot simply transpose the vision of the New Testament writers into our very different global context today, not if one understands God's inspiration to be mediated in human history. It should give Christians pause to realize that Matthew in 28:19 was thinking of the Gentile nations that needed to be taught God's will. Jews who already possessed the gift of the Torah, even if not the definitive Torah of Jesus that Matthew espoused, were clearly in a different category than pagans. For Christians today who affirm Jewish covenanting with God, it is plain that Judaism's long life with God's Torah has continued to produce a harvest of holiness. Jews do not need to be made disciples of Jesus to be introduced to the covenanting God. Instead, Christians and Jews can instruct each other about how they understand God's commands to them and help each other to overcome their covenantal failures.

If Jews do not need to be baptized to be in relationship with the God who saves, then what about the rest of humanity? First-century Jews (including baptized Jews like Matthew) grouped humanity into Jews and undifferentiated Gentiles. Jews knew the revelation given to Moses, but the "nations" were pagan idol worshippers. However, theirs was a smaller world than ours, and the ancient and complex religious systems of the Far East were unknown to Jews.

If today's Christians believe that God accommodates divine revelation to the perceptions of humanity, and if the world religions "often reflect a ray of that truth which enlightens all men and women," as the Second Vatican Council expresses it,[6] then the presence of many great religious traditions in the world is a reflection of God's grandeur. After all, "salvation is offered to all nations, as was already shown by the covenant with Noah, testifying to the universality of God's manifestation and the human response in faith."[7] This does not mean that Christians must conclude that all religions are relatively equal. Nor should Christians deny that God's incarnate Word is linked to everyone's salvation. It *does* mean that Christians need to develop theologies that acknowledge that God is at work everywhere, not only in Christianity and Judaism.

The idea that all religions should disappear into Christianity is also theologically problematic, because it risks equating the church with the kingdom of God. However, the church is the servant of God's kingdom, not the kingdom itself, as is evident when Christians pray the Lord's Prayer, "Thy kingdom come." We acknowledge that, although we are baptized, we are sinners. We pray that God will forgive us when the kingdom dawns. Christian tradition does not suppose that God will postpone the new creation until all humanity is baptized.[8]

Evangelization: In the Service of God's Kingdom

It follows that the purpose of evangelization is not to baptize the world, but to prepare for God's kingdom of justice and peace. Therefore, evangelization involves both the inner life of the Christian community as well as its outreach to others. John Paul II has noted in this regard that "The Church's mission is to foster 'the kingdom of our Lord and his Christ' (Rev. 11: 15), at whose service she is placed. . . . [Interreligious] dialogue is expressed in the common efforts of all believers for justice, solidarity and peace."[9]

Evangelization is the entire life of the church: praying, teaching, promoting human dignity, living the good news, proclaiming our hope in Jesus Christ, and engaging in interreligious dialogue. All these activities help prepare for God's kingdom. Naturally, persons who come to share our Christian faith are welcomed, encouraged, and celebrated, but this is not why Christians approach other religions with respect. Again, John Paul II has put it this way:

> Drawing upon the riches of our respective religious traditions, we must spread awareness that today's problems will not be solved if we remain ignorant of one another and isolated from one another. . . . We must do all that we can to turn awareness of past offenses and sins into a firm resolve to build a new future in which there will be nothing but respectful and fruitful cooperation between us.
>
> Dialogue is not an attempt to impose our views upon others. What it demands of all of us is that, holding to what we believe, we listen respectfully to one another, seek to discern all that is good and holy in each other's teachings, and cooperate in supporting everything that favors mutual understanding and peace.[10]

Christians must always witness through word and deed to our covenanting with God through Christ. That is our covenantal obligation. And we do so for the sake of the kingdom.

Conclusion

Our covenanting through Christ requires, if we are truly to praise and thank God for the unmerited graces we continue to receive, that we convert our own hearts. We now better appreciate that we Christians are not the only people covenanting with God. Therefore, we should honor God's wishes and foster among the Christian people attitudes of religious respect especially for the covenanting faith community of the Jewish people. Such respect must include preserving their distinctive relationship with God in the world, intended by the Holy One to endure until the end of days.

Notes

1. Delegates of the Bishops' Committee on Ecumenical and Interreligious Affairs and the National Council of Synagogues, "Reflections on Covenant and Mission," *Origins* 32, no. 13 (September 5, 2002): 221.

2. Committee on Inter-Church and Inter-Faith Relations, United Church of Canada, "Bearing Faithful Witness: United Church-Jewish Relations Today," at www.united-church.ca/bfw/pdf/bfw.pdf, 83.

3. Pontifical Biblical Commission, "The Interpretation of the Bible in the Church," *Origins* 23, no. 29 (January 6, 1994): 497–524, I, A.

4. Walter Cardinal Kasper, "The Commission for Religious Relations with the Jews: A Crucial Endeavor of the Catholic Church," November 6, 2002, III, at www.bc.edu/research/cjl/meta-elements/texts/articles/Kasper_6Nov02.htm

5. The full PBC text can be found at www.vatican.va/roman_curia/congregations/cfaith/pcb_documents/rc_con_cfaith_doc_20020212_popolo-ebraico_en.html.

6. Second Vatican Council, *Nostra Aetate*, 2, in Austin Flannery, ed. *The Conciliar and Post-Conciliar Documents* (Collegeville: Liturgical Press, 1984), 738–742.

7. John Paul II, General Audience, November 29, 2000, at www.bc.edu/research/cjl/meta-elements/texts/documents/johnpaulii/audience_29_Nov_00.htm.

8. Also relevant to this question is Paul's hymn in Philippians 2:1–13. See the chapter by Clark Williamson in this volume for discussion of this important passage.

9. John Paul II, General Audience, November 29, 2000.

10. John Paul II, Address at Jerusalem Interreligious Meeting, March 23, 2000, at www.bc.edu/research/cjl/meta-elements/texts/documents/johnpaulii/interreligiousmeeting32300.htm.

Further Reading

Delegates of the Bishops' Committee on Ecumenical and Interreligious Affairs and the National Council of Synagogues, "Reflections on Covenant and Mission," *Origins* 32, no. 13 (September 5, 2002): 221, at www.bc.edu/research/cjl/meta-elements/texts/documents/interreligious/ncs_usccb120802.htm.

Federici, Tommaso. "Study Outline on the Mission and Witness of the Church" (1977), at www.bc.edu/research/cjl/meta-elements/texts/articles/Federici.htm.

Fitzgerald, Michael. "Evangelization and Interreligious Dialogue" (October 25, 2003), at www.bc.edu/research/cjl/meta-elements/texts/articles/fitzgerald_Oct03.htm.

Kasper, Walter Cardinal. "The Commission for Religious Relations with the Jews: A Crucial Endeavor of the Catholic Church" (November 6, 2002), at www.bc.edu/research/cjl/meta-elements/texts/articles/Kasper_6Nov02.htm.

McGarry, Michael. "Can Catholics Make an Exception? Jews and 'The New Evangelization'" (1994), at www.bc.edu/research/cjl/meta-elements/texts/articles/mcgarry.htm.

14

CHAPTER

Targeting Jews
for Conversion:
A Contradiction of
Christian Faith and Hope

Joann Spillman

"A SACRED OBLIGATION" states, "In view of our conviction that Jews are in an eternal covenant with God, we renounce missionary efforts directed at converting Jews. At the same time, we welcome opportunities for Jews and Christians to bear witness to their respective experiences of God's saving ways." This goes to the very heart of Jewish-Christian relations. If Christians seek to convert Jews, they can hardly claim to respect Judaism; by such efforts, they are saying that Judaism ought to be eliminated. If Christians say that Jews need to be converted, then Christians are implying that Judaism is not salvific.

Moreover, I will argue in this chapter that a mission to convert Jews actually implies a denial of central Christian teachings.

Missions to the Jews take many forms. Some evangelize simply by spreading the gospel and are respectful of the Jews whom they address. Others try to convert Jews by attacking Judaism, often on the basis of misinformation, particularly about the Talmud. These groups prey on ignorance by targeting Jews who are unschooled in Judaism. Some who evangelize misrepresent themselves in various ways, including by calling themselves rabbis, as I discovered when a new "rabbi" in town visited my office in the hopes of being invited to lecture in my classes. A few groups engage in truly revolting tactics, such as a group that sent a sympathy card to a bereaved Jewish friend of mine, expressing regret that her recently deceased father is in hell. I reject all such missionary efforts, whatever their form, whether respectful or obnoxious, and I do so on theological grounds. The central doctrines of Christianity—including teachings about God, revelation, salvation, and Christ—provide compelling reasons why Christians should not seek to convert Jews. Indeed, a mission to convert Jews is actually inconsistent with major elements of the Christian message, because such a mission denies the very grace on which Christians rely. I ground my argument firmly in the Bible and complement it by personal experiences of contemporary Christians. Moreover, an end to efforts to convert Jews opens up the opportunity for genuine dialogue between Christians and Jews.

This argument draws on beliefs that are widely shared by Christians, both Catholic and Protestant. The ecumenical character of this chapter, however, does not presume to include Jewish theological perspectives. Although closely linked, Judaism and Christianity are in fact different religions; we misrepresent both if we exaggerate their similarity. Our theology must reflect the reality that the Hebrew Scripture has given rise to two of the religions that serve the one God.

Throughout this discussion, we must keep in mind that doctrines about God, revelation, salvation, and Christ all deal with mystery. This does not imply that the beliefs are irrational, but rather that they transcend our ability to comprehend them fully. These profound teachings invite our sustained reflection, even as we realize that we can never plumb their depths.

Christian Teaching

At the heart of the great good news of Christianity is the recognition that God's love is faithful, unconditional, and inclusive. We must not presume to suggest that there are limits to God's love. Divine love has no such boundaries: God does not promise to love us only if we are worthy; rather God reaches out to sinners. It is on this love that Christians must rely.

The Bible teaches that God made a covenant with the Jewish people (see chapters in this volume by Mary Boys and Philip Cunningham). According to that scripture, God repeatedly affirmed and renewed this covenant. God does not break promises, but rather, "He is mindful of His covenant forever, of the word that He commanded for a thousand generations" (Ps 105:8). While the people may be faithless, God is always faithful. If God were to renege on the covenant with Israel, then Christians could not rely on God with any confidence.

Christians affirm that God has acted to reveal who God is and what God wills. Indeed, in order for Christianity to make sense, Christians must be able to give some account of how they know God's message—a challenging task made more difficult by varying understandings of revelation across the different denominations. Christians, however, generally agree that revelation happens at God's own initiative. Revelation is analogous to interpersonal communication: God meets us person to person. God is a someone, not a something. Furthermore, revelation of God is always revelation of mystery; even as God communicates, God remains mystery to us. We must be careful not to describe revelation in a way that suggests that Christians have a clearer way of knowing God than we actually have.

Christians affirm that revelation, as mediated in the Bible, comes not only through Christ but also through the history of Israel: The God who is in Christ is also the God of the Exodus; the God of the apostles is also the God of the prophets. Given this reality, it necessarily follows that Christians must recognize and accept the validity of God's revelation to the Jewish people. Christians must realize that the Hebrew Bible contains a message intended for Jews as well as for Christians—indeed a message given first to Jews and then to Christians. Furthermore, the New Testament would be virtually impossible to understand without the Hebrew Scripture because it constantly links the life and teaching of Jesus Christ with the history of Israel.

Christians live in the hope of salvation. The Christian concept of salvation includes many elements: release, deliverance, forgiveness, holiness, justification, victory, reconciliation, restoration, fulfillment, and eternal life. Nearly all Christians understand salvation to include deliverance from evils, both personal and collective, forgiveness for sin, and the restoration of all—and of the whole universe—to God. Salvation is best thought of as a process, not a "once-for-all achievement." Many Christians envision eternal life as an unbroken communion with God and, with others, in God. While we cannot say exactly what eternal life with God will be like, Christians know that the clearest indication of what God will do in heaven is what God has done in the past.

When the Christian Scholars Group used the term "salvific" in relation to Judaism, we were aware that Jews do not think of salvation in the same way as Christians. The term itself is rarely used in Jewish theology, and there are no direct parallels in Jewish theology to many aspects of Christian doctrines of salvation. This chapter deals with Christian theology and concerns how Christians should view the salvation—as understood in the context of Christianity—of Jews. It is addressed to Christians, not Jews, and is phrased in terms of Christian, not Jewish, theology. Were Jews to address these issues, they would have different questions. Because Jews and Christians approach these doctrines so differently, some of the issues that most concern Christians are of little concern to Jews. Jewish thinkers do not focus on an afterlife, and many Jews have no specific expectations of a life to come. Indeed the great rabbis whose ideas helped shape Judaism were generally quite content to leave open questions about the life to come.

Recent Reconsiderations

In the last fifty years, many church leaders and theologians have reconsidered Christian teaching about Jews and Judaism. Christian organizations and even entire denominations have issued major statements about Jewish-Christian relations. Such statements generally express a genuine appreciation of and respect for Judaism and reject the prejudices and polemics of the past. Some of this new thinking views Jews and Christians as partners in God's work. Recent Christian theology stresses the intimate relationship between Judaism and Christianity; official Catholic documents have been especially insistent on this point. Catholic documents and Vatican policy do not view the dialogue between Christians and Jews as an interreligious dialogue. According to recent Catholic teaching, the relationship between Judaism and Christianity is so intimate and so central to the Catholic faith that the dialogue between Christians and Jews is part of an internal conversation within the church. "The problem of Jewish-Christian relations concerns the Church as such, since it is 'when pondering her own mystery' that she encounters the mystery of Israel."[1]

Many factors have prompted these recent reconsiderations: Christian scholars, in the last fifty years, have given much attention to the Hebrew

Scripture (see the chapter by Walter Harrelson in this volume) and have come to better appreciate this scripture. As more Christians seriously study Judaism, they have a better understanding of Jewish teaching and a greater appreciation of the power and beauty of the tradition. Christians have come to an increasing awareness of how the teaching of contempt helped lay the groundwork for the Shoah, as Eva Fleischner explains in her chapter in this volume. The recognition that many Christians were perpetrators in the Shoah as well as bystanders has given urgency to this reconsideration. In addition to these considerations, a growing number of theologians and church leaders have come to see the relationship between Judaism and Christianity as a central theological question, at the very heart of faith.

Salvation: An Essential Question

However respectful of the Jewish faith this new theology is, it is inadequate unless it affirms that God does in fact bring salvation through Judaism as well as through Christianity. Christians cannot genuinely see Judaism as part of God's plan if Jews are not called to eternal life. In blunt terms, Christians cannot claim to see Judaism as a genuine part of God's plan if they teach, explicitly or implicitly, that Judaism leads in the end to separation from God—to hell rather than to heaven.

Still it must be acknowledged that asking whether or not Jews are saved is an incongruous question because it asks a question that Jews themselves would not ask. We must recognize that the questions we Christians ask about Jews and Judaism are shaped by our own faith perspective and may not be questions that arise in Jewish theology.

Christ

Christians proclaim that salvation is given through Christ; we rejoice in the grace given us through Christ. Yet that does not necessarily mean that those who are not Christians are separated from grace. Indeed, the good news of Christianity would hardly be good news if it implied that the vast majority of human beings are cut off from salvation. Christians can fully rejoice in the work of Christ only if Christ offers salvation to all, to both Christians and to those who know God apart from Christianity. How God extends the grace, given through Christ, to those who are not Christians is not for Christians to determine. It is a matter for God's love. But we can be confident that God does extend grace to all, because God's love is unconditional and inclusive. This interpretation of the role of Christ as Savior, often called "inclusivism," is growing in popularity among many Christians. According to this approach, God extends grace through Christ not only to Christians but to all. No other interpretation does justice to the biblical understanding of God's love.

This reasoning applies to members of all the world's religions, not only to Jews. However, from the perspective of the Christian faith, Judaism is not just "another religion." Rather, Judaism has a unique relationship with Christianity. Christians affirm the revelation manifest in the biblical account of the history of Israel as part of the core of Christian faith. The God who reaches out through Christ is also the God of the covenant at Sinai. In fact, Christians link Christ's role as universal Savior to his descent from Abraham, in whom "all the families of the earth shall be blessed" (Matt 1:2 and Luke 3:34; both refer to Gen 12:3).

How might Christians envision the role of Christ in the salvation of those who are not Christians? There is no easy solution to this theological puzzle. However, several approaches are promising, as Peter Phan and Clark Williamson develop in their chapters in this volume. We might think of Christ as the one who mediates grace to all, whether the recipients know of his role or not. We might also speculate that all who know God, by whatever means or in whatever religious tradition, are experiencing Christ, the Word. Both of these approaches could be used to describe Christ's relationship to those in any religious tradition other than Christianity. However, when dealing specifically with Judaism, we have several additional options. We might think of Christ as reaffirming the Jewish covenant while extending the message of the God of Israel to Gentiles. We might see the life, death, and resurrection of Christ as an act of redemption in the tradition of the Exodus. In making this connection, we are following the example of the many passages in the New Testament that present the story of Christ by using the imagery of the Exodus. We might even see Christ as reaffirming, or recapitulating, or duplicating the Exodus.

Bible

The conclusion that Christians should not try to convert Jews is not only consistent with an interpretation of the scriptures, but is also rooted in biblical teaching. Whatever else they may teach, Protestants, Catholics, and Orthodox Christians agree that Christians must be faithful to their biblical foundations, both in teaching and in practice. Because the following observations are written from an ecumenical perspective, every effort is made to provide an argument that is credible to both Protestants and Catholics. The argument is based on broad themes in the Bible, on the "thrust" of the biblical narratives. Another chapter in this collection will deal with specific biblical passages.

The Christian Bible, of course, is composed of two testaments, the first of which is also the Bible of Judaism. This sharing of scripture is unique among the major world religions. Since we embrace the Hebrew Scripture as our First Testament, the teachings of that testament are foundational for Christian life. The Hebrew Scripture is focused on the Exodus, an event that provides the main paradigm for understanding God in the Hebrew Scripture and in much of the New Testament as well (see the chapter by Walter Harrelson in this volume). The Hebrew Scripture repeatedly affirms God's love for and relationship with the Jews. This is emphasized so strongly that any Christian who takes the Hebrew Scripture seriously must acknowledge it. Of course, reading the scripture is never simple, and all reading is interpretation. We never have scripture in itself; it is always scripture interpreted. We often struggle to find meaning in the Bible and to find its relevance to our pressing problems. However we interpret the Bible, we cannot be responsible interpreters if we simply ignore the meaning of the text of the Hebrew Scripture in its historical context.

Christians commonly read the Hebrew Scripture through the lens of the New Testament. This has led Christians to interpret the Hebrew Scripture as the foundation for Christianity and to understand Jesus Christ as fulfilling some of the expectations of the Hebrew Bible, a point especially emphasized by the Gospel according to Matthew. Reading the Hebrew Scripture in light of the New Testament is certainly a legitimate Christian practice, one shared by Christians of various denominations. However, Christians must also read the Hebrew Scripture on its own terms by drawing upon historical tools for situating texts in their historical, literary, and religious contexts.

While Christians often differ concerning how to interpret scripture, they commonly insist on beginning with the most obvious meaning of biblical texts. Many Christians are suspicious, and rightly so, of any approach that ignores the meaning of a biblical passage within its historical context. Such interpretations distort the meaning of a text in ways that cease to be readings *from* the text and become readings *into* the text. If Christians read the Hebrew Scripture as referring directly and solely to Jesus Christ and read the promises of God to Israel only as promises to the church, they distort the meaning of the Hebrew Scripture and ignore its primary meaning in its historical context.

The importance of Christian acceptance of the Hebrew Scripture as part of the Christian Bible cannot be overstated. The simple fact that Christians accept the Hebrew Scripture, with its teaching about the permanency of God's covenant with the Jewish people, provides a solid starting point for the argument that Christians should not target Jews for conversion.

But what about those parts of the New Testament that speak of Christ as the only way to the Father, the one mediator, and the only name by which people are saved (John 14:6; Acts 4:12; and 1 Tim 2:5)? Such passages are certainly in the New Testament, but so also are other passages that take a broader view of God's salvific will. These state that God finds acceptable people from every nation; that God is worshiped—unknowingly, even in pagan shrines; that God desires everyone to be saved; and that God is the Savior of all people (Acts 10:34; Acts 17:23; 1 Tim 2:3–4; 1 Tim 4:10). In addition to these passages, there are passages that directly link Christ with the salvation of all (John 3:17; Rom 5:18; Col 1:19–20). Given all of these passages, we must recognize that the biblical witness is, at very least, complex (see the chapter in this volume by Clark Williamson). Moreover, a close look at the passages that seem to assert that salvation is possible only through faith in Christ shows that they are more nuanced than they first appear. And, of course, one can believe that Christ is the mediator of salvation and still claim that he mediates salvation to all, whether Christian or not.

Any attempt to rethink the relationship of Jews and Christians must give careful attention to the history of biblical commentary. It was early Christian commentators, such as Barnabas, Justin Martyr, Irenaeus, Augustine, and others, who introduced some of the teachings that are most hostile to Judaism. It is unlikely that the most virulent forms of Christian anti-Judaism would have emerged without the impetus given by these early writers. While these early writers seem very distant from Christians today, we are influenced by them, directly and indirectly, whether we are aware of them or not. It is especially important for Catholics to confront these early writings, because Catholic theology gives considerable attention and weight to the teachings of early theologians—the Fathers of the Church.

In sum, there is a great deal at stake in the question of the legitimacy of a Christian mission to Jews, not only for Jewish-Christian relations but also for the coherence of Christian theology itself. A Christian theology that supports efforts to convert Jews is not faithful to the Christian message because it replaces the biblical understanding of a faithful God with a faithless God. It tries to put limits on the love of God, the love on which Christians rely. In so doing, it contradicts Christian faith and contravenes Christian hope.

Experiences of Contemporary Christians

In recent decades, increasing numbers of Christians have come to study Judaism in a variety of contexts—universities, church study groups, interfaith dialogue groups, and elsewhere. In my own university, a Catholic institution in the Midwest, where most students identify some form of Christianity as their religion or, at least, their religious heritage, courses on Judaism fill rapidly and generate waiting lists. Christians and Jews also find themselves working together on efforts to promote peace and justice, sometimes on projects jointly sponsored by churches and synagogues. In such situations, Christians encounter Judaism as a living religion, not a mere precursor to Christianity, not an old covenant that has been replaced, not a shadow, not a fossil, but rather a vital faith. Such experience contradicts the picture of Judaism as either dead or dying. In such situations, Christians encounter the beauty and the power of Jewish teachings and the devotion these teachings inspire. In this context, Christians find the teaching that Jews must convert to Christianity in order to serve the God of Israel very dubious.

If Christians can come to study Judaism rather than try to eliminate it, to dialogue with Jews rather than try to convert them, Christians will discover, in Judaism, another way of living the biblical faith. As often happens when people encounter a way of thinking other than their own, Christians may be stimulated and enriched by the encounter with another theology. The results can be momentous, as the experience of Paul van Buren demonstrates.

In the mid-1970s Paul van Buren was appointed chair of the large religion department of Temple University. At the time he was struggling intensely with problems in philosophy of religion and was dissatisfied with the results of his work. Although he had a superb education in Christian theology and was a recognized scholar in the field, he found himself on the fringes of the Christian community. He was unable to make sense out of— much less affirm—central teachings of Christianity. As chair of his department, he was responsible for leading a search for two new professors of Judaism. In order to prepare for the search, he immersed himself in the study of Judaism. The results transformed his thinking.

At that point, serendipitously, the *Christian Century* asked him to write a brief autobiographical essay. In response, he wrote an account of his change. "Jews and Judaism opened my eyes," he wrote. Christian stereotypes of Judaism "came tumbling down like the house of cards they were. . . . In their place, actual Judaism, the living faith of this living people of God came into view." This compelled him to rethink his entire understanding of Christianity. As a result, many of his earlier difficulties "simply receded into the background."[2] He spent the rest of his life struggling to formulate a "theology of the Jewish-Christian reality." Readers can judge the results for themselves. The titles of his three-volume work are cited in the accompanying endnote.[3]

Respecting the Differences

This chapter stresses that Christianity has close ties to Judaism, has doctrines rooted in Judaism, and shares part of its scripture with Judaism. However, it is important not to exaggerate the closeness of the ties between Judaism and Christianity or the similarities between the two. To do so would fail to respect the integrity of both religions. Such respect is a precondition of genuine dialogue

However closely tied, they have evolved into two quite different religions, with sometimes sharply different teachings. For example, Jewish teaching about God is inextricably linked to the Jewish understanding of Torah: God is the God of Torah. While the Christian understanding of God is rooted in biblical Judaism, most Christians affirm a doctrine of the Trinity, a doctrine both different from and unacceptable to Jewish teaching. Differences extend even to their shared scripture. While the Tanakh, or Jewish Bible, is also the Christian First Testament, the order of books is different. The Jewish Bible is organized into three parts: Torah, Prophets, and Writings; the Christian order of the books eliminates the distinction between the Prophets and Writings and tends to focus attention on the Prophets, as a kind of climax to the First Testament. Placed at the end of the First Testament and thus immediately before the Second Testament, the Prophets can and often do serve Christian readers as a bridge to the Second Testament, thus playing a role in Christianity strikingly different from that in Judaism. Moreover, Catholic and Orthodox Christians—together the majority of Christians—have books in their First Testament that are not in the Jewish Bible (also omitted from the Bible of Protestants, or placed in a separate section as the "Apocrypha"). Jews and Christians, moreover, interpret the Hebrew Scripture differently. They tend to identify different passages and themes as most important. Both communities read the Hebrew Scripture with the help of and through the lens of later developments. Jews read it with the guidance of the Talmud and Rabbinic Judaism (see the chapter in this volume by Peter Pettit and John Townsend); Christians with the guidance of the New Testament and the history of the Christian Church. These examples of differences could be multiplied and extend to both teachings and practice. No genuine dialogue is possible unless such differences are recognized and taken into account.

A Broader Question

In exploring the Christian understanding of Judaism, the question of the relationship between Christianity and Judaism is an inevitable one, because the God made known in Christ is the God of Israel. But we cannot be content to limit our theological inquiry to the relationship between Christianity and Judaism. After all, we do not live in a world of only Jews and Christians, but rather in a world that includes Hindus, Buddhists, Muslims and many others—including millions of people who profess no faith in God. What is the relationship of Christianity to these other religions and peoples? The inclusive view of Christ's role as Savior presented here may provide a partial answer, but this broader question goes beyond the scope of our work as Christian scholars dedicated to exploring our relationship to Jews and Judaism.

A Final Comment

However Christians approach this broader issue, we must always remember that the relationship between Christianity and Judaism is unique. Christian recognition of Judaism as revelatory and salvific is based not only on an inclusive Christology but also on teachings about God, revelation, and salvation. Moreover, targeting Jews for conversion actually contradicts Christian faith and contravenes Christian hope. What is at stake here is nothing less than the coherence of the Christian message.

Notes

1. "Guidelines and Suggestions for Implementing the Conciliar Declaration *Nostra Aetate*." This document has been published in many forms. A convenient source is Helga Croner, ed., *Stepping Stones to Further Jewish-Christian Relations* (New York: Stimulus Books, 1977), 15.

2. Paul M. van Buren, "Probing the Jewish-Christian Reality," *Christian Century* 98 (June 17, 1981): 665–67.

3. Paul M. van Buren, *A Theology of the Jewish-Christian Reality*, part I, *Discerning the Way* (New York: Seabury, 1980); part II, *A Christian Theology of the People Israel* (New York: Seabury, 1983); part III, *Christ in Context* (San Francisco: Harper and Row, 1988).

Further Reading

Boys, Mary C. *Has God Only One Blessing? Judaism as a Source of Christian Self-Understanding.* New York: Paulist, 2000.

Lofink, Norbert. *The Covenant Never Revoked: Biblical Reflections on Christian-Jewish Dialogue.* New York: Paulist, 1991.

Williamson, Clark M. *A Guest in the House of Israel: Post-Holocaust Church Theology* Louisville, KY: Westminster / John Knox Press, 1993.

———. *Has God Rejected His People? Anti-Judaism in the Christian Church.* Nashville: Abingdon, 1982.

Williamson, Clark M., and Ronald J. Allen. *Interpreting Difficult Texts: Anti-Judaism and Christian Preaching.* London: Trinity Press International, 1989.

IX
PART

Christian Worship that Teaches Contempt for Judaism Dishonors God

15

CHAPTER

The God of Israel and Christian Worship

John C. Merkle

The God of Israel and Christian Theology

Christianity, like Judaism, is first and foremost a monotheistic faith, claiming that there is but one true God. And the one God whom Christians worship is the Holy One of Israel, the same God worshiped by Jews. But one of the ways by which Christian theologians have attempted to demonstrate the superiority of Christianity over Judaism has been to advocate the idea that the Christian view of God is superior to the Jewish view. For example, following the lead of the second-century theologian Marcion, many Christian thinkers have claimed that Judaism teaches a God of wrath, Christianity a God of love. This claim is obviously false. Not only does it fail to acknowledge the fact that in the Hebrew Bible God is repeatedly referred to as loving and compassionate, it also ignores the fact that Jewish views of God have developed well beyond those found in ancient Israelite religion. Postbiblical Jewish understandings of God, no less than developed Christian understandings, call into question some of the accounts of God's action found in both the Hebrew Bible and the church's apostolic writings.

Although Marcion was excommunicated by the church at Rome in 144 C.E. for, among other things, teaching that the God of Jesus Christ was other than and superior to the God of Jewish faith, his spirit penetrated Christianity—both East and West—and has persisted throughout the centuries. While rejecting Marcion's radical dualism, traditionally, Christian theologians have espoused the idea that Christianity has a view of God superior to that of Judaism, all the while misrepresenting the latter. Of the countless examples that could be given, a few from the modern era will suffice.

Friedrich Schleiermacher, acknowledged as the father of modern theology and the most influential Protestant theologian of the nineteenth century, claimed that Christianity represents "the purest form of monotheism which has appeared in history," and that "Jewish monotheism . . . was everywhere tinctured with materialistic conceptions" and betrayed "a lingering affinity with fetishism."[1] Karl Barth, the twentieth century's most influential Protestant theologian, implicitly denied validity to the Jewish view of God by claiming that "apart from and without Jesus Christ we can say nothing at all about God."[2] Do we not hear an echo of Marcion in Barth's claim that if God's presence "is sought and supposedly found apart from Jesus Christ, it can signify in practice only our enslavement to a false god"?[3]

Karl Rahner, the most acclaimed Catholic theologian of our time, held that only through God's revelation in Christ do we have "a criterion for distinguishing in the concrete history of religion between what is a human misunderstanding of the transcendental experience of God, and what is the legitimate interpretation of this experience."[4] This clearly discounts the Jewish perspective (and other perspectives). Even worse, Rahner speaks of "the Jews who rejected Jesus" as typical of "those who try to direct God according to their own little categories, those who only see God in images . . . that they themselves have constructed."[5] Another eminent Catholic thinker, Leslie Dewart, has conveyed the spirit of Marcion in suggesting that "it would be inexact . . . to suppose that the Christian theos is the same as the Yahweh of the Old Testament."[6] In tune with Dewart, Gustavo Gutiérrez, the pioneer of "liberation theology," has claimed that "the presence of Jesus is the epiphany of this new and different God—not a God of fear and punishment, distant from us and delighting in sacrifices but instead a God who is close."[7]

Later, by focusing on Jewish understandings of God, we will note how these assertions by Christian theologians grossly distort Jewish perspectives. But before doing that, let us turn to how Christian worship distorts Jews and Judaism, including Jewish views of God.

The God of Israel and Christian Worship

Christian liturgical prayers have not denigrated Jewish understandings of God as explicitly as have the theological claims cited above. In fact, some ancient Jewish prayers, the psalms of the Hebrew Bible, have been incorporated into Christian liturgies. Yet this appropriation of Jewish prayers has not usually been accompanied by an appreciation of their essential Jewishness. Instead, their significance has been thought to consist only in relation to the Christ of Christian faith they have been perceived to anticipate. And the imagined Christ of this perceived anticipation has borne little resemblance to the Jesus who lived—and prayed—within Israel's covenant with God. To be sure, Christians have every right to read and pray the psalms from a christological perspective (which is, after all, the perspective of Christian faith), but they should also appreciate the Jewishness of the psalms and recognize the right of Jews to read and pray them from a nonchristological perspective.

Moreover, while the inclusion of psalms from the Hebrew Bible in Christian liturgies has the potential to inspire appreciation for Judaism, the use of some psalms not representing Israel's more inspired vision of the divine-human relationship will not ignite such appreciation. Since Christian liturgies include Israel's ancient prayers (as also other parts of the Hebrew Scriptures), it would be appropriate, as recommended by some recent church documents, for preachers to learn to draw inspiration from postbiblical Jewish sources in preparing their homilies—and to share those sources of inspiration with their congregants. This would drive home the point that Judaism is not, as is often presumed by Christians, simply the "religion of the Old Testament."

Something else worth noting about the use of the psalms and other parts of the Hebrew Bible in Christian liturgies is that some of these scriptural portions point to the failings of Israelites to live up to their covenantal responsibilities. Instead of appreciating the fact that the Hebrew Scriptures are honest about the sins committed by Israelites, many Christians have turned this prophetic self-criticism into a condemnation of Jews and Judaism in general. Christian preachers have a moral responsibility to counter such moves by showing that the church needs to heed the criticism of the prophets.

Despite the Jewishness of Jesus and the Jewish origins of Christian worship, the liturgical prayers of the churches have not fostered appreciation among Christians for Jewish approaches to God. To the contrary, they have either ignored Jewish covenantal life with God or, worse, have promoted the idea that, by not accepting Christ, the Jews have rejected God. The most notorious of such prayers was the Good Friday prayer for the Jews that Pope John XXIII removed from the liturgy in 1959: "Let us pray for the unfaithful Jews, that our God and Lord may remove the veil from their hearts; that they may also acknowledge our Lord Jesus Christ." Still present in some editions of the Liturgy of the Hours is this prayer, contrasting Jewish "lack of faith" with the "faithful" church: "Lord God, your only Son wept over ancient Jerusalem, soon to be destroyed for its lack of faith. He established the new Jerusalem firmly upon the rock and made it the mother of the faithful. Make us rejoice in your Church, and grant that all people may be reborn into the freedom of your Spirit."[8]

Fortunately, this kind of prayer is not at the heart of the church's public worship; that is, it is not in the church's various eucharistic prayers. But, unfortunately, the eucharistic prayers, intended as thanksgiving prayers for "all that God has done for the worshipers from creation on to its climax in Jesus Christ,"[9] are nearly devoid of reference to Israel's covenant with God. Noting this absence (in Orthodox, Roman Catholic, and Anglican eucharistic prayers), Paul van Buren writes:

> Generally, it appears that the church does not think it need give thanks for the long history of God's dealing with Israel, or of Israel's life with God prior to the coming of Christ. It seems to be content with creation and "the fall," apparently not thinking that the story of what God then did about the situation by calling Abraham and his heirs, and in calling Moses and giving the Torah, is a matter that should concern the church.[10]

According to van Buren, this shows that, despite the church's condemnation of Marcion's view that the God of Jesus Christ is other than the God of Israel, Marcion remains "firmly in control of the heart of the church's worship, his thesis accepted that the coming of Jesus Christ was a radical novelty."[11]

Marcion's (or Marcion-like) influence is apparent not only in the eucharistic prayers but also in the Liturgy of the Word, which often includes readings from the Hebrew Bible Marcion excluded from his canon. The very structure of the lectionaries that assign scriptural readings for the Liturgy of the Word in Christian eucharistic services promotes the impression that the Hebrew Scriptures have value merely as a prelude to the New Testament and its proclamation of Jesus Christ. "A key way in which christocentrism operates in the Lectionary of the Mass lies in the pairing of the Gospel and the Old Testament lections by the concept of salvation history," which teaches that "what God revealed in promise and in a veiled way to Israel is fulfilled and fully manifest in Jesus."[12] While some recent church documents have insisted that the Hebrew Scriptures should be appreciated in their own right and not simply as background for the New Testament, the promise-fulfillment paradigm operative in the lectionaries used by both Catholics and Protestants fails to convey the spiritual richness and the abiding significance of the Hebrew Scriptures.

As distressing as it is that the Jewish covenant with God is virtually ignored in the church's eucharistic prayers and that Hebrew Scriptures are not given the respect they deserve, more troubling are the ways Jews are depicted in so many New Testament texts used in liturgical contexts. For example, Jews are depicted as preoccupied with the letter rather than the spirit of the law, and as guilty of the death of Christ, and homilies based on these texts often reinforce such negative portrayals. Robert Bullock correctly observes that the most recent lectionary for the Mass, which went into use on the first Sunday of Advent 1998, "does not regard the depiction of Jews and Judaism in the texts as a concern."[13] He goes on to detail the problems arising from this lack of concern. Clearly, the very structure of the lectionary and many of the readings from the New Testament it assigns promote a distorted view of Jews and Judaism, including a distorted view of Jewish approaches to God. A number of recent church documents, including statements by Pope John Paul II, have warned Christians against erroneous depictions of Jews and Judaism. But these warnings obviously have not been heeded by those who have created the lectionaries for Christian worship—nor by many preachers who continue to place Jesus in opposition to Judaism, to misrepresent Jewish groups (especially the Pharisees), to suggest that Jews were responsible for the death of Christ, and to foster the impression that Judaism has been superseded by Christianity. Bullock's overall assessment of how Jews and Judaism are portrayed in Christian worship is chilling. "Millions go to churches every Sunday. They enter a sacred environment of word, song, prayer, and art. How Jews and Judaism are depicted in this environment, in the lectionary, hymns, prayers, and art is highly problematic. In the liturgical environment, supersessionism is endemic."[14]

Jewish Understandings of God

Ironically, the denigration of Jews and Judaism in Christian theological texts and liturgical contexts persists at a time when many Christians have rediscovered the spiritual grandeur of Judaism. This rediscovery reveals that Jewish approaches to God can be a source of inspiration for Christians. When we read the sages of Israel—whether ancient, medieval, modern, or contemporary—we discover that what Jews understand about God's closeness to us and love for us is every bit as profound as what Christian theologians usually claim can only be known through faith in Christ. When we move from a spirit of disputation to a spirit of dialogue with Jews, we Christians learn that our belief in the Incarnation of God in Christ has not led us to feel that God is any closer to human beings than faithful Jews have always assumed.

To begin with, the God of the Hebrew Bible is the God of covenant, the God who enters into intimate partnership with the people of Israel. As "the Holy One," God is indeed transcendent. But as "the Holy One of Israel," God is known not simply as a transcendent *reality* but as a transcendent *presence*. And God's presence is not limited to the people of Israel; rather, it "fills all the earth" (Isa 6:3). But more important than God being everywhere is that "God draws close to those whose hearts are broken" (Ps 34:18) and "loves the alien who lives among you" (Deut 10:18).

How absurd for Christians to contrast the New Testament's God of love with the supposedly remote and wrathful God of the Hebrew Bible! Catholic theologian Padraic O'Hare corrects such a mistaken notion by pointing out that "when Christians read and pray the moving lines from John's Gospel, 'God is love,' they are encountering a basic tenet of Judaism, not a 'Christian' novelty or innovation."[15]

As much as ancient Israelite faith celebrated the presence and love of God, it signaled only the beginning of an abiding and developing Jewish appreciation of God's presence and love. Concerning the rabbis of early postbiblical Judaism, David Wolpe writes: "The Rabbis delighted in developing the concept of God's love for humanity in general and for Israel in particular." This was "the central truth of their lives: the existence of a good and caring God, enmeshed in the trials and triumphs of human life, who looked on them and the world with love."[16]

God's love has its consequences, not only for those loved but also for God. It means, as many Jewish sages have taught, that God is affected by the plight of creatures, even to the point of suffering. Abraham Heschel goes so far as to say that the idea of divine pathos is "the central idea in prophetic theology" because "God's participation in human history finds its deepest expression in the fact that God can actually suffer."[17]

Many Christians may think this talk of God's suffering is nothing new, since we Christians focus on the suffering of Christ, whom we believe to be God incarnate. But, in fact, classical Christian theology, having assimilated the Aristotelian idea of suffering as an imperfection unworthy of God, refutes the idea that God suffers. The traditional view is that Christ suffers in his human nature, not in his divine nature. To be sure, there are Christian theologians nowadays who do speak of the suffering of God, claiming that for God to be unmoved by the plight of creatures would indicate not perfection but deficiency on God's part. And, indeed, there have been Jewish thinkers who have tried to explain away the biblical and rabbinic allusions to God's suffering because they, like many Christians, have been influenced by Aristotelian philosophy. But the idea of God's suffering can be found in abundance within the Jewish tradition. And even if we reject the classical Christian theological view that God cannot suffer, it is good for us Christians to realize that others, without any doctrine of Incarnation, affirm the suffering of God, suffering born of love.

Learning from Jews that God suffers *with us*, rather than focusing solely on how Christ suffers *for us*, can have a profound effect on our own understanding of God and on our way of relating to God. It can help us overcome our tendency to blame God for the evils that befall us, and it can save us enormous spiritual energy that might otherwise be spent in the attempt to solve the insoluble problem of how God, thought to be not only all-good but also all-powerful, either causes or permits evils to occur. Focusing on God's suffering, we may be inclined to question the idea of divine omnipotence, just as Heschel did by claiming that this idea, "holding God responsible for everything, expecting God to do the impossible, to defy human freedom, is a non-Jewish idea."[18] Perhaps the idea of divine omnipotence should become a non-Christian idea as well. If we stop thinking of omnipotence as an essential characteristic of the divine, then we will be free to appreciate as never before that the true mark of divinity—what makes God divine and therefore worthy of our worship—is not absolute power and control, but infinite compassion, unending love.

Such an understanding of God is bound to have a profound effect on our way of relating to God. If, with Heschel, we believe that "God's mercy is too great to permit the innocent to suffer," but that "there are forces that interfere with God's mercy, with God's power," we may be moved to have "compassion for God,"[19] which Heschel regards as a component of faith in God. Moreover, we may become convinced, or more convinced, that our supreme responsibility is to let the divine mercy flow through our lives to help God alleviate suffering.

Reforming Our Liturgies

Among the many sufferings we Christians are called upon to help God alleviate are the sufferings of Jews—sufferings so often caused by Christian anti-Judaism and antisemitism. Pope John Paul II and other church leaders have acknowledged the suffering that many Christians have brought upon Jews, and they have called for repentance and a new Christian attitude toward Jews and Judaism. During the Great Jubilee Year of 2000, at the Basilica of St. Peter and again at the Western Wall in Jerusalem, John Paul prayed publicly for God's forgiveness for the sins of Christians against Jews. Recalling those solemn events, Walter Cardinal Kasper said, "We are all called to share in our inner attitudes, prayers, and actions in this same journey of conversion and reconciliation," because it must not be "limited merely to a few authoritative, meaningful gestures" such as the pope's or to "high level [church] documents."[20] Surely one of the most effective ways to promote such conversion and reconciliation is by reforming our liturgies so that they express and foster the newfound appreciation for Jews and Judaism already articulated in some recent church documents and dramatically represented by John Paul's gestures.

Already twenty years ago David Berger pointed out that "all the ringing denunciations of antisemitism and progressive reassessments of Judaism have little importance if they are confined to an activist elite and have no resonance among ordinary Christians." He therefore challenged Christians to embark upon "liturgical reform . . . in the effort to exorcise the impact of historic Christian anti-Judaism."[21] The Christian Scholars Group on Christian-Jewish Relations concurs with Berger, and, thus, article 8 of "A Sacred Obligation" includes these lines: "We urge church leaders to examine scripture readings, prayers, the structure of the lectionaries, preaching and hymns to remove distorted images of Judaism. A reformed Christian liturgical life would express a new relationship with Jews and thus honor God."

While purging our liturgies of anti-Judaism must be done to help reduce Jewish suffering caused by antisemitism, it must also be done for the spiritual health of Christians and for the integrity and credibility of Christianity. For far too long, Christians defined Christianity over against a misrepresented Judaism. Even today, far too many Christians have a distorted understanding of Judaism and think that its validity came to an end with the emergence of Christianity as the one valid pathway to God. But those of us who have been spiritually enriched through interfaith encounters with Jews and Judaism cannot but agree with Cardinal Kasper that, "although the contrasting concept—of an Israel *once* chosen but later rejected by God forever and now replaced by the Church—may have had widespread dissemination for almost twenty centuries, it does not in reality represent a truth of the faith," and, in fact, the church's rediscovered bond with the Jews allows "a new springtime for the Church" to bloom.[22] But most Christians will only be able to enjoy this new springtime after the fruits of liturgical reform have enabled them to perceive the spiritual grandeur of Judaism and to discover, in the spirit of friendship with Jews, an enhanced way of worshiping God.

Notes

1. Friedrich Schleiermacher, *The Christian Faith*, English translation of second German edition (1830), edited by H. R. Mackintosh and J. S. Stewart (Edinburgh: T. and T. Clark, 1928), 38, 387, and 37.

2. Karl Barth, *Church Dogmatics*, vol. IV, pt. I (Edinburgh: T. and T. Clark, 1957), 45.

3. Barth, *Church Dogmatics*, vol. II, pt. I, 319.

4. Karl Rahner, *Foundations of Christian Faith: An Introduction to the Idea of Christianity* (New York: Seabury, 1978), 157.

5. Karl Rahner, *Spiritual Exercises* (New York: Herder and Herder, 1956), 235.

6. Leslie Dewart, *The Future of Belief in a World Come of Age* (New York: Herder and Herder, 1966), 138.

7. Gustavo Gutiérrez, *Sharing the Word through the Liturgical Year* (Maryknoll, NY: Orbis Books, 1997), 128–29.

8. *Christian Prayer: The Liturgy of the Hours* (New York: Catholic Book Publishing, 1976); cited in Mary C. Boys, *Has God Only One Blessing? Judaism as a Source of Christian Self-Understanding* (New York: Paulist, 2000), 202.

9. Paul M. van Buren, *According to the Scriptures: The Origins of the Gospel and of the Church's Old Testament* (Grand Rapids, MI: Eerdmans, 1998), 77.

10. Buren, *According to the Scriptures*, 78.

11. Buren, *According to the Scriptures*.

12. Boys, *Has God Only One Blessing?* 208.

13. Robert W. Bullock, "After Auschwitz: Jews, Judaism, and Christian Worship," in Carol Rittner and John K. Roth, eds., *"Good News" after Auschwitz? Christian Faith within a Post-Holocaust World* (Macon, GA: Mercer University Press, 2001), 74.

14. Bullock, "After Auschwitz," 73–74.

15. Padraic O'Hare, *The Enduring Covenant: The Education of Christians and the End of Antisemitism* (Valley Forge, PA: Trinity Press International, 1997), 131.

16. David J. Wolpe, *The Healer of Shattered Hearts: A Jewish View of God* (New York: Henry Holt, 1990), 70.

17. Abraham Joshua Heschel, *The Prophets* (New York: Harper and Row, 1962), 227.

18. Abraham Joshua Heschel, "Teaching Jewish Theology," *Synagogue School*, fall 1969, 13.

19. Abraham Joshua Heschel, "On Prayer," *Conservative Judaism*, fall 1970, 4; *A Passion for Truth* (New York: Farrar, Straus, and Giroux, 1973), 301.

20. Walter Cardinal Kasper, "Antisemitism: A Wound to be Healed" (Reflections for the Fourth European Day of Jewish Culture, September 5, 2003, at www.bc.edu/research/cjl), 2.

21. David Berger, "Jewish-Christian Relations: A Jewish Perspective," *Journal of Ecumenical Studies*, winter 1983; reprinted in Naomi W. Cohen, ed., *Essential Papers on Jewish Christian Relations in the United States* (New York: New York University Press, 1990), 345.

22. Kasper, "Antisemitism," 1, 3.

Further Reading

Boys, Mary C. *Has God Only One Blessing? Judaism as a Source of Christian Self-Understanding*. New York: Paulist, 2000. See especially chapter 12, "The Liturgy: A Call to Conversion," 199–222.

Fisher, Eugene J. *The Jewish Roots of Christian Liturgy*. New York: Paulist, 1990.

Kee, Howard Clark, and Irvin J. Borowsky, eds. *Removing Anti-Judaism from the Pulpit*. New York: Continuum, 1996.

Williamson, Clark M. *A Guest in the House of Israel: Post-Holocaust Church Theology*. Louisville, KY: Westminster / John Knox Press, 1993. See especially chapter 8, "The God of Israel and the Church," 202–32.

Williamson, Clark M., and Ronald J. Allen. *Interpreting Difficult Texts: Anti-Judaism and Christian Preaching*. London: SCM; Philadelphia: Trinity International Press, 1989.

16

CHAPTER

A Matter of Perspective: An Alternative Reading of Mark 15:38

Rosann M. Catalano

SINCE THE beginning of the church, Jesus' life, death, and resurrection have formed the core of the church's teaching and preaching, shaped the structure of Christian worship, figured prominently in Christian piety and prayer, and provided the subject matter for a considerable portion of Christian hymnody. Christians believe that Jesus' life, death, and resurrection are an inseparable unity that together discloses both the mystery of God and the meaning of being made in God's image. And yet, it is his crucifixion and death that have exercised the greatest influence on the Christian imagination. In many Christian traditions, the beaten and broken body of Jesus has played a central role in both the structure and content of Christian prayer, and has dominated the history of Christian art, at least since the ninth century. From Matthias Grünewald's image of the twisted and bloody Jesus that forms the center-piece of his Isenheim Altarpiece,[1] to the nineteenth-century hymn "Nothing but the Blood,"[2] to the sorrowful mysteries of the Roman Catholic rosary,[3] to the cross of Jesus hung in churches and found in the homes of most Christians, Jesus' suffering and death are seared deeply into the Christian imagination. The passion of Jesus shapes Christian consciousness in ways both subtle and profound.

The suffering and death of Jesus have also played a central role in the church's theological formation. In particular, the church has, from its begin-ning, struggled with two distinct, but related, questions. What do Jesus' cru-cifixion and death mean for his followers? What do they mean for those who do not profess Jesus as the Messiah, the Anointed of God? In regard to the latter question, the church has been particularly preoccupied with the Jewish people. Throughout its history the church has wrestled with their steadfast fidelity to the God of Israel independent of the church's procla-mation that Jesus is the long-awaited Messiah. To this day, the Jewish peo-ple remain the single greatest theological challenge to the church.

As many chapters in this volume have detailed, a deeply embedded teaching of contempt has marked the history of the church's struggle to give a theological account of the Jewish people. In the aftermath of the Holocaust, many Christian theologians and church bodies initiated a self-critical theological reexamination that chronicled the clear relationship between the church's teaching regarding Jesus' crucifixion and death and its teaching concerning Judaism and the Jewish people. What also became increasingly apparent is the direct link between the church's claim that the Jewish people were and remain responsible for the death of Jesus and the vit-riol of its teaching concerning the Jewish people. Rooted in its preoccupa-tion with Jewish responsibility for Jesus' crucifixion and death, the church's anti-Jewish teaching too often demonized the Jewish people, with tragic and deadly consequences.

The theological reassessment began by thinking anew about the impli-cations of St. Paul's teaching that "the gifts and the calling of God are irrev-ocable" (Rom 11:29). If God's gifts and God's call *are* binding, then God has never revoked either the covenant with the Jewish people or the Torah given them at Sinai. The Jewish people were from their beginning, are now, and will forever remain God's most beloved. The implication of this insight is clear: if the church is to regain its credibility, it is essential that it take responsibility for the deadly consequences of its longstanding anti-Jewish teaching and that it develop a more adequate theological understanding of Judaism and the Jewish people. It is in this spirit that the Christian Scholars Group issued "A Sacred Obligation."

This chapter concerns itself with article 8 of that statement, which asserts that "Christian worship that teaches contempt for Judaism dishonors God." This assertion condemns any anti-Jewish teaching in either the church's public worship or the private devotional practices of its faithful, and it calls for a reassessment of every facet of Christian worship—its structure and its theology, its preaching and its prayers, its hymnody, and its ritual gestures—in order to eliminate teaching that denigrates the Jewish people.

Because I assume that the church's public worship profoundly influences private prayer and devotion, I am particularly interested in what the church teaches in the week that begins with Passion/Palm Sunday and concludes on Easter Sunday. During worship services of this most solemn week the church reads long portions from the gospel accounts of Jesus' crucifixion and death. Because the death of Jesus is an intensely powerful symbol, the importance of what Christian worship teaches during this holiest of liturgical seasons about Jesus' death—its significance and implications, and especially why it happened and who bears responsibility for it—is a matter of great urgency.

In order to give sufficient depth to this concern in so brief a chapter, I focus on one detail in the biblical account of Jesus' last hours as an example of the urgent need to find alternative understandings of texts that the church has traditionally read in ways that show contempt for Judaism. The detail is the tearing of the Temple curtain at the moment of Jesus' death, which appears, virtually identically, in three of the four canonical gospels: Matthew 27:51, Mark 15:38, and Luke 23:45b. I will focus on the account found in Mark's gospel: "Then Jesus gave a loud cry and breathed his last. And the curtain of the temple was torn in two, from top to bottom. Now, when the centurion, who stood facing him, saw that in this way he breathed his last, he said, 'Truly, this man was God's Son!'" (Mark 15:37–39). The church has traditionally understood this detail as an unambiguous sign from God heralding both the end of the Temple in Jerusalem and the end of Judaism. In turn, this interpretation provided a biblical justification for the church's teaching of contempt for Judaism and the Jewish people.

In the face of this longstanding tradition of interpretation, and in the spirit of "A Sacred Obligation," I propose to interpret Mark 15:38 in ways that are faithful both to the gospel and to the church's commitment to rid itself of its anti-Jewish theology. My goal in this chapter is to offer a viable, alternative reading of Mark 15:38 that will provide readers an opportunity to think anew about the significance of Jesus' crucifixion and death, especially in relation to their understanding of Judaism and the Jewish people.

I develop my argument in three sections: introductory observations on how to determine the meaning of a biblical text, an overview of the church's traditional teaching of Mark 15:37–39, and an alternative interpretation.

What Does a Text Mean?

The first clue to understanding what a text means requires acknowledging the complex relationship that exists between the world of a text—especially its literary and historical context—and the world of the reader. In particular, the assumption regarding what kind of literature we are reading exercises an enormous influence on our understanding of what a text means. We read fiction differently from biography. We understand a newspaper editorial differently from an article on the front page. We comprehend the true meaning of the feature story "Dryer Eats Socks" only when we read that its author is Erma Brombeck.

This principle of the dynamic relationship between literary genre and meaning is equally true of the Bible. Like fiction or biography, "gospel" is a specific literary genre with a particular purpose and set of assumptions regarding how it is to be interpreted. The followers of Jesus created this genre out of a deep desire to preserve for the community of believers the meaning of Jesus' life, death, and resurrection, and the impact of that claim on how they were to live. As such, the gospels are neither histories of the early church nor biographies of Jesus, at least in the modern sense of these genres. They are instead *theological* documents whose primary purpose is to advance a claim about God, about God's relationship to the world, about God's desire for humankind, and most especially, about the role of Jesus in God's hope for the world (see the chapter in this volume by Philip Cunningham). Thus, the rules governing the interpretation of a gospel text differ from those that pertain to historical documents or to biographies. The most important clues to the meaning of a gospel passage do not reside primarily in the literal historicity of the event or in the literal meaning of its words. These clues lie first and foremost in an acknowledgment that the intent of the gospel is to instruct its readers that the God of Israel has spoken a definitive word to the world through Jesus, a Jew from Nazareth.

Composed between the years 70 and 125 C.E., the gospels preserve four accounts with distinctive emphases, written to four different communities of Jesus' followers, each facing its own unique questions and challenges. We might think of these earliest communities as wondering what God intended to teach through the life and death of Jesus of Nazareth. In particular, they must have pondered what God was teaching them by raising the dead man Jesus to new life. They surely hungered to understand the significance of Jesus for them, and must have questioned how they were to live and behave if they professed Jesus to be the Christ of God.

Traditional Understandings of Mark 15:38

Mark 15:38 highlights a single detail in the narrative account of Jesus' last hours. It is one of several immediate "responses" to the death of Jesus recorded in the gospels.[4] What is the "big story" that readers might infer, and what is the role of this verse in teaching that story? In explaining Mark's distinctive interpretation of the meaning of this verse, the late New Testament scholar Raymond E. Brown directs our attention to two linguistic clues embedded in verse 38.[5] The first is the verb used to describe what happens to the Temple curtain; the second is the use of, and connections made with, the word "Temple."

The verb used to describe what happens to the curtain of the Temple immediately following Jesus' death is a form of the Greek word *schizein*, to tear. It is in the passive voice, a biblical literary convention frequently used to indicate that God is the agent of the action, the so-called "divine passive." This same verb appears in only one other place in the entirety of Mark: 1:10–11. Immediately after John baptizes Jesus, the heavens are torn (the first use of the "divine passive") and a voice (God's) declares of Jesus, "You are my beloved son." In Mark 15:38, God acts again, this time tearing not the heavens, but the Temple curtain. By employing the divine passive in this latter instance, the gospel seems to teach two lessons. First, it evokes the beginning of the gospel; a declaration concerning Jesus follows. In this instance, however, it is not God who utters the declaration, but a Roman centurion, an "outsider," who both recognizes and confirms what God has declared at the beginning of Jesus' public ministry: "Truly this man was God's son."

The second claim Mark 15:38 seems to make by its use of the divine passive is that what happens to the Temple curtain immediately following Jesus' death is neither a natural disaster nor an odd coincidence. The curtain of the Temple is torn in two as a deliberate act of *God*, a point to which I shall return in the third section.

One additional detail makes clear the full import of the use of the verb *schizein* in the second gospel. A close reading of Mark's passion narrative reveals a carefully crafted account of Jesus' last days that makes clear who is responsible for Jesus' suffering and death. Mark 14 begins with the Jewish authorities in Jerusalem conspiring for ways to arrest and kill Jesus (14:1). It continues with these same authorities seeking testimony against Jesus to justify their putting him to death (14:55); mocking his identification as the Christ, the son of the Blessed, at his trial (14:61–64); and consulting together regarding his fate. It concludes with these same authorities having Jesus bound and led away to Pilate to be crucified (15:1–3).[6] So a traditional reading of Mark identifies three claims about the Jews: (1) the Jewish authorities in Jerusalem refused to acknowledge Jesus' identity as God's beloved son; (2) they were responsible for Jesus' suffering and death; and (3) God responded by violently tearing the Temple curtain as an clear sign of God's anger with their actions.

Brown explains that the verb *schizein* in Mark 15:38 functions to bring to mind its earlier use in 1:10–11—to make clear that God, from the moment of Jesus' death, will turn to and rely on "outsiders" to recognize God's beloved son. Brown's assessment of the linguistic evidence regarding the use of the verb *schizein* in both 1:10–11 and 15:38 is this: "The centurion who recognizes Jesus' true identity may represent the Gentiles ready to acknowledge what the Jews denied" (1,109).

The second linguistic clue to the traditional understanding of Mark 15:38 is to be found in the *object* of God's violent act of tearing. It is not *any* curtain that God tears in two from top to bottom, but the curtain of the *Temple*, the dwelling place of the Most High and the primary locus of God's *Shekinah*, the most profound expression of the divine presence. The traditional interpretation of this divine gesture argues that God has passed judgment on the Jewish people and on their Temple because they refused to acknowledge the true identity of Jesus and because they conspired to bring about the death of God's son. By tearing the curtain of the Temple, God has for all time removed the "barrier" that once separated the divine presence from the people. God's presence is set free; it is no longer confined to the Temple, but available to all who follow Jesus. Henceforth, nothing will separate God from God's people.[7]

This overview of Mark 15:38 discloses one of the more intractable problems facing New Testament interpreters. We can infer that the author of the second gospel did not write this passage in order to teach contempt for Judaism and the Jewish people, but rather crafted it in light of the complex identity struggles after the destruction of the Temple in 70 C.E. In the centuries after the death of Jesus, however, when Christianity and Rabbinic Judaism were in the prolonged process of becoming two distinct traditions, Christian interpreters initiated what became a far more toxic move that over time became the linchpin of Christian replacement theology. What had been in Mark's time an internal debate about the significance of the life and death of Jesus among the Jewish followers of Jesus and those Jews who were not followers of the Way became in the hands of later interpreters a lethal critique of Jewish fidelity to their covenant with the God of Israel. Because this interpretive tradition achieved a broad consensus among Christian scholars, it found its way into seminary teaching and, through the clergy, into churches everywhere, where it contributed to the ways in which millions of Christians thought about the death of Jesus and about the Jewish people. As such, it helped support and sustain the church's virulent anti-Jewish teaching. In subtle, although no less toxic ways, it has helped to shape the piety and devotional practices of Christians everywhere.

Brown's analysis of *schizein* is a clue to a larger pattern in Mark. Within the broader context of the gospel's teaching regarding the meaning and consequences of Jesus' passion and death, Mark 15:38 seems to claim that the Jewish refusal to acknowledge Jesus as God's beloved son and Jewish complicity in Jesus' death evoked a violent and definitive response from God. Given the way in which the Gospel of Mark structures its account of Jesus' crucifixion and death, it is difficult to argue with Brown's conclusion that the narrative has embedded within it an anti-Jewish bias. In that sense, he is right to claim that an explanation of Mark 15:37–39 is "relatively simple" (1,098).

It becomes more complicated when we acknowledge that over the centuries the church has read passages such as Mark 15:38 against the backdrop of a larger anti-Jewish framework that can be summarized as follows:

- The Jerusalem Temple is no longer the repository of God's presence, which is now to be found among the followers of Jesus.
- Because of their refusal to acknowledge the true identity of Jesus, Judaism and the Jewish people have been replaced as God's beloved by a "new" Israel, the church, with whom God has made a "new" and everlasting covenant.
- All that is "old" has passed away.

Thus, we must do more than explain what Mark meant. We must probe the consequences of our reading of texts. A biblical text that can be read as contributing to a theology of contempt for the Jewish people can never be "relatively simple." Nor can there be anything "simple" about the fact that subsequent generations used this anti-Jewish interpretation as one of the pillars upon which they constructed their teaching of contempt for the Jewish people. There is nothing "simple" about a reading that has been used throughout most of the church's history to justify unspeakable acts of horror toward women and men who knew what the church forgot all too quickly: that "the gifts and the calling of God are irrevocable" (Rom 11:29).

A traditional reading of Mark 15:38 illustrates how intractable a problem Christian supersessionism is, precisely because an anti-Jewish reading has been understood as the "intended" meaning of the text. Against the backdrop of the church's tragic history with the Jewish people, New Testament scholars must acknowledge more readily the complicity of this traditional reading of Mark 15:38 in the church's anti-Jewish teaching; they must be held accountable for perpetuating such readings; and they must seek alternative interpretations that do not denigrate Judaism and the Jewish people.

Brown implicitly offers a way forward in his phrase "what the Gospel(s) narrate." By expressing himself in this way, Brown underscores the folly of searching for the author's intent in our quest for meaning. Specifically, any attempt to determine what the author of Mark "intended" by writing the events narrated in 15:37–39 as he did is fraught with difficulty because what the gospel writer "intended" is available *only through the preserved text*. Thus, to focus on "what the gospel narrates" rather than on what the author intended avoids the pitfall of suggesting that one can know with any degree of certainty what lies in the author's mind. Freed from that illusion, the reader is directed back to the text itself, and from there, to a deeper exploration of what the text narrates. Because the gospels are the living word of the living God, I believe they offer a "solution" to the anti-Jewish problem they help create. The text itself invites multiple interpretations precisely because it is a living word animated by a God who is everpresent to the church in the texts the church calls "sacred."

How then might readers access other interpretations? How might they go about constructing a non-supersessionist interpretation of Mark 15:38? Can the indisputable anti-Jewish polemic that characterizes the traditional interpretation of this text be countered by alternative readings that honor both the gospel *and* the Jewish people? What clues might Mark 15:38 offer to help construct an alternative interpretation? What more might await us if we were to return to Mark 15:38 open to the possibility of being "once more surprised"? Might the text itself surprise us if we took the time to linger over it awhile longer, listening for additional voices that may be awaiting our hearing? To the reader with ears to hear, what more might the text say?[8]

An Alternative Interpretation of Mark 15:38

Earlier in this chapter, I observed that the rhetorical device of the "divine passive" implies that it is God who tears the curtain of the Temple in two from top to bottom. If we turn our attention away from the Temple curtain per se to the One who tears it, what more might the text reveal? What might the divine action of tearing teach us? This shift in perspective becomes my starting point for exploring the possibility of an alternative interpretation of Mark 15:38.

Brown provides a clue to assist in this quest when he writes, "If wrath is the dominant symbolism of the tearing in Mark 15:38, is there also an element of sorrow at what has happened to Jesus and/or what is happening to the sanctuary and to Jerusalem? . . . The evidence is not conclusive, but one should not discount the added motif of sorrow" (1,101).

Taking my clue from Brown's observation, I ask: What more might Mark 15:38 disclose if the reader were to focus on the tearing of the Temple curtain as an expression of God's *sorrow* rather than as an expression of God's anger? What more might the reader learn from this shift in focus concerning the meaning and significance of Jesus' death, about Christianity's relationship to Judaism and the Jewish people, and about how Christians are to live in the world?

Three ideas converge to guide my response to these questions. The first is the Jewish notion that the attribute of empathy is among the chief characteristics of the God of Israel. The Tanakh/Old Testament is replete with texts that describe God as one who feels sorrow, who weeps, who mourns, who grieves (see, e.g., Ps 34:18; Isa 30:19; Jer 31:8–9; Zech 12:10). Later rabbinic writings continue this line of teaching. For example, *Berakhot* 3a in the Babylonian Talmud preserves an exquisite image of the *bat qol* (the divine voice) mourning over the ruin of Jerusalem. Post-Holocaust Jewish writers return to this same theme, most notably, Abraham Joshua Heschel, who writes of God's capacity and willingness to "suffer with" those who suffer.[9]

The second idea that contributes to an alternative interpretation of Mark 15:38 is the biblical custom of tearing a garment as a sign of grief or mourning. Known as "cutting *q'riah*," this custom is found throughout the Tanakh/Old Testament. For example, 2 Kings 2:12–13 recounts that Elisha is inconsolable after the prophet Elijah is taken up to heaven. As a sign of his sorrow, he "took hold of his own clothes and tore them in two pieces." In 2 Samuel 13:31, we read that the king "tore his garments" when he heard that Absalom had killed all his sons.

The third idea comes from later rabbinic law, which designates a hierarchy of mournful occasions and assigns to each mournful occasion the degree to which a garment is to be torn in response to that mourning. This is especially significant for my inquiry because certain mournful occasions call for the garment to be torn in such a manner that it can never again be used. Among the mournful occasions that mandate the tearing of the garment so that it is beyond repair are the destruction of the Temple and the destruction of Jerusalem (*Mo'ed Qatan* 26a).

Bringing these biblical and rabbinic traditions to bear upon Mark 15:38, I would make the following observations:

- The Temple curtain is God's "garment."
- God tears the curtain as a gesture of cutting *q'riah*, a sign of mourning and of a grief beyond consolation at the death of Jesus.
- The extent of the tear—in two from top to bottom—suggests that the curtain is beyond repair.
- In the hierarchy of mournful occasions, Jesus' death is on a par with the destruction of the Temple and the destruction of Jerusalem.

If we allow the motif of sorrow rather than anger to govern the interpretation of God's tearing the curtain of the Temple, the question the text occasions is not "Why is God angry?" but "What is God mourning?" What occasions divine sorrow at this moment in the narrative? If we return to the text, "making room" for contemplating God's action as a sign of mourning, if we take to heart the depth of God's grief signaled by the irreparable tearing of the Temple curtain, what more might we learn?

If we return to Mark 15:38, this time listening for God's voice to answer our questions, might we not hear God saying to the church and to the followers of Jesus:

> I tore the curtain of the Temple as a sign of my profound sorrow over the death of this beloved, righteous son of the Torah. I split it beyond repair as a sign of my grief over the complicity of some religious leaders in his death. I am overcome by anguish in anticipation of the sorrow my beloved Israel has yet to bear because of the pain the followers of Jesus will inflict upon them. I have not rejected the Jewish people.

My love for them, like theirs for me, will endure forever. I did not abandon the Temple, but was driven out when Rome destroyed it. I mourn the destruction of my Temple, and I weep at the site of my holy city, Jerusalem, destroyed by imperial Rome. With my Temple and my holy city in ruins, I shall accompany into exile those whom I first called and will always love (*Midrash Rabbah, Lamentations, proem* XXXIV). I have not transferred my love for the Jewish people to the church any more than a parent abandons its first child at the birth of its second. Israel is my people and I am their God. And I am your God, for I am the God of Jesus through whom you have come to know and love me.

If Christians were to adopt these words as the preferred reading of Mark 15:38, what would they learn? How would they be required to live?

First, the above text teaches that God's immediate response to the death of Jesus is grief for the suffering and death of yet another Jew at the hands of an imperial power. If Christians were to pattern their behavior after God's, they would be among the first to mourn the death of every Jew and of every human being who is tortured, suffers, and dies at the hands of state-sanctioned, abusive power. They would be among the first to protect and shelter the homeless, the poor, the hungry, and those who suffer for the sake of justice. They would be among the first to speak out against the powers that slaughter the innocent and brutalize the unprotected. Because Christians are signed by the cross of Jesus, they would be among the first to commit themselves to repairing a world in which people continue to be crucified.

Second, the text teaches that God does not abandon those whom God has chosen. If the church were to take this teaching to heart, it would have to rethink its own religious identity vis-à-vis the Jewish people, whom God has never abandoned. It would rejoice that God is faithful to all God's promises. And it would acknowledge that God invites whomever God desires to God's holy mountain by whatever means God chooses.

Third, the text teaches that Christians ought to learn to live with the possibility that the meaning of a biblical event is anything but self-evident. Precisely because the texts embody a surplus of meanings, many voices inhabit their sacred texts. At times those voices may be contradictory and dissonant. Christians must learn the discipline of living with the unsettling tension that accompanies multiple interpretations. They need to acquire the aptitude for living in those uncomfortable places where there are no easy answers, no single authoritative voice, but only a lasting promise: "And remember, I am with you always, to the end of the age" (Matt 28:20).

And finally, because of the church's longstanding teaching of contempt for Judaism and the Jewish people, Christians are especially obligated to search for alternative meanings whenever the dominant understanding of a biblical text diminishes, disparages, or demonizes any of God's beloved children, most especially the Jewish people.

When Christians come to the foot of the cross of Jesus, they need a piety that honors God and all those whom God loves. Such a piety will go a long way to restore the Jewish people to their rightful place as a people created, loved, and chosen by God to be recipients of God's own Torah. Such a piety will go a long way in drawing Christians more deeply into the mystery of the One made known to them in and through the life, death, and resurrection of Jesus of Nazareth.

Notes

1. See www.kfki.hu/~arthp/index1.html for a summary description and photographs of the Isenheim Altarpiece.

2. See www.cyberhymnal.org/htm/n/b/nbtblood.htm for the words to this hymn.

3. See www.rosary-center.org/sorrow.htm for a detailed list of each of the mysteries contemplated in this devotional practice.

4. These "responses" can be divided into two groups: those that involve external effects and those that record the reactions of witnesses. The tearing of the Temple curtain into two from top to bottom falls into the first category: external effects.

5. For this overview of Mark 15:38 I have relied on what is perhaps the most important exegetical study of Jesus' passion and death, that of Raymond E. Brown, *The Death of the Messiah, from Gethsemane to Grave: A Commentary on the Passion Narratives in the Four Gospels*, 2 vols. (New York: Doubleday, 1994), 2:1097–140. All references to Brown are to the second volume; to simplify notation, I have placed further citations in parentheses in my text.

6. Throughout Mark's account of Jesus' passion, he refers to these Jewish authorities variously as chief priests, scribes, elders, or the whole Sanhedrin council.

7. Thus, the image of God tearing the curtain of the Temple conjures up powerful associations and implications. Allusions to God's departing the Temple sanctuary would not be altogether foreign to Mark's Jewish readers. Late Second Temple literature includes similar imagery. For example, Ezekiel 9–10, written just prior to the destruction of the First Temple in 587 B.C.E. by the Babylonians under Nebuchadnezzar, records that the glory of God departs the Temple in anger as a consequence of the idolatries practiced there. 2 Apoc Bar 6, written in the latter half of the first century C.E, describes the destruction of the Second Temple in 69–70 C.E by the Romans (portrayed as the Babylonians); in this account an angel takes away

the curtain of the Temple and all the contents of the Holy of Holies before the voice says, "Enter—he has left" (8:2).

8. See Mark 4:25.

9. Abraham Joshua Heschel, *The Prophets* (New York: Harper and Row, 1962), vol. II, "The Theology of Pathos," 1–12.

Further Reading

Brown, Raymond E. *The Death of the Messiah, from Gethsemane to Grave: A Commentary on the Passion Narratives in the Four Gospels*, 2 vols. New York: Doubleday, 1994.

Heschel, Abraham Joshua. *The Prophets*. Perennial Classics edition. New York: HarperCollins, 2001.

17

CHAPTER

Translations of the
New Testament
for Our Time

Norman Beck

Translation as Interpretation

In our statement "A Sacred Obligation," we write that the "New Testament contains passages that have frequently generated negative attitudes toward Jews and Judaism." We urge leaders of churches to scrutinize their use of scripture in lectionaries, hymns, and preaching so as to eliminate distorted images of Judaism. Less apparent, but of utmost importance, is the translation of scripture that the churches use.

There can be no translation of the New Testament or of any other communication without interpretation. Because of this, Muslims insist that the only accurate form of their sacred scriptures, the *Qur'an*, is the Arabic original, and Jews prefer to use their sacred scriptures in their original "holy language," the Hebrew and Aramaic forms, in order to reduce the interpretive element. Most Christians within our Western Christian churches, however, read and hear the New Testament in translations into their own modern languages rather than in its original Greek form.

Unless everyone within our Western Christian churches becomes proficient in the Greek language in which the New Testament was written and transmitted, we shall have to continue to translate the New Testament into modern languages. So it is imperative that we educate and sensitize ourselves about the interpretive element inherent in the process of translation. My purpose in writing this chapter is to explain some of the complexities of interpretation and, in particular, to show how anti-Judaism has implicitly shaped translation of New Testament texts. I will also provide alternative translations that will contribute to a reformed Christian liturgical life that expresses our new relationship with Jews.

To reduce the interpretive element as much as possible, many Christians have preferred to have their translations prepared in what is often called "formal equivalence" form. Formal equivalence translations attempt to translate "word for word." This is, of course, never possible; thus, when it is attempted, the translation is in many instances incoherent. A translation has to make sense to the readers and hearers. Nevertheless, until recently most translators of the Greek New Testament into English have tried as much as possible to use formal equivalence.

During the past two decades, however, many of us have moved to what Eugene A. Nida of the American Bible Society and others call "functional equivalence." This often includes the use of paraphrase, that is, a restatement using additional appropriate words in the target language in order to communicate more clearly what is written in the original Greek. Functional equivalence translation requires much more work and skill of the translator than is required of the formal equivalence translator. Functional equivalence translators, more than their formal equivalence counterparts, recognize that words, like people, are products of their heredity (root or stem meanings), as well as of their environment (usage within a specific situation by a specific speaker and writer). For example, in American English words such as "gay," "cool," and "hot" have acquired additional or altered meanings. A good functional equivalence translation, therefore, will rarely be "word for word."

The use of functional equivalence provides more latitude for the translator. Consequently, it also offers more opportunities to translate statements within the New Testament about Jews and Judaism with appropriate sensitivity. Of course, functional equivalence also makes it possible to translate the Greek New Testament with greater insensitivity than when using formal equivalence methods. Even formal equivalence translations of the New Testament have frequently been more anti-Jewish than the Greek original, especially many of those made into English during the twentieth century of our common era, as I shall show in this chapter.

Barriers into Bridges

Our Christian tradition, though wholesome and positive in most respects, has been disparaging and negative with regard to Jews and Judaism in three highly significant ways. It is our sacred obligation to transform these three barriers that we as Christians have placed between ourselves and the Jews into bridges over which we can pass to learn from each other.

The first of these barriers is the biased "prophecy-fulfillment" use of the Jewish scriptures. Simplistic interpretations of Israel's prophets give the inaccurate impression that they were predicting events that would occur centuries later rather than giving a bold proclamation of God's messages of merciful judgment. The prophets addressed issues of their own time. Christians must respect the context in which the prophetic word was uttered. That we see Christ reflected in prophecy is a second layer of meaning.

The second barrier is the narrow "exclusivistic Christ" concept. When Christians understand Jesus as the Messiah (Christ) in a one-dimensional and inadequate way as the one who fulfilled Jewish messianic expectations, they cannot understand why Jews do not accept Christ. Were we to understand how the concept of Messiah in Judaism is dynamic and complex, we would grasp that the way of Jesus Christ is not the only way to God.

The third barrier is the virulent Christian "teaching of contempt," in Jules Isaac's term (see also the chapters in this volume by Eugene Fisher and Eva Fleischner). In the New Testament, the teaching of contempt involves the claim that Christianity has superseded Judaism and that Jews are Christ-killers, offspring of poisonous snakes and of the Devil, hateful and hypocritical. Both Jews and Christians have problematic texts within their sacred scriptures. In the "Old Testament" (First Testament, what Jews call "Tanakh"; see the chapter in this volume by Walter Harrelson) we find an especially troubling passage in 1 Samuel 15:2–3: "Thus says the Lord of hosts, 'I will punish the Amalekites for what they did in opposing the Israelites when they came up out of Egypt. Now go and attack Amalek, and utterly destroy all that they have; do not spare them, but kill both man and woman, child and infant, ox and sheep, camel and donkey.'" Such problematic passages require (and receive) commentary, lest they rationalize harm. Only our Christian texts, however, have contributed to the suffering and death of millions of other people. I have examined these barriers elsewhere.[1]

Prerequisite for eradicating the barrier of the teaching of contempt is our frank acknowledgment of its existence.[2] We then can proceed by avoiding the use of the texts that express this contempt within our specifically Christian scriptures in our private devotions and in our public worship services. A very important aspect of avoiding the use of such texts in public worship services is the sensitive revision of our lectionaries—preselected texts in one-, three-, or four-year cycles read within most of our congregations.[3]

The most challenging task in reducing our teaching of contempt is that of educating and sensitizing the approximately two billion Christians living today, who speak hundreds of languages. This educational process is facilitated when the relatively few persons making new translations of the Greek New Testament into modern languages are sensitive to the tragic consequences of anti-Judaism and reflect this sensitivity in their translations. One sensitive translator can reach millions of other Christians. For example, Lydie Huynh changed and improved her translation of the Greek New Testament into French in 128 places after she had read an article by Roger Omanson, "Anti-Jewish Bias of the NT," and my *Mature Christianity in the 21st Century*. The effects of her rethinking are very significant, since Huynh's work is used by tribal translators who produce African-language translations of the New Testament in some seventeen countries in sub-Saharan Africa.[4]

A Test Case: Translation of Romans 11:11–32

Romans 9–11 is the principal section within the letters of Paul included in the New Testament in which Paul writes about Jews as Jews. That is, Paul is concerned here with Jews who have remained in the ambit of Judaism and have not been drawn, as some others were, into the circle of Jesus' followers. Formal equivalence translations give inadequate attention to the environment (context) of words. Followers of Jesus from Jewish backgrounds should be identified as such in our translations, especially in texts such as Romans 2:17 and Galatians 3:28. Early Christians who wanted to require Gentile followers of Jesus to submit to Jewish dietary requirements and, if male, to be circumcised should be specified as Judaizing Christians, not as Jews.

Within these three vitally important chapters, we shall examine a series of translations of Romans 11:28 and then of the larger section 11:11–32. I want to show how theological assumptions shape translations, whether they be formal or functional. To lay out the problem clearly, I begin with two English translations of 11:28, the first from the New Revised Standard Version (NRSV), and the second from my own translation, *The New Testament: A New Translation and Redaction*:

- As regards the gospel they are enemies of God for your sake; but as regards election they are beloved, for the sake of their ancestors (NRSV).
- With respect to the good news that we proclaim they are temporarily alienated in deference to you, but with respect to their being chosen they remain dearly loved in deference to their ancestors (Beck translation).

Two issues are at stake: who the enemies are, and whether the enmity is permanent or temporary. The problem arises with the contrasting adjectives *echthroi* (ἐχθροί) and *agapētoi* (ἀγαπητοί). The NRSV translates the former as "enemies of God," whereas I render it "temporarily alienated." (Note that the "of God" is not in the text of Romans 11:28.) The translations of the latter are similar: "beloved" and "dearly loved." Let us probe the differences more closely.

As I have indicated in *Mature Christianity in the 21st Century*, in many contexts the adjective *echthroi* (ἐχθροι) has the connotation of persons who are "hated" or, when it is used as a substantive—an adjective used as a noun—are "enemies" of someone. When, however, we consider the environment of the word in Romans 11:11–32, in which Paul offers the profound metaphor of the olive tree, we see that in 11:28 Paul uses *echthroi* in the sense of persons who are "temporarily estranged" or "temporarily alienated" until God grafts them back into the olive tree. Functional equivalence translations can indicate this, as mine does above. The key here is attention to the environment surrounding the word, in this case the metaphor of the olive tree.

The two adjectives contrasted in 11:28 appear from the context of Romans 11:11–32 to refer to Jews contemporary with Paul. They seem to have heard the proclamation of Jesus as *the* Messiah. Seeing no evidence, however, of the conditions that they associated with the Messianic Age, they had not joined Paul's developing Christian community in Rome, with its mix of Christians from both Jewish and Gentile backgrounds. The Greek text of 11:28 is not explicit about from whom they are "temporarily estranged" or "temporarily alienated," though "because of their ancestors they remain dearly loved."

Martin Luther's German translation (1522), the Rheims-Douay Roman Catholic translation (1582–1610), and the King James Version (1611) all retain the ambiguity of the Greek text as to the nature of this temporary alienation. During the twentieth century, however, most English translations add some form of interpretive qualifier, such as "of God" (not in the Greek texts), as indicated in table 17.1.

In the next six examples the word "they" is replaced by the words "the Jews," which is also not in the Greek texts, thus subjecting readers and hearers to two interpretive anti-Jewish additions. The result is an anti-Jewish statement that goes far beyond the Greek original, even in translations that are driven by the formal equivalence methodology, as illustrated in table 17.2.

The Contemporary English Version (CEV), prepared and published by the American Bible Society in 1995, uses the functional equivalence methodology. Though appropriately sensitive to the anti-Jewish polemic in the fourth gospel, unfortunately the CEV translators rendered Romans 11:28a as "The people of Israel are treated as God's enemies, so that the good news can come to you Gentiles." They continue with sensitivity and grace, however, in 11:28b–29, with "But they are still the chosen ones, and God loves them because of their famous ancestors. God doesn't take back the gifts he has given or forget about the people he has chosen."

Table 17.1

Translation and Date	Translation of Romans 11:28
James Moffatt, 1913	they are enemies of God
Edgar J. Goodspeed, 1923	they are treated as enemies of God
Revised Standard Version, 1946, 1971	they are enemies of God
New Revised Standard Version, 1990	they are enemies of God
J. B. Phillips, 1958	they are at present God's enemies
New English Bible, 1961	they are treated as God's enemies
William F. Beck, 1963	God's rule in telling the good news is to treat them as His enemies.
Revised English Bible, 1989	they are God's enemies

Table 17.2

Translation and Date	Translation of Rom 11:28
Amplified Bible, 1965	they [the Jews, at present] are enemies [of God]
Good News for Modern Man, 1966	the Jews are God's enemies
Jerusalem Bible, 1966	the Jews are enemies of God
New American Bible, 1970	the Jews are enemies of God
The Living Bible, 1971	Now many of the Jews are enemies of the Gospel. They hate it…
New Century Version, 1986	The Jews refuse to accept the Good News, so they are God's enemies
Good News Bible— Today's English Version, 1992	the Jews are God's enemies

The New American Standard Bible (1960), the Modern Language Bible (1969), the New International Version (1978), the American Holy Bible (1984), and the New American Bible (1989) do not add the words "of God" to their translation of *echthroi* in 11:28a, but they do translate *echthroi* as "enemies." The repeated use of one, and in many instances two, of these interpretive anti-Jewish additions indicates that many of these twentieth-century translators were heavily influenced by interpretive choices previously made by other translators. They should, rather, have engaged in the more difficult work of giving adequate attention to the environment (context) of the words that they were translating.

That many of the twentieth-century translators were heavily influenced by interpretive choices made by other translators can be seen also in the repeated translation of *echthroi* as if it were a substantive that can be expressed in English as "enemies." Yet, in most instances they did not render the adjective *agapētoi* with which it is paired in Romans 11:28 as a substantive. This interpretive choice, which can be seen already in the King James Version, is grammatically incorrect. Both Greek words are adjectives used as adjectives and paired with each other. It is an anti-Jewish bias to give the negative adjective *echthroi* the additional force and substance of rendering it as a noun while not doing the same with the positive adjective *agapētoi*.

A comparison of these translations in the larger segment of Romans under consideration here (Romans 11:11–32) indicates that again there is little evidence of a heightened anti-Jewish bias in Martin Luther's German edition, the Rheims-Douay edition, the King James Version, the New King James Version, the New American Standard Bible, or the American Holy Bible. The other twentieth-century translations, however, replaced pronouns and unexpressed subjects of verbs in the Greek text with the specific noun "Jews" or "Israel" in pejorative situations in at least one instance in 11:11–32, as table 17.3 indicates.

The result is an unnecessary, constant bombardment of the readers and hearers of this crucial New Testament text with the idea that the Jews are people who stumble, are jealous, are disobedient, do not believe God, have left God, have set themselves as enemies against the gospel, are full of ungodliness, refuse God's gifts, and are rebels against God.

The Living Bible is included in these comparisons because of the popularity it attained within a decade of its publication, even though it is not a translation from the Greek texts. According to Bruce M. Metzger, the Living Bible produced by Kenneth N. Taylor "enjoyed the most phenomenal distribution in publishing history," having "captured 46 percent of the total sales of the Bible in the U.S.A." by the "mid-1970s."[5] Metzger indicates that by the end of the twentieth century "it had been translated into nearly one hundred languages, together spoken by 90 percent of the world's population, and forty million copies had been printed." Taylor accomplished this by paraphrasing the American Standard Version "into simple, modern English" designed "to help his ten children understand the Scriptures during daily family devotions."

Much of the market that the Living Bible once held has been lost to the New International Version and to other translations. The popularity of the Living Bible, however, which according to my analysis of Romans 11:11–32 is the most anti-Jewish of all twentieth-century Bibles published in the English language—at least in this crucial text from Romans—is a clear indication of how important it is for us to be conscious of the way in which bias may influence translation.

It should be noted that in neither of the two instances in which the word "Israel" is used in the Greek text of Romans 11:11–32 is Israel presented in an unfavorable position. Since within our biblical tradition the "hardening" of certain people is accomplished by God as part of God's amazing plan of salvation, Paul follows his reference to the refusal of many

Table 17.3

Translation	Replacement of Pronouns and Unexpressed Subjects of Verbs in Greek with the Noun "Jews" or "Israel"
James Moffatt, Edgar J. Goodspeed, J. B. Phillips, New English Bible, Modern Language Bible, New International Version, Revised English Bible	once
Revised Standard Version and New Revised Standard Version	twice
William F. Beck	three times
Jerusalem Bible and New American Bible	four times
Amplified Bible	five times
Contemporary English Version	six times
Good News for Modern Man	eight times
Good News Bible— Today's English Version	nine times
New Century Version	eleven times
Living Bible	thirteen times

of his people to accept the freedom from the bondage of sin and death until the time when the full number of the Gentiles have accepted it (11:25) immediately with his joyful statement that then all of his people (Israel) will be set free from sin and death (11:26). The reflections by which Paul was inspired to write his magnificent conclusion (11:33–36) to Romans 9–11 were not triggered by his concentration on Jewish intransigence, but by his understanding of God's glorious plan of salvation. Insensitive interpretive translations of Romans 11:11–32 such as those cited above obscure the reason for Paul's exclamation that follows the passage: "O the depth of God's riches and wisdom and understanding! How unfathomable are God's judgments! How untrackable are God's paths!" Even worse, insensitive translations such as those that have dominated the twentieth century give the false impression that Paul is praising God for condemning Paul's own people.

When the Greek texts of Romans 9–11 are translated without anti-Jewish biases, these three chapters, which more than any other portion of the New Testament relate directly to the Jews and Judaism, are not virulently anti-Jewish. To the contrary: in these chapters the good olive tree is the Jewish one into to which we Christians are grafted.

The examples of translations of Romans 11:11–32 given in this section illustrate how much translators, as well as other interpreters of sacred texts, are influenced by their presuppositions and biases, as well as by the political and spiritual conditions in which they function. These analyses could easily be extended to hundreds of other New Testament texts.

Translations of the New Testament for the Twenty-First Century

The twentieth century produced a proliferation of translations of the Greek New Testament and the entire Christian Bible into modern languages. Translations in this next century should be characterized by more careful attention to the environment (context) of words in the texts. Although this makes translation a much more difficult task, it honors our sacred obligation to rethink our Christian faith in relation to Judaism and the Jewish people.

I intend my own translation, published in 2001—the full title of which is *The New Testament: A new translation and redaction that dares to be sensitive, sensitive to anti-Jewish polemic and to sexism, and dares to be innovative for our time by moving back into the past of early church development and forward into the future of the church that is still to come*—to provide a model for other twenty-first-century translations. The trend toward this type of sensitivity in translation is evident in the work of the American Bible Society teams that produced the Contemporary English Version near the end of the twentieth century. Their translation of the fourth gospel, in which the Greek words *hoi Ioudaioi* (the Jews) are translated with excellent sensitivity, must be continued and extended to the entire New Testament, as I have done, in this new century.

In the translations into modern languages of the most virulently anti-Jewish New Testament texts and of the texts that relegate all women to subordinate roles in the church, I suggest not only sensitive translation but also the statement of repudiation of the harmful racist and sexist elements in these texts by printing these elements in small-print form, which I have done, for example, in 1 Thessalonians 2:13–16; Matthew 23:29–33, 38; 27:1–26; John 8:37–59; Acts 7:51–8:1a; and 1 Timothy 2:11–15. The virulently anti-Jewish materials in such texts are not essential to the message of the New Testament and of Christianity. In fact, they seriously detract from it. By printing such texts in small-print form, we can make it clear that we realize that the problem of the teaching of contempt is present in our sacred texts themselves and not merely in our interpretations of them.

There will be many changes in the ways in which the New Testament and the entire Bible will be translated and distributed within our new century. None of us can predict the magnitude of these changes. The changes will certainly go far beyond the few that I can suggest here. May the changes be to the glory of God. May they be a fulfillment of our sacred obligation to rethink our Christian faith in relation to Judaism and the Jewish people.

Notes

1. Most recently, my "Replacing Barriers with Bridges," in John C. Merkle, ed., *Faith Transformed: Christian Encounters with Jews and Judaism* (Collegeville, MN: Liturgical, 2003), 71–89. The third barrier is the subject of my *Mature Christianity in the 21st Century: The Recognition and Repudiation of the Anti-Jewish Polemic in the New Testament*, rev. ed. (New York: Crossroad; Philadelphia: American Interfaith Institute / World Alliance, 1994).

2. See Jules Isaac, *The Teaching of Contempt: Christian Roots of Anti-Semitism* (New York: Holt, Rinehart and Winston, 1964).

3. See my "Removing Anti-Jewish Polemic from our Christian Lectionaries: A Proposal" at http://jcrelations.net/articl1/beck.htm, and "Appendix A: A New Four Year Lectionary," in my *The New Testament: A New Translation and Redaction* (Lima, OH: Fairway, 2001), 622–81, the only lectionary available in the English language that is "for Christ" without being "against the Jews." Only my "A New Four Year Lectionary" is fully sensitive to this problem, avoiding anti-Jewish texts. Interdenominational and international revision of lectionaries to avoid the "teaching of contempt" is urgently needed.

4. See Lydie Huynh, "The Next 2,000 Years . . .," *Explorations* 9, no. 3 (1995): 5; Roger Omanson, "Anti-Jewish Bias of the NT," *Bible Translator*, July 1992.

5. Bruce M. Metzger, *The Bible in Translation: Ancient and English Versions* (Grand Rapids, MI: Baker, 2001), 179.

PART

We Affirm the Importance of the Land of Israel for the Life of the Jewish People

The Land of Israel in the Cauldron of the Middle East: A Challenge to Christian-Jewish Relations

Michael B. McGarry

MANY WILL eagerly look to this chapter to see how "they" (the Christian Scholars Group) come down on the contemporary dilemma of the Israeli-Palestinian conflict. My own role is more modest: to offer a context for our affirmation in the ninth point of "A Sacred Obligation" of the importance of the land in the life of the Jewish people, and to explore the implications for relations between Jews and Christians today.

In today's political climate, however, where thoughtful consideration of complex realities often descends into scoring debating points or where listening to the other functions as a pretext for shoring up support for "our side," my contribution may be both challenging and disappointing. For some, siding wholeheartedly and unquestionably with current Israeli (political) policies is the litmus test of whether we Christians have truly overcome the centuries of antisemitism that have plagued Christian communities. Others, more sympathetic to a Palestinian perspective on the past sixty years, will wonder whether we have succumbed to the logic that those who passionately work for Christian-Jewish understanding, as we do, must, therefore, be willing to ignore Palestinian suffering and cries of injustice. Readers who hope that my chapter will make a "final pronouncement" in either direction (I hope) will be disappointed. I wish to go beyond either-or positions. In my experience, too many on all sides say, in effect, "If you wish to be my friend, you must hate the people I hate."

Our Christian faith should make us love more generously while we keep our ears open to the beleaguered and suffering voices—from whichever side. Therefore, what I propose in this chapter is more programmatic than definitive, more exploratory than polemical. I wish to offer our Christian and Jewish colleagues considerations for dialogue rather than conclusions.

What moves me in this direction, providentially, is the robust internal political and religious debates in Israel, where I now live. Here passionate voices debate on a daily basis the religious and existential meaning of the Jewish return to the land in various forums: in print and electronic media, at academic gatherings, and over dinner tables. Inspired by their openness and their ardor, I wish to engage my Christian brothers and sisters on this topic.

From the beginning, however, I wish to lay out two fundamental assertions. First, the centrality of the land in the Jewish self-understanding is for us not up for debate. This, the centripetal idea in the ninth point of our statement; it is an affirmation I believe all Christians need to make, because land is a fundamental dimension of Judaism. Second, we do not equate recognition of this central Jewish self-understanding with heeding the views of one party or one side in the current political situation. Rather, affirming the centrality of the land comes from paying attention to the *many* Jewish sides of the conversation. Furthermore, committed as we are to recognizing "that both Israelis and Palestinians have the right to live in peace and security in a homeland of their own," we are firm in our resolve to listen and respond to the perspectives of our Christian and Muslim Palestinian brothers and sisters. Moreover, our commitment to pay attention to many sides bears similarity to the complex views *some* of our Jewish brothers and sisters hold. Indeed, many Jews throughout the world insist that their history of suffering opens them to others' suffering, including that of the Palestinian people. They ask that we Christians be attentive to the many voices about political options in the region.

I believe that listening to both sides will in the end be the best guarantee for an Israel that is secure and at peace with its neighbors. Tragically, for many in the Holy Land, one casualty of the second Intifada has been the death of empathy among Israelis and Palestinians for the other. But this must not be the price of solidarity with our Jewish or Palestinian interlocutors. If empathy for the other dies, then the death of hope for a land where Jews can live in safety and peace will soon follow.

As they discern where God's Spirit is leading them in a post-Shoah world, Christians must move beyond the supersessionist "Christian theology [that] charged that the Jews had condemned themselves to homelessness by rejecting God's Messiah." We must retrieve neglected or forgotten parts of our tradition to understand ourselves anew in God's salvific plan as partners alongside Jews. And we must reject those aspects of our tradition that have proved so harmful to the Jewish people. The project of writing "A Sacred Obligation," a result of recent decades of dialogue, has yielded new appreciation for Jewish self-understanding that fundamentally includes attachment to the land.

So we begin with that datum and go back in time.

Christian Thinking about the Land

After the destruction of the Temple in 70 C.E. and the expulsion of the Jews from Jerusalem that followed the Bar Kochba revolt (132–35 C.E.), both the Jewish faithful and Jewish followers of "the Way"—as Jesus' Movement first designated itself—sought to make sense out of these defeats. In the first century, the Romans did not make fine distinctions between Jews who followed Jesus and those (the vast majority) who did not. The Romans rooted out any they perceived to be a threat to their imperial rule (see the chapters in this volume by Joseph Tyson and Jean-Pierre Ruiz).

Jews who did not follow Jesus had a ready paradigm to understand this catastrophic loss of their Temple and Jerusalem: exile. Memory of a previous exile in Babylon many centuries before (ca. 587–540 B.C.E.) had been kept alive in their scriptures, as Psalm 137 testifies vividly. In this new exile they drew upon the heritage bequeathed by the Pharisaic revolution of Second Temple Judaism, which they then expanded into the Mishnah, Talmud, and other writings, as Peter Pettit and John Townsend explain in their chapter in this volume. Even with the rise of the synagogue and the rich tradition of studying, commenting on, and arguing about Torah, the Jewish people never lost their attachment to the land. Every year at Pesach (Passover), in every household, they prayed "next year in Jerusalem."

After the destruction of the Temple and of Jerusalem, those first-century Jews who followed Jesus—the nascent church—intensified their quest for self-understanding vis-à-vis those who remained wholly under the ambit of Judaism. They "remembered" certain sayings from Jesus that helped them to interpret those terrible events. Some sayings, based on interpretations of Isaiah that promised destruction and dispersion for infidelity, predicted the destruction of the Temple and the fall of Jerusalem. Other sayings "spiritualized" and relativized any attachment to a particular place, whether the Temple or Jerusalem. Especially important for the followers of the Way in this regard were the following New Testament passages (see also Luke 19:17–18, 41–44; Acts 7:44–55):

- John 4:21–24: "Jesus said to her, 'Woman, believe me, the hour is coming when you will worship the Father neither on this mountain nor in Jerusalem. You worship what you do not know; we worship what we know, for salvation is from the Jews. But the hour is coming, and is now here, when the true worshipers will worship the Father in spirit and truth, for the father seeks such as these to worship him. God is spirit, and those who worship him must worship in spirit and truth.'"
- Hebrews 12:22–26: "But you have come to Mount Zion and to the city of the living God, the heavenly Jerusalem, and to innumerable angels in festal gathering, and to the assembly of the firstborn who are enrolled in heaven, and to God the judge of all, and to the spirits of the righteous made perfect, and to Jesus, the mediator of a new covenant, and to the sprinkled blood that speaks a better word than the blood of Abel. See that you do not refuse the one who is speaking; for if they did not escape what they refused the one who warned them on earth, how much less will we escape if we reject the one who warns from heaven!"

Early Christians theologized about Jewish attachment to the land of Israel for two reasons: as a reaction to the crises of the late first century, and as a polemic against those Jews who did not accept Jesus as their Messiah. Jerusalem's fate in particular figured prominently in early Christian apologetics to affirm the rightness of the path of those Jews who followed the Jew Jesus over against those who did not. By the fourth century, Christian apologists pointed to the Jewish diaspora around the then-known world, in tandem with their expulsion from Jerusalem, as "proof" that God had abandoned them and that God had adopted the Christian people. Moreover, by now the Christian church was overwhelmingly Gentile. The great theologian and saint from northern Africa, Augustine, believed that the punishment for Jewish rejection of Jesus was that God had condemned them to be perpetual wanderers—to be "wandering Jews" without a land *(Reply to Faustus the Manichean)*.

Nevertheless, the move into a Christian appropriation of the "Holy Land" was not easy. Once Emperor Constantine made Christianity a licit religion in the Roman Empire early in the fourth century, some Christians, led by his mother St. Helen, began to travel to Palestine. They ventured to Jerusalem, only to see it in ruins. To them this was evidence that God had taken away the Jewish land as punishment for the Jewish people's failure to recognize the Messiah. At the same time, inspired by walking in the footsteps of Jesus, these Christians "found" the places associated with Jesus' earthly ministry. There they began to "worship with their lips and fingertips," as it were: to touch the tomb where Jesus' body had lain was to touch the One who had been raised from the dead. Thus Christian practice aided a promising "theology of place," if not a "theology of land."

A Christian understanding of the "Holy Land" was neither univocal nor without opposition. Christians like Origen, Eusebius, and Gregory of Nyssa, relying heavily upon John 4 and other passages cited above, countered, "We do not go to a shrine like pagans to seek God. God does not dwell in particular places."[1] Indeed, early Christian controversies over a "holy land" are both fascinating and complex. To this day, many Christians refuse to see the religious value of attachment to any land, even if they lack awareness of the centuries-old Christian charge that God's revenge on the Jewish people for "rejecting" their Messiah was their removal from any land.

The iconoclastic controversies of the eighth and ninth centuries over the permissibility of veneration of visual representations of Christ also challenged expressions of faith such as pilgrimages, pictures, and other tangible sacramentals. But with the final acceptance of icons and pilgrimages, Christians emerged all the more committed to the land. Tragically, this commitment found bloody expression in the crusades of the eleventh to thirteenth centuries. The Protestant Reformation of the sixteenth century again challenged the notion of holy places, viewing devotion to them as superstitious and a sign of works righteousness. Evangelical Protestantism of the past two centuries typically has reflected on the heavenly Jerusalem, thereby relativizing or even replacing an earthly Jerusalem (see Heb 12:22–29). The legacy of some of those controversies might be summed up in the observation that "Catholics come to the Holy Land on pilgrimage, and Protestants, more committed to the Word of God, come on study tours." The point is not which tradition has the correct understanding of the "Holy Land," but rather to note that some Christian traditions display ambivalence about the very notion of any land that is called holy. This ambivalence has its roots in interpretations of the Bible, including those noted above.

In the evolution of their varied attitudes toward the Holy Land, Christians also made Jewish relation to the land part of their arsenal of anti-Jewish teachings. Once Christianity became a legal religion, and then in the late fourth century the official religion of the Roman Empire, Christian apologists hardened in their negative assessment of Jews who had not followed Jesus. In their view, God had abandoned the Jews, replacing them with a new people, the Christians. To prove that God no longer favored the Jewish people, Christians, now in a position of power, kept the Jewish people landless by enacting legislation that banned them from owning property. Obviously, these laws had a self-fulfilling dimension to them, "proving" that God had abandoned the landless Jews in favor of the Christians. Augustine's earlier formulation of the theology of the landless or "wandering" Jew now had the force of law.

Such hostility to the Jewish connection to the land of Israel has shadowed the Christian world for centuries. In fact, the theological judgment that God kept the Jews landless as punishment for refusing their Messiah continued into the twentieth century. When Theodore Herzl, the father of modern Zionism, approached Pope Pius X in 1904 to seek his support for the Jewish return to the land, the pope responded: "We cannot encourage this movement. We cannot prevent the Jews from going to Jerusalem—but we could never sanction it. . . . The Jews have not recognized our Lord, therefore we cannot recognize the Jewish people."[2] The pope here is echoing centuries of supersessionist theology—a theology that eclipsed the centrality of the land to Judaism.

Now, in the wake of the Shoah, as Western Christians abandon other dimensions of this supersessionist theology, they have begun to suspect that perhaps Christians should not theologize about the land at all—certainly, not *for* the Jews, who vigorously do it for themselves. Indeed, among Jews there is hardly a uniform "theology of land" with which Christians may agree or disagree. But Christians must acknowledge that the land of Israel is important for Jews, whether they live in Tel Aviv, London, Los Angeles, Istanbul, or Sydney. Moreover, Jewish liturgy and literature are filled with references to the land. Simply put, the land of Israel is a vital aspect of Judaism. Recognizing this fundamental reality enables Christians to begin a dialogue with Jews. It is certainly not the last word in the cauldron of the Middle East, but it is an essential first word.

Nevertheless, Christians must not confuse a support of the Jewish return to the land with an unquestioning support of a particular political expression of Zionism or of particular borders of that land. Some enemies of Israel and some enemies of the Jewish people eagerly seek ammunition from Christians who criticize particular Israeli policies in order to delegitimize the political reality of Israel. Others, particularly evangelical lovers of Zion, draw upon a particular theological position—the premillennial return of the people to Israel—to justify a sort of Christian theological domino game in which the Jewish return to Israel is a necessary but temporary prelude to the Jewish people's conversion to Christianity. As Daniel Levitas has characterized it, "According to this view, history unfolds in a series of distinct preordained periods or 'dispensations' and the return of the Jews to Israel will not only bring about Christ's return, but also their destruction."[3]

Christians should neither delegitimize nor sacralize the State of Israel. Rather, we must recognize the importance of the land to the Jewish people and commit ourselves both to dialogue with them and exploration of what we may have to learn for our own tradition. Neither the Bible nor a particular Christian theology enables us to conclude what Israel's borders should be. Our Christian faith, however, should lead us to encourage political leaders to rededicate themselves to working out a just and lasting peace for all who inhabit the land. As the Vatican's Commission for Religious Relations with the Jews judiciously advises:

> Christians are invited to understand this [Jewish] religious attachment [to the land] which finds its roots in Biblical tradition, without however making their own any particular religious interpretation of this relationship (cf. *Declaration* of the U.S. Conference of Catholic Bishops, November 20, 1975).
>
> The existence of the State of Israel and its political options should be envisaged not in a perspective which is in itself religious, but in their reference to the common principles of international law.

The permanence of Israel (while so many ancient peoples have disappeared without trace) is a historic fact and a sign to be interpreted within God's design. We must in any case rid ourselves of the traditional idea of a people *punished*, preserved as a *living argument* for Christian apologetic. It remains a chosen people, "the pure olive on which were grafted the branches of the wild olive which are the gentiles" (John Paul II, 6th March, 1982, alluding to Rm 11:17–24).[4]

Jewish Thinking about the Land

Rabbi Harold Kushner writes:

Over the years, I have found that the issue that puzzles non-Jews the most about Judaism is the role that Israel plays in our minds and souls. It has no analogue in the Christian world. . . . Moreover, the [Jewish] attachment [to the Land] is emotional, not nostalgic or theological. It cuts across all religious and social borders. Religious and nonreligious Jews, orthodox and liberal, rich and poor are more united by their love for Israel than by any other single subject on the Jewish agenda (except perhaps for antisemitism). How shall we understand this?[5]

Indeed, how shall we *Christians* understand this?

For almost two millennia until 1948, Jews had lived without a land of their own. To be sure, Jews had always inhabited portions of the land west of the Jordan River. But despite the annual expression of longing for "next year in Jerusalem," Jews around the world had neither a leader nor the political power to act on their yearning. In the nineteenth century, extraordinary leaders arose from European communities to begin a search for a land where they could be safe as Jews. As Christians may be surprised to learn, the earliest leaders advocating a return to the land were far from religious. They sought Zion not for biblical purposes, but for security: protection for the Jewish people from the regular, violent antisemitic attacks of European Christians. Indeed, some of the most vigorous Jewish opposition to Zionism came from their communities' *religious* thinkers, many of whom felt that there were too many physical hurdles to overcome. Some also believed that the return to the land was a sign of messianic times, and that therefore it must be at divine, not human, initiative. Nonetheless, in the wake of the antisemitism stirred up in France in the Dreyfus Affair (1894–1906), in which a Jewish army officer was falsely accused of espionage, the visionary leader Theodor Herzl concluded that Christian Europe was not a safe place for Jews. So he traveled throughout Europe in a passionate call to the Jewish people to return to Zion. Thus began the modern Zionist movement. It entailed purchase of land in Ottoman-ruled Palestine and then more assertive means under the British Mandate (1920–1948). The Zionist movement, primarily secular in origin but later garnering religious support and justification, is both fascinating and complex.

For most Jews the return to the land and the establishment of the State of Israel in 1948 are modern miracles of their identity. The land of Israel is a dearly cherished tenet of most Jewish self-understanding, even if observant and nonobservant Jews put forward different reasons for it. And it is simply this phenomenon of the land's centrality for Jewish self-understanding that Christians must acknowledge and engage. Discarding supersessionist theology makes it possible for Christians, without imposing their own theological categories, to begin to understand the religious and cultural foundations for the Jewish longing for Zion. Various political configurations and border disputes, although critically important, should not obscure an attentive Christian engagement with our Jewish brothers and sisters.

Contemporary Christian Perspectives: A Spectrum of Viewpoints

Today Christians find themselves on many places of the political and theological spectrum with regard to the Jewish return to the land. Although what follows is a sweeping generalization, it is nonetheless helpful to identify three broad points of view.

Evangelical Christians often rejoice with the Jewish return to the land. They hail the Zionist enterprise not so much because they want the Jews to survive and thrive as Jews, but because they believe that the Jewish return to the land is part of God's larger plan for the ultimate triumph of Christ. They believe that the return of the Jews to the land of Israel will precede Christ's return to earth. Their view usually stands on a fundamentalist view of certain passages in the scriptures, particularly a predictive understanding of prophecy. Thus we see vigorous support politically, religiously, and socially for the Jewish return to all the land west of the Jordan River as part of this Christian theological template that the founding of the state precipitated in 1948. Many evangelicals ignore the fate of

Palestinians, whether Christian or Muslim, whether in Israel proper or the West Bank. Ultimately, however, their vigorous support for Jewish return to all the land west of the Jordan River results in the end of the Jewish people *as Jews*, since their theology requires that Jews convert to Christianity as a prelude to the Second Coming of Christ.

Other Christians, who have a different interpretation of the Bible (see Philip Cunningham's chapter in this volume) view with some ambivalence the establishment of the state in 1948. They criticize the subsequent policies of some Israeli governments, especially as these policies have negatively impacted Palestinians. While granting the profound effect of the Shoah on Jews, they wonder about the solution to this European problem by a move to the Middle East. They eschew millennial or fundamentalist readings of biblical prophecy, whether in the New or Old Testaments, and choose to evaluate the Jewish return to the land simply and solely by Western standards of human rights. Their own reaction against fundamentalist readings of the Bible makes them recoil from geopolitical arguments based on biblical texts. Often, Latin American liberation theologies or Continental postmodern and postcolonial assumptions have profoundly shaped their views. Whatever the reason, these Christians express their religious convictions by siding with "the underdog," in this case, from their viewpoint, the Arabs who were the majority in the land before 1948. Vigorously denying any anti-semitism, they claim that the place of the Christian is to stand with the oppressed and resist the oppressor, no matter from which religious or ethnic background that person may come. These Christians often appeal to a universalism that precludes any particularistic expression, such as "the chosen people" or the land of Israel. While they may feel uneasy about Christian complicity in the Shoah, they feel that such guilt does not justify European Jewry's "confiscation" of another people's land.

Still others, humbled and horrified by the Shoah, recognize the human need for a safe place for the Jewish people as well as the Christian responsibility to support them with a secure homeland, most meaningfully expressed in the State of Israel. They see that Christians have little right to preach to the Jews about justice and fairness in the light of centuries of persecution. Thus, they support the Jewish return to the land, not so much out of religious conviction as out of moral solidarity with the victims of Christian persecution. At the same time, they do not turn a deaf ear to Palestinian suffering; rather, they seek ways for both Jews and Palestinians to live safely in their respective homelands.

Conclusion

The Christian Scholars Group's affirmation of the importance of the land for Jewish self-understanding requires careful attention. But the *legitimacy* of the State of Israel is not our agenda item. I believe it is dangerous, and ultimately ineffective, to provide a warrant for Israel's political legitimacy on theological grounds. If political legitimacy depends on theology, then it can be lost by countervailing theologies. So one finds some Christians charging that Jews do not have a right to the land of Israel because, in their judgment, most contemporary Israelis are not living according to the covenant. Or one finds the position that Jews lost their right to the land when they denied their Messiah (remember Pope Pius X to Herzl and much of Christian tradition). On the other side of the spectrum, one finds those dispensational Christian theologies that base the Jewish return and right to the land on a predictive understanding of prophecy that will, in the end, lead to the annihilation of the Jewish people as Jews.

Most member nations of the United Nations are younger than Israel. Like Israel, many have border disputes and other difficulties with national aspirations of native peoples or other marginalized groups. However much some Jews and Christians may want Israel to play a theological or transcendent role in history, Israel ultimately must find its meaning and legitimacy in the same way as other national states do, within the global family of countries (as the Vatican Commission's statement rightly suggests; see n. 3). But we Christians must address the *religious* question of the Jewish attachment to the land without Israel's legitimacy being the conclusion of the discussion. Otherwise, both friend and foe of Israel will have an arsenal of *theological* tools to either excuse and ignore Israel's sometimes unjust behavior or deny its sometimes morally superior behaviors, neither of which allows Israelis their humanity.

We Christians need to acknowledge and address the centrality of the land to Jewish self-understanding. When we seek in respectful dialogue to understand the meaning of the land in Judaism, we Christians will learn something not only about Jews but also about ourselves.

Notes

1. This is a summary of the argument. For a discussion of the issue, see Brouria Bitton-Ashkelony, "The Attitudes of Church Fathers toward Pilgrimage to Jerusalem

in the Fourth and Fifth Centuries," in Lee I. Levine, ed., *Jerusalem: Its Sanctity and Centrality to Judaism, Christianity and Islam* (New York: Continuum, 1998), 188–203; Robert Wilken, *The Land Called Holy: Palestine in Christian History and Thought* (New Haven: Yale University Press, 1992), 101-25; and Karen Armstrong, *Jerusalem: One City, Three Faiths* (New York: Ballantine Books, 1997), 171–3.

2. Pope Pius X, quoted in Sergio I. Minerbi, *The Vatican and Zionism: Conflict in the Holy Land, 1895–1925* (New York: Oxford University Press, 1990), 100ff.

3. Daniel Levitas, "A Marriage Made for Heaven," *Reform Judaism*, summer 2003, 38–46, 81; 39.

4. Vatican Commission for Religious Relations with the Jews, "Notes on the Correct Way to Present the Jews and Judaism in Preaching and Catechesis in the Roman Catholic Church" (June 24, 1985), in Eugene J. Fisher and Leon Klenicki, eds., *In Our Time: The Flowering of Jewish-Catholic Dialogue* (New York: Paulist, 1990), 38–50, 49. See a similar statement from the Department for Ecumenical Affairs of the Evangelical Lutheran Church in America, "Jewish Concern for the State of Israel," at www.elca.org/ea/interfaith/jewish/tp6.htm.

5. Harold Kushner, *To Life! A Celebration of Jewish Being and Thinking* (New York: Little Brown, 1993), 243ff.

Further Reading

Brueggemann, Walter. *The Land: Place as Gift, Promise and Challenge in Biblical Faith*. Philadelphia: Fortress, 1977.

Burrell, David, and Yehezkel Landau, eds. *Voices from Jerusalem*. New York: Paulist, 1992.

Immanuel 22/23 (1989): The whole issue is devoted to the topic "People, Land and State of Israel: Jewish and Christian Perspectives"; but see, especially, Petra Heldt and Malcolm Lowe, "Theological Significance of the Rebirth of the State of Israel—Different Christian Attitudes," 133–46.

March, W. Eugene. *Israel and the Politics of Land: A Theological Case Study*. Louisville, KY: Westminister / John Knox, 1994.

Merkley, Paul Charles. *Christian Attitudes towards the State of Israel*. Montreal: McGill and Queens University Press, 2001.

Sennott, Charles M. *The Body and the Blood: The Holy Land's Christians at the Turn of a New Millennium*. New York: Public Affairs Books, 2001.

Wilken, Robert. *A Land Called Holy: Palestine in Christian History and Thought*. New Haven, CT: Yale University Press, 1993.

XI

P A R T

Christians Should Work with Jews for the Healing of the World

19

CHAPTER

The Challenge of *Tikkun Olam* for Jews and Christians

John T. Pawlikowski

WHEN SPEAKING of ethics in the context of the Christian-Jewish dialogue, the term *tikkun olam* frequently surfaces as a way of defining joint moral obligation incumbent on the two faith communities. The term has Jewish origins, meaning "repairing the world" in Hebrew; its roots lie in the Jewish covenantal tradition going back to Sinai. For all Jews, whatever their particular denominational affiliation, it represents the continuing covenantal obligation to make God's mercy and love visible throughout the world. Jesus himself in the gospel of Matthew, the most Jewish of the four gospel accounts, appears to draw upon this tradition of *tikkun olam* when he urges his followers to be "salt of the earth" and the "light of the world" (Matt 5:13–16). Hence, many within the Christian-Jewish dialogue have seen it as a most appropriate image for expressing a shared Jewish-Christian mandate for enhancing justice and mercy in global society.

Jewish and Christian Ethics: Refining the Distinctions

Any discussion of ethics in the context of the Christian-Jewish dialogue must begin with a discussion of the law-gospel distinction that has been a centerpiece of classical, and even current, Christian ethics. This distinction is used to argue for the basic inferiority of Jewish ethics in contrast to Christian moral theory on the grounds that the former is rooted entirely in law while love stands at the heart of Christian ethics. This perspective dominated Christian thinking for many centuries, despite the fact that Catholic canon lawers often studied the Jewish legal tradition to aid in making concrete moral decisions within the framework of Catholic case law. This distinction has been especially strong in Protestant ethics, often cast in terms of Paul's contrast between law and spirit.

Christian ethicists have often argued for the superiority of their ethical perspective because they believe a vengeful notion of God dominates Jewish moral thinking. S. Daniel Breslauer shows the inadequacy of this assumption in his argument that divine compassion constitutes the principal divine attribute. God still remains Judge, but a Judge whose decisions are tempered by mercy. In the Jewish tradition, God's prerogative as ultimate Judge "moderates and limits the extent of arbitrary human judgment."[1] Breslauer sees this emphasis on divine judgeship as a caution for Christians, who may too easily conflate human understandings of government and justice with God's will.

Breslauer enables Christians to correct another stereotype of Jewish ethics: that Jews lack a coherent model for imitating God because Judaism has no doctrine of the Incarnation. This is simply false. The Hebrew Bible and later rabbinic writings contain numerous examples of merciful deeds on the part of God. These examples undergird a realistic ethic rooted in the imitation of God. Breslauer shows that this supposed differentiation between Christian and Jewish ethics in terms of *imitatio Dei* is clearly exaggerated. In fact, an ethic of divine imitation serves to strengthen Jewish-Christian collaboration in the process of *tikkun olam*.

The classical basis for distinguishing Christian ethics—love—from Jewish ethics—law—within the moral tradition of the churches is a gross distortion. While Jewish ethics may not speak of love in the abstract as much as Christian ethics, an examination of the *halakhic* (legal) tradition that has served as the basic of Jewish moral decision making throughout the centuries clearly reveals that love and compassion have in fact permeated its concrete ethical judgments. Ronald Green, a Jewish ethicist who has studied in depth the relationship between Jewish and Christian ethical thought, provides a good example of how compassion shapes Jewish ethics. The rabbis, confronted with the question of whether an adolescent who committed suicide could be buried in hallowed ground, responded positively, arguing that parents should not endure the torment of exclusion from a deceased child. They defined adolescent death in such a way that it could never fall within the category of suicide. Green insists that we can find numerous examples of such humane and progressive reasoning tempering or even obliterating the letter of outdated laws.[2]

While Jewish ethics cannot be stereotyped in the manner of the classical Christian law-love distinction, nevertheless, Judaism gives somewhat greater emphasis to concrete legal decisions than does its Christian counterpart. (Catholicism, however, has a casuistic or case-based moral tradition that draws somewhat on talmudic ethics.) The moral life in Judaism has to be pursued through the development of legal reasoning. Generic neighbor love, so central in much of Christian ethical thought, does not take on the same importance in Judaism.

Green attributes the centrality of legal reasoning in Jewish tradition to two principal causes: (1) The fundamental goal within Jewish ethics is to create a "holy community" in all aspects of life. (2) Communal practices are the principal way of communicating and instilling ethical ideals. Some Jewish scholars have even questioned the propriety of speaking of Jewish ethics in the same way as Christians understand ethics as a theological discipline. Clearly, Jewish and Christian ethics show considerable difference in terms of their basic modality. Christianity has traditionally accorded overarching ethical principles a certain primacy in morality, the exception being the Catholic casuistic approach, while Judaism has been far more concerned with practical reasoning.

Another distinction between Jewish and Christian ethics concerns the particularity-universality polarity. The same tension has existed in both traditions over the centuries. In terms of fundamental orientation, however, Ronald Green argues that Christianity has generally favored the universalistic pole while Judaism has leaned more toward the particularistic dimension. As an example, he notes the central role the parable of the Good Samaritan has played in the Christian ethical heritage. Parallel stories in Judaism do not elicit the same profound response. Jewish ethics certainly prescribes concern for the sojourner in one's midst, as the story of Ruth shows. Yet, for Jews the highlight of the story of Ruth occurs when Ruth identifies her fate with that of the Jewish community and becomes a true "daughter of Israel."

Jewish scholars have noted that Christian and Jewish ethical systems differ significantly in the respective value they place on suffering. Christianity generally places a much higher value on the meaning of suffering than does Judaism, due in major part to the theological centrality of Christ's death. Christians often regard suffering as redemptive and morally purifying, both personally and in terms of the struggle for social justice. Liberation ethics in Christianity has often placed a central emphasis on Christ crucified, something that would find little resonance in Jewish ethics, with rare exception. Important talmudic scholars have, in fact, denounced any glorification of suffering and urged the foregoing of future reward if it meant enduring suffering in the process. *Halakhic* thinking normally suspends any legal requirement if it jeopardizes human life and health in a particular situation. We have seen this flexibility operative in discussions relative to abortion, homosexuality, and genetics, in which Jewish ethics shows considerable willingness to embrace new technologies, in contrast to the pervasive moral reserve of many ethicians within the Christian community.

A final point of contrast between Jewish and Christian ethics has been the notion of natural law, the existence of basic moral laws within the human condition that can be apprehended through the use of human reason. Natural law, coming in significant part out of the Thomistic tradition, has been a core element in Christian ethics, especially in Catholic ethics. The classical emphasis on natural law has waned somewhat, particularly in post-Vatican II Catholic ethics stressing a more experiential and biblical approach. Nonetheless, natural law still remains an important feature of Christian ethics that has little parallel in the Jewish tradition, with the exception of David Novak, one of the few Jewish scholars to have embraced it. The Christian focus on natural law renders its ethical system less open to major reformulation than is the case in Judaism; sexual ethics and genetic ethics are two current examples of such a contrast.

United in Struggle

Christian-Jewish dialogue in the United States in particular had its origins in the struggle for *tikkun olam*. This was particularly the case for Catholics and Jews, who shared the experience of being discriminated against in terms of housing and employment during the latter part of the nineteenth century and into the first half of the twentieth. Both were targets of the notorious Ku Klux Klan. This shared experience of discrimination led to a willingness on the part of American Jews and Catholics to join with socially progressive Protestants in an important coalition that had a major impact on social conditions in this country.

Around 1920 Catholic leaders joined their counterparts in Jewish organizations, the Central Conference of American Rabbis in particular, and in the Protestant Federal Council of Churches to address jointly some of the major social issues of the period. There was tri-faith involvement, for example, in the enginemen's strike on the Western Maryland Railroad in 1927 and in the investigation into the Armistice Day Tragedy in 1919 in Centralia, Washington, in which worker lives were lost.

On the level of federal labor policy, several important interventions were undertaken by representatives of the three faith communities. December 1929 saw a joint Protestant-Catholic-Jewish statement on conditions in the textile industry, followed by one on unemployment in January 1932. The previous year had seen tri-faith sponsorship of a national conference on "Permanent Preventives of Unemployment" in Washington. And in June 1932, when unemployment in the United States had risen to alarming proportions and the federal government seemed reluctant to take any decisive action to remedy the situation, Rabbi Edward L. Israel, Fr. R. A. McGowan, and the Rev. James Myers joined representatives of the American Federation of Labor and national farmers organizations in testifying before the House and Senate. In their presentations, broadcast on a nationwide radio hookup, they demanded an adequate response to the unemployment crisis from government at both the federal and local levels. Their testimony is credited with significant influence in bringing about congressional approval of the first federal funds for meeting this crisis later on that year.

Joint efforts continued in 1933. In July, after passage of the National Industrial Recovery Act (NIRA), the Central Conference of American Rabbis and the Federal Council of Churches, in conjunction with the National Catholic Welfare Conference, issued a public statement outlining the social implications of this historic legislation. Signing for the Catholic Bishops' Conference was Msgr. John A. Ryan. Msgr. Ryan headed the Catholic Bishops' Conference office on social action for some twenty-five years, during which he had a major impact on social legislation in the United States. He was also the driving force behind the formation of the national interreligious coalition on social issues. He was eventually succeeded by Msgr. George Higgins, a protégé of Ryan's, who combined a deep involvement in social issues with an abiding interest in Catholic-Jewish relations. Higgins was an important behind-the-scenes personality at the Second Vatican Council; he exercised considerable influence on the formation and passage of the conciliar declaration *Nostra Aetate*, with its crucial article 4 on the church's relationship with Judaism, as well as the parallel declaration on religious liberty, *Dignitatis Humanae*. After the council he was instrumental in the establishment of the U.S. bishops' office on Catholic-Jewish relations, and he chaired its national advisory committee until his death in 2002. The ministry of George Higgins exemplified the profound connection between the issues of social justice and Catholic-Jewish relations.

In December 1933 representatives of the three major faith communities testified before the Committee of Ways and Means of the House of Representatives, calling for tax laws that would ensure a more equitable distribution of wealth and income in the nation. The National Conference of Christians and Jews, founded during the 1928 U.S. presidential election, countered anti-Catholic attacks on the first Catholic candidate for president, Alfred E. Smith. The NCCJ continued to work against prejudice in American life during subsequent decades. In the 1960s important Catholics, Jews, and Protestants joined Dr. Martin Luther King Jr.'s struggle for human rights, including such prominent leaders as Rabbi Abraham Joshua Heschel. This civil rights coalition eventually led to an interfaith coalition against the Vietnam War, Clergy and Laity Concerned about Vietnam. Among key players were Fr. John A Sheerin, c.s.p., then editor of the *Catholic World* magazine. Fr. Sheerin, an early member of the Christian Scholars Group (then called the Israel Study Group, as described by Alice Eckardt in her chapter in this volume), combined a commitment to social justice with considerable involvement in Catholic-Jewish relations in ways similar to Msgr. Higgins.

Such activities had a lasting effect. They broke down barriers among the representatives of religious groups in the United States, which carried over into the deliberations of Vatican II on the Jewish-Christian issue as well as on religious liberty. The American bishops were certainly not as progressive overall as some of their European counterparts, yet they became strong supporters of *Nostra Aetate* and of the declaration on religious liberty. Their experience of these interreligious coalitions taught them that interfaith relations were a positive reality in terms of Catholic faith, not a threat, as had been the case in many parts of Europe. Similarly, the positive experience of these coalitions enabled sectors of American Protestantism to reexamine the churches' relationships with Jews and Judaism in a manner parallel to that of the Second Vatican Council.

Moreover, these activities had an important impact on the social setting in this country. Social researchers Claris Silcox and Galen Fisher explicitly attribute the abolition of the twelve-hour day in the steel industry, for example, "in considerable measure" to these trilateral efforts. Overall they conclude that "this close collaboration by these three agencies, speaking for tens of thousands of churches and synagogues, is considered by thoughtful men to have done much toward educating the conscience of the nation and towards demonstrating the courageous concern of all the creeds with justice and the good life."[3] The historic National Conference on Religion and Race in Chicago, convened in the midst of the civil rights struggle of the 1960s, had an impact on the passage of comprehensive civil rights legislation in this country.

During the last two decades, growing internal disagreements on issues related to sexual and gender issues have negatively impacted the effort to undertake a joint Jewish-Christian pursuit of *tikkun olam*. Fundamental perspectives on change and continuity within each community have generated Jewish-Christian coalitions on varied sides of the political spectrum. Certain Jews feel closer to certain Christians (and vice versa) on selected issues than they do to other members of their own community. Despite these differences, there have been some attempts to rebuild the successful interreligious cooperation of previous decades in such areas as workers' rights and ecology. The latter issue was even taken up within the official international dialogue between the Vatican and the International Jewish Committee for Interreligious Consultation.

Caring for Creation: A Fundamental Moral Question

The fundamental moral question facing both Jews and Christians after the Shoah is how we understand the divine and human roles in caring for creation. Some influential Jewish scholars, such as Irving Greenberg, have spoken of a basic "role reversal" in terms of responsibility after the experience of the Shoah. He has argued that moral responsibility for the world has now been transferred to an unprecedented degree to the human community.[4] While both Jewish and Christian scholars have critiqued Greenberg's "role reversal" thesis as too drastic, without question that responsibility has passed to the human community in ways never before imagined.

One critical dimension of this current moral challenge certainly comes in the area of ecology. We are becoming increasingly aware that continued destruction of our biosphere may reach the point where any possibility of *tikkun olam* has effectively vanished. The Christian-Jewish dialogue may provide important resources for coming to grips with this fundamental challenge to continued creational survival. For one, the Jewish tradition has far more of a liturgical tradition highlighting the dignity of all creation than does Christianity. Jewish scholars may help us overcome the basic thesis of Lynn White, who argued at the outset of the ecological movement that the perspective on creation found in the book of Genesis is inherently destructive. My late colleague at the Catholic Theological Union, Rabbi Hayim Perelmuter, shows how the rabbinic tradition has interpreted the creation stories in Genesis in more ecologically friendly ways than White's perspective would allow.[5]

Human rights constitute another central challenge facing Jews and Christians, particularly in light of the Holocaust. The Third Reich regarded certain peoples as "vermin," "unfortunate expendables," and biologically unfit for continued existence. Human rights must become part of the self-definition of each religious community, since the failure to have a clear policy of human rights impeded the Christian institutional response to the Holocaust. Christianity and Judaism cannot survive meaningfully today if they allow the death or suffering of other people to become a by-product of their legitimate efforts at self-preservation as religious communities. The church must see the survival of all persons as integral to its own authentic survival. The Nazis viewed Jews, Poles, the Roma, gays, and the disabled as "unfortunate expendables," to use the term of Nora Levin. To regard any persons as "unfortunate expendables" is inimical to Christianity and Judaism.

Jews and Christians also need to turn their attention to the question of the severe, and growing, economic disparity in contemporary society. They must recognize how people in charge of global institutions are "sucked up" into the system and completely lose their moral edge. Historian Peter Hayes has produced a brilliant study of how the German business community, at first quite leery of the Nazi movement, eventually became intimately involved with its policy of human annihilation. Most alarming about this development, says Hayes, was not even the complicity in murder, but a sense of innocence about such complicity on the part of the businessmen. They were able to subdue any moral hesitation they may have experienced with the response "What else can I do?" They lost sight of the far more important question, "What must I never do?"[6] This is an area particularly well developed in Christian ethical literature that might constructively enhance Jewish thinking.

Another fruitful area for discussion in the Christian-Jewish dialogue is the connection between ritual/spirituality and social responsibility. Our communities are increasingly aware of the necessity of public ritual to inculcate a sense of moral responsibility; without it, the possibility of making moral responsibility integral to global consciousness remains rather remote. Related to this is the connection between spirituality and social justice. The Jewish tradition, with its understanding of mysticism, might enhance the considerable discussion of this issue in Christian circles in the past forty years. As Max Kadushin has shown in his volume *Worship and Ethics: A Study in Rabbinic Judaism*, the real problem in mystical experience for the Jew is not the going out, but the *shuv*, the return.[7]

The Ethical Challenge: War and Peace

The final point I raise in connection with a joint Jewish-Christian effort at *tikkun olam* is that of war and peace. In recent years the Christian tradition has been moving more and more into making peace a major priority. Even the Catholic Church at the institutional level appears to be moving away from its classical "just war" doctrine into a mode where any form of warfare seems morally questionable. We have certainly seen this in the speeches and writings of Pope John Paul II during the Gulf War and more recently the war in Iraq. In U.S. Catholicism, the process began with the issuance of the Bishops' Peace Pastoral in 1983. In the Protestant community, the World Council of Churches, the National Council of Churches, and specific denominations, such as the Methodists, have pursued an increasingly antiwar line. This has certainly been the case in the public discussions leading up to the war in Iraq, where practically every major Christian denomination had grave misgivings about a preemptive military response to the dangers posed by the Hussein regime.

The Jewish community has tended to support recent military action. After they issued their pastoral letter, "The Challenge of Peace," the Bishops' Conference and the Union of American Hebrew Congregations produced a joint study guide on the pastoral letter.[8] Since then, however, Jews and Christians seem to be drifting apart on the war/peace issue. The situation in the Middle East is significantly responsible for this growing division.

Certainly, Judaism has significant peace movements, such as the Tikkun community, American Friends of Peace Now, and the Shalom Center. Individuals such as Yehezkel Landau are prominent spokespersons for the Jewish peace perspective. In fall 2003 leaders of Reform, Conservative, and Reconstructionist Judaism joined Christian and Muslim counterparts in publicly endorsing a set of concrete recommendations in support of the "Roadmap to Peace in the Middle East"--by the United Religions Initiative and *A Different Future*—which the U.S. Interreligious Committee for Peace in the Middle East released at the National Press Club in Washington.

While this most recent action represents some upgrading of the Jewish institutional response on the issue of Middle East peace, the peace voices within the Jewish community have not thus far impacted in a significant way on the Jewish institutional approach, whether religious or secular, to the continuing conflict in Israel/Palestine. The overriding concern within Judaism at present is without doubt the safety and security of the State of Israel. Given past history and present reality this is certainly a valid concern. But I do not think it serves the Jewish community well, nor the pursuit of *tikkun olam* in general, for the war/peace issue to be taken off the table within the Christian-Jewish dialogue (see the chapter in this volume by Michael McGarry).

One of America's leading thinkers on war and peace questions, Michael Walzer, has suggested that the Jewish community has much to gain in terms of its own understanding on war and peace questions from dialogue with the Catholic community, particularly with the Bishops' Pastoral Letter "On the Challenge of Peace." While recognizing the profound institutional differences between Catholicism and Judaism, he has called for a Jewish effort to prepare a parallel letter or even letters, now that Jews carry political responsibilities denied them for centuries. "If we were to do all that," says Walzer, "we would have at the end the basis for a new kind of Jewish-Catholic dialogue, concretely focused on issues and cases. We could see where we differ, or where we have differed, and where the two traditions overlap or even coincide."[9]

I detect a growing frustration among Christians deeply involved with the dialogue for many years, people who have strongly supported Israel in times of crisis, about the lack of any public discussion within the Jewish leadership over certain measures being taken by the Israeli government in the West Bank and Gaza. While Christians in the dialogue recognize the precarious condition in which Israel finds itself with the continuing terrorist bombings, they feel "in bello" questions, to employ language from the Catholic "just war" tradition, are not being asked by the Jewish leadership. I am pleased that the ongoing dialogue between the National Council of Synagogues and the Catholic Bishops' Committee for Ecumenical and Interreligious Affairs has begun to consider such issues as part of their ongoing meetings.

In the final analysis, one cannot build a peaceful and just society in the Middle East or any other region of serious social conflict unless there is some retention of the humanity of the other, even at those times when military force may prove necessary for survival. One of the most profound moral lessons that Christians have learned from a study of the Holocaust is how ecclesial self-definitions rendered Jews "unfortunate expendables" who could be cast aside in a situation in which the churches felt under dire threat. If we see any beginnings of a post-Holocaust morality in the churches, it is the movement toward an ecclesiology that has no room for "expendables," even in circumstances where the challenge to group survival is indeed real.

From the above discussion it ought to be clear that the effort to achieve a joint Christian-Jewish witness to *tikkun olam* will face a rocky road at times, especially at this moment in terms of issues related to war and peace, abortion, genetics, and homosexuality. But, despite the boulders we may have to confront, no other alternative is viable for Jews and Christians, given our joint bonding in the ongoing covenant with the Creator God.

Notes

1. S. Daniel Breslauer, "Justice: The Jewish View," in Leon Klenicki and Geoffrey Wigoder, eds., *A Dictionary of the Jewish-Christian Dialogue* (New York: Paulist, 1983), 109.

2. Ronald Green, "Jewish and Christian Ethics: What Can We Learn from One Another?" in John Kelsay and Sumner B. Twiss, eds., *The Annual of the Society of Christian Ethics* (Washington, DC: Georgetown University Press, 1999), 3–18.

3. Claris Silcox and Galen Fisher, *Catholics, Jews and Protestants: A Study of Relationships in the United States and Canada* (New York: Institute of Social and Religious Research, 1934), 301–31.

4. Irving Greenberg, *For the Sake of Heaven and Earth: The New Encounter between Judaism and Christianity* (Philadelphia: The Jewish Publication Society, 2004), esp. 162–185.

5. Hayim G. Perelmuter, "'Do Not Destroy'—Ecology in the Fabric of Judaism," *The Ecological Challenge: Ethical, Liturgical and Spiritual Responses,* Richard Fragomeni and John T. Pawlikowski, eds. (Collegeville: The Liturgical Press, 1994), 129–38. Cf. Lynn White, Jr., "The Historical Roots of Our Ecological Crisis," *Science* 155 (1967): 1203–1207.

6. Peter Hayes, "Conscience, Knowledge and 'Secondary Ethics': German Corporate Executives from 'Aryanization' to the Holocaust," in Judith H. Banki and John T. Pawlikowski, eds., *Ethics in the Shadow of the Holocaust: Christian and Jewish Perspectives* (Franklin, WI: Sheed and Ward, 2001), 313–35.

7. Max Kadushin, *Worship and Ethics: A Study in Rabbinic Judaism* (Evanston, IL: Northwestern University Press, 1964).

8. Annete Daum and Eugene Fisher, eds. *The Challenge of Shalom for Catholics and Jews: A Dialogical Guide to the Catholic Bishops' Pastoral on Peace and War* (New York: Union of American Hebrew Congregations; Washington: National Conference of Catholic Bishops, 1985).

9. Michael Walzer, "Reflections on a Man and his Dialogue," in Hayim Goren Perelmuter, *Harvest of a Dialogue: Reflections of a Rabbi/Scholar on a Catholic Faculty*, ed. John Pawlikowski and Dianne Bergant (Hoboken, NJ: KTAV, 1997), 232–37. Walzer makes the same assertion with regard to the "Catholic Bishops' Letter on the Economy."

Further Reading

Banki, Judith H., and John T. Pawlikowski, eds. *Ethics in the Shadow of the Holocaust: Christian and Jewish Perspectives*. Franklin, WI: Sheed and Ward, 2002.

Bemporad, Jack, John Pawlikowski, and Joseph Sievers, eds. *Good and Evil after Auschwitz: Ethical Implications for Today*. Hoboken, NJ: KTAV, 2001.

Dorff, Elliot N., and Louis E. Newman, eds. *Contemporary Jewish Ethics and Morality*. New York: Oxford University Press, 1995.

Green, Ronald. "Jewish and Christian Ethics: What Can We Learn from One Another?" *The Annual of the Society of Christian Ethics*. Washington, DC: Georgetown University Press.

Maguire, Daniel C. *The Moral Core of Judaism and Christianity*. Minneapolis: Fortress, 1993.

Roth, John K., ed. *Ethics after the Holocaust: Perspectives, Critique, and Responses*. St. Paul, MN: Paragon House, 1999.

PART

Christian-Jewish
Relations after the Shoah:
Historical Reflections

20

CHAPTER

The Road to Reconciliation: Protestant Church Statements on Christian-Jewish Relations

Franklin Sherman

OFFICIAL STATEMENTS of the mainline Protestant churches reflect a sea change in their attitude toward Judaism and the Jewish people in the past fifty years. Less clear is the impact of this dramatic change on the pulpit and pew. Despite this perennial problem, the statements indicate a major "turning," what the Hebrew term *teshuvah* denotes, at the official level. These statements have helped to shape the work of our group of scholars, as we make explicit in the introduction to "A Sacred Obligation."

Statements from the World Council of Churches

Other chapters in our book reveal how, in the years immediately following World War II, the churches of Europe gradually awakened to the horror of the Holocaust and to their complicity in it. The World Council of Churches, founded in 1948 in Amsterdam, spoke to this realization at its First Assembly: "We call upon all the churches we represent to denounce anti-Semitism, no matter what its origin, as absolutely irreconcilable with the profession and practice of the Christian faith. Anti-Semitism is a sin against God and man [humankind]."[1] To this the World Council's 1961 Third Assembly in New Delhi added the admonition: "In Christian teaching, the historic events which led to the Crucifixion should not be so presented as to impose upon the Jewish people of today responsibilities which must fall on all humanity, not on one race or community. Jews were the first to accept Jesus and Jews are not the only ones who do not yet recognize him."[2]

The World Council's 1967 Faith and Order Commission report, known as the "Bristol Report" because the commission met in Bristol, England, reflected the longstanding debate about whether it is theologically legitimate to direct evangelizing efforts to the Jewish people. The report noted that the differing views on this are related to different conceptions of the church. If the church is viewed as the "Body of Christ," and, as such, the definitive community of salvation, then the Jews clearly are outside it, and need to be brought in. But if the church is thought of as the "People of God," then Jews as Jews can also be viewed as sharing in this role. From this standpoint, the report states, "it is possible to regard the Church and the Jewish people together as forming the one people of God, separated from one another for the time being, yet with the promise that they will ultimately become one." The practical implication of this view, the report notes, is that the church's relation to the Jewish people "should be thought of more in terms of ecumenical engagement in order to heal the breach than of missionary witness in which she hopes for conversion."[3]

The 1988 meeting of the World Council of Churches Consultation on the Church and the Jewish People in Sigtuna, Sweden, reviewed the preceding statement and summarized their basic affirmations as follows:

- The covenant of God with the Jewish people remains valid.
- Antisemitism and all forms of the teaching of contempt for Judaism are to be repudiated.
- The living tradition of Judaism is a gift of God.

- Coercive proselytism directed toward Jews is incompatible with Christian faith.
- Jews and Christians bear a common responsibility as witnesses to God's righteousness and peace in the world.[4]

Lutheran Statements

Meanwhile, individual Protestant denominations had also begun to come to terms with the incubus of anti-Judaism. The Lutheran Church—of which I am a clergy member; I have been a participant in some of the dialogues discussed here—bears a special responsibility because of Luther's infamous tract "On the Jews and Their Lies" (1543). The Lutheran World Federation (LWF), representing some sixty-five million Lutherans around the world, held a series of international conferences devoted to this theme, starting with a meeting at Løgumkloster, Denmark, in 1964, and extending to one in Dobogokö, Hungary, in 2001. The Løgumkloster report, citing the commandment "Thou shalt not bear false witness against thy neighbor," urges the LWF member churches "to examine their publications for possible anti-Semitic references, and to remove and oppose false generalizations about the Jews," and adds: "Especially reprehensible are the notions that Jews, rather than all mankind, are responsible for the death of Jesus the Christ, and that God has for this reason rejected his covenant people."[5]

At a meeting cosponsored by the Lutheran World Federation and the International Jewish Committee on Interreligious Consultations in Stockholm in 1983, the Lutheran participants issued a statement deploring and rejecting Martin Luther's writings against the Jews. "The sins of Luther's anti-Jewish remarks," they state, "the violence of his attacks on the Jews, must be acknowledged with deep distress. And all occasions for similar sin in the present or the future must be removed from our churches."[6] In a statement issued jointly by the Lutheran and Jewish participants, they note their agreement on the following points:

- We affirm the integrity and dignity of our two faith communities and repudiate any organized proselytizing of each other.
- We pledge to combat all forms of racial and religious prejudice and express our solidarity with all who suffer the denial of full religious freedom.
- Sharing in the common patrimony of the Prophets of Israel and inspired by their vision, we commit ourselves to strive for a world in

which the threat of nuclear warfare will be ended, where poverty and hunger will be eradicated, in which violence and terrorism will be overcome, and a just and lasting peace will be established.[7]

In the United States, a series of developments in the early 1990s made American Lutherans keenly aware of their own responsibility to distance themselves from Luther's anti-Jewish writings, as had been done on the world level in 1983. Several books and television programs on the history of antisemitism featured Luther as one of the chief figures in that doleful history, as did the brief film on the same subject shown at the United States Holocaust Memorial Museum, which opened in April 1993. A proposal to renounce Luther's views was brought to the national assembly of the Evangelical Lutheran Church in America (ELCA) in Kansas City that summer and met with vigorous debate, in which some maintained that such an apology was both unnecessary and unseemly. But when proponents of the measure read out some of Luther's hateful words, the delegates—most of whom had been completely unaware of this aspect of their heritage—were shocked into voting overwhelmingly for the preparation of such a statement. It was issued in April 1994 under the title "Declaration of the Evangelical Lutheran Church in America to the Jewish Community."

Frankly acknowledging the reality of Luther's views, the declaration states: "We reject this violent invective, and yet more do we express our deep and abiding sorrow over its tragic effects on subsequent generations. . . . We recognize in anti-Semitism a contradiction and an affront to the Gospel, a violation of our hope and calling, and we pledge this church to oppose the deadly working of such bigotry, both within our own circles and in the society around us." Looking forward, the declaration states "our urgent desire to live out our faith in Jesus Christ with love and respect for the Jewish people."[8]

In 1998, the ELCA issued a further document, "Guidelines for Lutheran-Jewish Relations," which reiterates some of these themes and presents practical suggestions for conversations, visits, joint study, and common action between Jews and Christians in local communities. The guidelines offer cautionary comments about holding "demonstration Seders" as well as suggestions about prayer in interfaith settings and other such practical matters. Particular attention is called to the Jewish concern for communal survival, which causes Jews to feel strongly about topics such as the security of the State of Israel, intermarriage, and conversion. "Lutherans are not obligated to adopt the same perspective on these matters," the document notes, "but it is vital for us to understand and respect our neighbors' concerns."[9]

Statements of Other Protestant Churches in the United States

In 1964, the House of Bishops of the Episcopal Church in the United States rejected the charge of "deicide" directed against the Jews in a statement that resembles and, it may be noted, antedates the similar declaration by the Second Vatican Council in 1965. The Episcopal bishops declare:

> The charge of deicide against the Jews is a tragic misunderstanding of the inner significance of the crucifixion. To be sure, Jesus was crucified by *some* soldiers at the instigation of *some* Jews. But this cannot be construed as imputing corporate guilt to every Jew in Jesus' day, much less the Jewish people in subsequent generations. Simple justice alone proclaims the charge of a corporate or inherited curse on the Jewish people to be false.[10]

The Episcopal General Convention adopted a resolution on Christian-Jewish Dialogue in 1979 that stresses Christians' spiritual indebtedness to Judaism; the convention elaborates on this in its "Guidelines for Christian-Jewish Relations" of 1988.[11] Ten years later, the Lambeth Conference, representing the worldwide Anglican communion (seventy million members), adopted a comprehensive statement on interfaith dialogue that deals with relations to both Judaism and Islam. Regarding the former, it notes that "Judaism is not only a religion, as many Christians understand the word, but a people and a civilization."[12] The Lambeth statement reviews the manifold contributions of Jews to modern culture and urges Christians to recognize the ongoing spiritual vitality of Judaism.

From the 1970s onward, most other mainline Protestant denominations in the United States also issued significant statements on Christian-Jewish relations. The United Methodist Church adopted "Bridge in Hope: Interreligious Dialogue between Jews and Christians" in 1972, updating it in 1996 with a revised document, "Building New Bridges in Hope." The latter is particularly clear regarding the ongoing validity of the Jewish covenant: "We believe that just as God is steadfastly faithful to the biblical covenant in Jesus Christ, likewise God is steadfastly faithful to the biblical covenant with the Jewish people. . . . Both Jews and Christians are bound to God in covenant, with no covenantal relationship invalidated by any other."[13]

Similarly, the United Church of Christ (UCC) in its 1987 General Synod affirmed "its recognition that God's covenant with the Jewish people has not been rescinded or abrogated by God, but remains in full force, inasmuch as 'the gifts and the promise of God are irrevocable' (Rom. 11:29)."[14] To be sure, this affirmation was not uncontested, in this or other church bodies. A study panel of the UCC reported in 1990 that discussion of the ongoing role of the Jews in the providence of God, including their relation to the land of Israel, had been the occasion of much "learning, passion, and growth." The panel concluded that two seemingly contradictory yet complementary truths must be held in tension: on the one hand, "the singular deed God has done to redeem all the world in the life, death, and resurrection of Jesus Christ," and on the other hand, "God's unrescinded covenant with Jewish people."[15]

The Presbyterian Church (United States) produced a lengthy paper in 1987 entitled "A Theological Understanding of the Relationship between Christians and Jews." Although not officially adopted by the General Assembly, but only "commended to the church for study and reflection," the paper has been widely influential. Affirming that "the church, elected in Jesus Christ, has been engrafted into the people of God established by the covenant with Abraham, Isaac, and Jacob," it boldly asserts: "Therefore, Christians have not replaced Jews." It sees the ongoing life of the Jewish people and their spiritual vitality as a sign of God's redeeming faithfulness.[16]

In a similar vein, the Theology Committee of the Christian Church (Disciples of Christ) submitted to the church its 1993 "Statement on Relations between Jews and Christians," decrying the "teaching of contempt" toward Jews and Judaism: "We confess that both the church and the Jewish people are elected by God for witness to the world and that the relation of the church and the Jewish people to each other is grounded on God's gracious election of each."[17]

European Protestant Churches

During these same decades, the various national and regional church bodies in Europe issued many similar statements. The 1988 "Declaration on the 50th Anniversary of *Kristallnacht* [the Night of the Shattered Glass]," issued jointly by the Protestant churches of both parts of the then still-divided Germany, is typical. The statement strongly rebuts the view that "nobody knew" what was happening to the Jews in Germany:

> What happened in the month of November 1938 was carried out in public, took place before the eyes of everyone. The persecution was directed towards all Jews. The race-madness displayed its humanity-despising brutality. No one could have denied all knowledge of it.

Those who planned and implemented these crimes were able to count on the majority of our people being either compliant, indifferent and looking the other way, or silent out of fear. Christians too—with a few exceptions—kept silent.[18]

"The Church," the document goes on to state, "failed to see the deep inner connection between Judaism and Christianity. It viewed the synagogue as something that had been rejected by God, rather than as the first loved and the chosen people."

Among the most scholarly and detailed documents to appear is the recent "Church and Israel: A Contribution from the Reformation Churches in Europe to the Relationship between Christians and Jews." It is the work of delegates of more than twenty European churches over the course of eight consultations from 1996 until its adoption by the Fifth General Assembly of the Leuenberg Church Fellowship, now known as the Community of Protestant Churches in Europe, in June 2001.

The question of the church's relation to the Jewish people follows from the Leuenberg Fellowship's previous study in 1994, "The Church of Jesus Christ: The Contribution of the Reformation towards Ecumenical Dialogue on Church Unity." The designation of the church as the "people of God" in that text invites further reflection on the tension between the church's closeness to and boundaries with Israel. The authors of the 2001 document note that Jews may believe it presumptuous of Christians to describe themselves as "the people of God." If the church is to use the term, "it cannot ignore its special relationship to and link with Judaism." This relationship, moreover, is "not marginal" for the church and Christian theology; it raises a "central element of Reformation ecclesiology which is derived from the action of God."[19] Nevertheless, a Christian theological statement on Israel as the people of God "must respect the fact that Israel describes itself as the 'people of God' in its own way." And these two statements about Israel need not necessarily agree (§ 1.3).

After addressing some of the historical factors in the relation between European churches and Israel—most notably, the Shoah—the study document identifies four contemporary theological concepts intended to clarify the church's relationship with Israel:

- Israel and the church as two parallel ways of salvation; there are two ways to the One God of Abraham: for Israel, the Torah, and for the nations, Christ.

- The "uncancelled covenant": God's covenant with Israel is not cancelled; the "New Covenant" is not a second covenant, but the covenant renewal promised in Jeremiah 31, "and thus a confirmation and a further development of the covenant God made with Israel that goes beyond the covenant with Israel" (§ 1.2.1).
- The "pilgrimage of the nations to Zion": Jews and Christians share the same tradition of promise and hope.
- The One People of God, comprising Israel and the church, attempts to hold together the sovereignty and mercy of God with the experience of the separation between Israel and the church.

All of these concepts avoid a serious problem in the past, in which Christian faith was viewed as a replacement for Israel. Yet none of the concepts is adequate, the report states. These contrasting positions represent "stages in an unfinished process of theological reasoning" (§ 1.5). Despite the shortcomings in each of the four formulations, the Leuenberg Church Fellowship document recognizes that they have enriched the theology and spirituality of Christians, offering stimuli for the internal dialogue of the churches and encouraging people to reflect more positively on Israel. "Therefore the church must continue this process and seek further possibilities for defining and understanding its identity in relationship to Israel" (§ 1.5).

Contrasting Baptist Statements

Returning to the U.S. scene, one may note that the Southern Baptist Convention, the nation's largest Protestant denomination, has caused great concern among those involved in Christian-Jewish relations by its explicit espousal of a mission to the Jews. A 1996 resolution committed the Southern Baptist Convention's "energies and resources toward the proclamation of the gospel to the Jewish people."[20] In contrast, the Alliance of Baptists, an association of progressive Baptist churches across the country, has issued a statement that forthrightly rejects "a theology which has valued conversion over dialogue, invective over understanding, and prejudice over knowledge." It calls for an acknowledgment of "the vibrancy, vitality, and efficacy of the Jewish faith," and pledges to

- Affirm the teaching of the Christian scriptures that God has not rejected the community of Israel, God's covenant people (Rom 11:1–2), since "the gifts and calling of God are irrevocable" (Rom 11:29).

- Renounce interpretations of scripture that foster religious stereotyping and prejudice against the Jewish people and their faith.
- Seek genuine dialogue with the broader Jewish community, a dialogue built on mutual respect and the integrity of each faith.
- Lift our voices quickly and boldly against all expressions of anti-semitism.
- Educate ourselves and others on the history of Jewish-Christian relations from the first century to the present, so as to understand our present by learning from our past.
- Commit ourselves to rigorous consideration of appropriate forms of Christian witness for our time.[21]

A Concluding Word

We can conclude this survey of Protestant statements on Christian-Jewish relations with reference to the most recent statement by the United Church of Canada. Following a six-year study, the church's general council adopted a resolution at its meeting in August 2003 that acknowledges the history of anti-Judaism and antisemitism within Christianity as a whole and the United Church of Canada in particular. The statement rejects all teaching of contempt toward Jews and any belief that Christians have replaced Jews in the love and purpose of God. It declares once more with St. Paul that "the gifts and calling of God to the Jewish people are irrevocable." Affirming the significance of Judaism as at once a religion, a people, and a covenant community, the Canadian statement calls on Christians and Jews to join in *tikkun olam*, mending the world.[22]

These are sentiments that well sum up the "road to reconciliation" that Christians and Jews have traveled over these past fifty years. Much work lies ahead, but the road to reconciliation is well established—if still missing on the maps of too many Christians.

Notes

1. World Council of Churches, 1948, text in Allan Brockway et al., eds., *The Theology of the Churches and the Jewish People: Statements by the World Council of Churches and Its Member Churches* (Geneva: WCC Publications, 1988), 5. Statements (some not readily available in print) cited in my chapter are also available at www.jcrelations.net.

2. World Council of Churches, Third Assembly, 1961, in Brockway et al., *Theology of the Churches*, 12.

3. World Council of Churches, Faith and Order Commission, "Bristol Report," 1967, in Brockway et al., *Theology of the Churches*, 81.

4. World Council of Churches Consultation on the Church and the Jewish People, "The Churches and the Jewish People: Towards a New Understanding," 1988, in *The New Relationship between Christians and Jews: Documentation of Major Statements* (Heppenheim, Germany: International Council of Christians and Jews, 1998), 60.

5. In Helga Croner, comp., *Stepping Stones to Further Jewish-Christian Relations* (London: Stimulus Books, 1977), 85. Also in Harold H. Ditmanson, ed., *Stepping Stones to Further Jewish-Lutheran Relationships: Key Lutheran Statements* (Minneapolis: Augsburg, 1990), 27.

6. Lutheran World Federation, 1983, in Ditmanson, *Stepping Stones*, 103.

7. Lutheran World Federation and the International Jewish Committee on Interreligious Consultations, 1983, in Ditmanson, *Stepping Stones*, 101–2.

8. ELCA, "Declaration of the Evangelical Lutheran Church in America to the Jewish Community," www.jcrelations.net.

9. ELCA, "Guidelines for Lutheran-Jewish Relations," 1998, www.jcrelations.net/en/?ed=995. Links to the 1994 declaration and 1998 guidelines, as well as other Lutheran materials, may be found at www.elca.org/ea/interfaith/jewish/index.html.

10. House of Bishops of the Episcopal Church, 1964, in Croner, *Stepping Stones*, 87.

11. In *The Blue Book: Reports of the Committees, Commissions, Boards and Agencies of the General Convention of the Episcopal Church, 1988* (Cincinnati: Forward Movement, 1989).

12. The Lambeth Conference, 1988, "Jews, Christians and Muslims: The Way of Dialogue," http://www.jcrelations.net/en/?id=1006.

13. General Conference of the United Methodist Church (USA), 1996, "Building New Bridges in Hope," http://www.jcrelations.net/en/?id=999.

14. United Church of Christ, 1987 General Synod, "Relationship between the United Church of Christ and the Jewish Community," *New Conversations* 12/3 (1990): 67-68. Also http://www.ucc.org/ecumenical/87-gs-jewish.pdf.

15. Theological Panel on Jewish-Christian Relations of the United Church of Christ, 1990, "A Message to the Churches."

16. Presbyterian Church (U.S.A.), "A Theological Understanding of the Relationship between Christians and Jews," 1987, in Donald G. Dawe and Aurelia T. Fule, eds., *Christians and Jews Together: Voices from the Conversation* (Louisville: Theology and Worship Ministry Unit, Presbyterian Church [U.S.A.], 1991), 47.

17. Theology Committee of the Christian Church (Disciple of Christ), "Statement on Relations between Jews and Christians," 1993, in Clark M. Williamson, ed., *The Church and the Jewish People: A Study Guide for the Christian Church (Disciples of Christ)* (St. Louis: Christian Board of Publication, 1994).

18 "Declaration on the 50th Anniversary of *Kristallnacht*," 1988. Many of the statements of the German and other European churches are posted on the website *http://www.jcrelations.net*. Their vast extent is shown by the nearly 1,800 pages of documentation collected in the two volumes *Die Kirche und das Judentum: Dokumente von 1945-1985* and *Die Kirche und das Judentum: Dokumente von 1986-2000* (Paderborn and Munich, 1988, 2001).

19. The Leuenberg Church Fellowship, 2001, "Church and Israel: A Contribution from the Reformation Churches in Europe to the Relationship between Christians and Jews," http://www.jcrelations.net/en/?id=1009. Further references to this document are in parentheses.

20. The Southern Baptist Convention, 1996, "Resolution on Jewish Evangelism," http://www.sbc.net/resolutions/amResolution.asp?ID=655.

21. "A Statement on Jewish-Christian Relations from the Alliance of Baptists," 2003, http://www.allianceofbaptists.org/christian-jewish.htm. Interestingly, the Alliance also adopted in 2003 a parallel statement on Christian-Muslim relations (see http://www.allianceofbaptists.org/muslims-christians.htm).

22. 38th General Council of the United Church of Canada, "Bearing Faithful Witness: Statement on United Church-Jewish Relations Today," 2003. See the full statement at http://www.jcrelations.net/en/displayItem.php?id=998.

Further Reading

Brockway, Allan, et. al. *The Theology of the Churches and the Jewish People: Statements by the World Council of Churches and Its Member Churches*. Geneva, Switzerland: WCC Publications, 1988.

Croner, Helga, ed. *More Stepping Stones to Jewish-Christian Relations: An Unabridged Collection of Christian Documents, 1975-1983*. New York: Paulist, 1985.

———, ed. *Stepping Stones to Further Jewish-Christian Relations: An Unabridged Collection of Christian Documents*. London: Stimulus Books, 1977.

www.bc.edu/research/cjl. The website of the Center for Jewish-Christian Learning of Boston College.

www.jcrelations.net. A site with articles, reviews, and reports on Jewish-Christian relations around the world, maintained by the International Council of Christians and Jews.

21

CHAPTER

Catholic Teaching
on Jews and Judaism:
An Evolution in Process

Eugene J. Fisher

I N 1943, the eminent French historian Jules Isaac went into hiding in France. A scholar, he used his time to research and put on
paper thoughts that would change the course of the ancient, too
often tragic, relationship between the Catholic Church and the Jewish people. He sought in history an answer, as Claire Hutchet Bishop puts it, to the
question "Why was there such silence and apathy in the Christian world concerning the fate of the European Jews?"[1] The results of Isaac's covert wartime
scholarship would deeply influence the Second Vatican Council's *Nostra
Aetate*, number 4,[2] the first statement by any council in the church's history
to consider directly the church's relationship with "the Mystery of Israel."
The council would focus the church's attention on the twin theological issues
at the heart of that long and painful history: the rejection of the deicide
charge[3] and the implications of God's "irrevocable" covenant with the Jews.

After the war in 1947, Isaac published the results of his research in a six-hundred-page volume, *Jesus and Israel*. The book had a great impact in France. Later that year, Isaac met in Paris with a group of French Christians and Jews that included three Catholic priests (Jean de Menasce, Paul Demann, and Jean Daniélou) and presented them with eighteen points aimed at the "purification of Christian teaching regarding the Jews." These became the basis for the "Ten Points of Seelisberg," issued internationally later that year from Switzerland.

In 1949, Isaac met with Pope Pius XII, presenting him with the Seelisberg points and arguing for the suppression of the term "perfidious" from the Good Friday Prayer for the Jews. Isaac noted that Catholics did not kneel for the Jews as they did for others during the prayer. Pius did authorize a milder translation of *perfidis* as "unfaithful" or "unbelieving," and restored kneeling for the Jews in 1955. But it was not until 1958 that *perfidis* was eliminated. And it was eliminated not by Pius but by his successor, Pope John XXIII. Indeed, consideration of the more fundamental Seelisberg points and their implications for the basic triumphalistic and conversionist tone of the church's theology and liturgy would only, as we shall see, be taken up by the Second Vatican Council itself.

Again, Isaac played a key role. After meeting with Isaac in 1960, John XXIII established a commission charged with developing a draft on the Jews for consideration by the Second Vatican Council. He entrusted leadership of this commission to Cardinal Augustin Bea, a Jesuit biblical scholar.

Nostra Aetate: In Our Time

The draft of the statement on the Jews (originally *De Iudais*) went through many adventures, first being attached to the ecumenical document and then separated and surrounded with statements on other world religions (Islam, Buddhism, Hinduism, native traditions), the latter to encourage votes from bishops in those regions where Christianity was (and is) a minority. The bishops of Europe, the scene of the Shoah, and North America, which after World War II had the world's largest Jewish population, pushed strongly for the document. Bishops in Arab countries opposed a document on Jews, as did some traditionalist bishops. In the end, however, the bishops offered overwhelming support: 1,763 affirmative votes, 250 negative ones, and 10 abstentions.

NA, promulgated on October 28, 1965, is distinctive among conciliar documents in not including any references to the Fathers of the Church or to previous ecumenical councils. This, as Cardinals Bea and Johannes Willebrands emphasized, was because no previous council had taken up the issue of the church's relationship with the Jewish people directly. Nor had the charge that the Jews were collectively guilty for the crucifixion of Jesus ever been seriously debated. First appearing in the late second century, and often embroidered, the charge of "deicide"—in killing Jesus, the Jews had killed God—had never really been challenged over the centuries; it was simply assumed. So *NA* represented a sea change. While acknowledging the historical involvement of some Jewish authorities of the time, *NA* affirms that "what happened in His [Christ's] passion cannot be blamed upon all the Jews then living, nor upon the Jews of today." Thus, "the Jews should not be presented as repudiated or cursed by God, as if such views followed from Sacred Scripture."

For a positive understanding of Judaism, *NA* turns to the New Testament itself: "The Jews still remain most dear to God because of their fathers, for He does not repent of the gifts he makes nor of the calls He issues" (Rom 11:28–29). It acknowledges as well the church's ongoing "spiritual bond" and "common spiritual patrimony" with Jews. Deploring any form of antisemitism, the council urges instead "that mutual understanding and respect which is the fruit above all of biblical and theological studies, and of brotherly dialogues."

Controversy and Growth in Understanding

The reception of *NA* was mixed, with both plaudits and substantive criticism extended. Critics asked whether the council had truly closed the door on proselytism and noted its failure to mention either the Shoah or Israel. They questioned the use of the weaker term "deplore" rather than "condemn" in reference to antisemitism. Such criticisms, among other issues, were taken up almost immediately in dialogues in the United States and Europe, and then in the official dialogue with the International Jewish Committee for Interreligious Relations (IJCIC), which held its first meeting in Paris in 1971.

Similarly, every subsequent document issued by the Holy See on Catholic-Jewish relations has received as much criticism as praise, sometimes for omissions, sometimes for ambiguous or misleading wording. Indeed, significant issues remain on the agenda of Catholic-Jewish dialogue. The 1985 Vatican *Notes on the Correct Way to Present the Jews and Judaism in Preaching and Catechesis in the Roman Catholic Church*, for example, calls typology the sign of "a problem unresolved." Yet the 1994 *Catechism of the Catholic Church* relies heavily on typology in its use of scripture.

These criticisms, however, have been and continue to be quite healthy for the church, since subsequent documents often, though not always, address them through clearer or fuller explorations than earlier ones. *NA*, for example, makes no mention of postbiblical Jewish thought or traditions. The 1974 *Guidelines and Suggestions* (see "Implementing *Nostra Aetate* Locally and Universally," below) notes simply that "the history of Judaism did not end with the destruction of Jerusalem but rather went on to develop a religious tradition." The 1985 *Notes* contains an entire section on "Judaism and Christianity in History" and states that Christians can "profit discerningly from the traditions of Jewish reading of Scripture."

Similarly, the insights of contemporary Catholic biblical and theological scholarship, in this area as in others, take time to be integrated into teaching and preaching for a billion people of diverse cultures. Hence the use of the image of "evolution" in the subtitle of this chapter. The official documents of the church with which this chapter deals may quite accurately be called "revolutionary," but fitting all the new insights into the old wineskins of preconciliar theological categories is impossible without rethinking the categories themselves. So following up on the implications of revolutionary insights in the magisterium will inevitably at best be "evolutionary."

Implementing *Nostra Aetate* Locally and Universally

The U.S. Catholic bishops in January 1967 were the first to come out with guidelines for the local implementation of the council's decree. Their "Guidelines for Catholic-Jewish Relations" point to the incompatibility of dialogue with proselytism, and urge the involvement of Catholic scholars and educators on all levels. In 1974 the Holy See's newly formed Commission for Religious Relations with the Jews (so named because the Vatican Secretariat of State handles all political relations with the State of Israel) issued its own, universal *Guidelines and Suggestions* for implementing *NA*. This document reflects the influence of statements from various national conferences of bishops, most notably that of the French bishops in 1973. "Deliberately practical" in nature, the 1974 *Guidelines* draws out some of the rich liturgical and educational implications of the dialogue, noting laconically that over the centuries "such relations as there have been between Jew and Christian have scarcely ever risen above the level of monologue." Key to the dialogue, of course, is "respect for the faith and religious convictions" of the other, "a common meeting in the presence of God, in prayer and silent meditation."

Noting "the existing links" between Christian and Jewish liturgies, the 1974 *Guidelines* reminds Christians that much in the Jewish scripture "retains its own perpetual value . . . [and] has not been cancelled by the later interpretation of the New Testament." While Christians believe that the biblical promises were in one sense "fulfilled with the first coming of Christ," it is equally the church's proclamation that "we still await their perfect fulfillment in his glorious return at the end of time." These two points reappear in even sharper language in the 1991 statement of the Pontifical Biblical Commission: teachers, preachers, liturgical translators and biblical commentaries are to have an "overriding preoccupation, taking scriptural studies into account," not to "distort" the meaning of the sacred texts, "especially when it is a question of passages which seem to show the Jewish people as such in an unfavorable light." As with virtually all of the Catholic documents, this Pontifical Biblical Commission statement urges joint social action and witness.[4]

Lex Orandi, Lex Credendi

The emphasis on liturgical and catechetical aspects of the relationship is characteristically "Catholic." In the liturgical reform of the 1970s following the council, the Good Friday prayer that had referred to "faithless Jews" and the "blindness of that people" was eradicated. The new prayer, instead of praying for the conversion of the Jews, reads:

> Let us pray for the Jewish people, the first to hear the word of God, that they may continue to grow in the love of his Name and in faithfulness to his covenant.
>
> Almighty and eternal God, long ago you gave your promise to Abraham and his posterity. Listen to your Church as we pray that the people you first made your own may arrive at the fullness of redemption.

The phrase "fullness of redemption" is not historical but eschatological. Like St. Paul in Romans 11, the prayer leaves the issue in God's hands, to be revealed at the end of time with the Second Coming of Christ. Since the Catholic community takes seriously the ancient principle *lex orandi, lex credendi* (the law of prayer is the law of faith), this change in the church's only prayer for the Jews has great significance.

The Role of John Paul II

The numerous addresses and reflections of Pope John Paul II during his remarkable pontificate bear great significance.[5] In meeting with Jewish leaders in Mainz, Germany, in 1980, for example, the pope built upon a statement of the German bishops issued earlier that year calling for respect for "the spiritual heritage of Israel for the Church." In his own statement, the pope emphasizes that this legacy is to be seen as "a living heritage, which must be understood and preserved in its depth and richness by us Catholic Christians." He boldly states that "the true and central dimension of our dialogue is [that] of the meeting between the people of God of the Old Covenant, never revoked by God (cf. Rom 11:29), and that of the New Covenant." This meeting, the pope continues, "is at the same time a dialogue within our Church, that is to say, between the first and second part of her Bible." This now frequently cited affirmation heightens the enduring character of God's covenant with the Jewish people. It also sharpens the understanding that in some way Christian-Jewish dialogue is for the church not so much an "interreligious" or "interfaith" exercise as an internal one between members of the one people of God, Jews and Christians.

As the 1974 *Guidelines* notes, paraphrasing the council, "It is when the Church delves into her own mystery that she encounters the mystery of Israel." Because of the shared scriptures, shared biblical history, and the fact that Jesus, Mary, and the apostles were all Jewish, the subsequent "parting of the ways" between the Jewish and (increasingly Gentile) Christian communities was in a real sense the first schism experienced by nascent Christianity. Thus, Catholic-Jewish dialogue may have as much in common with the ecumenical movement as it does with the interfaith agenda. Nevertheless, it differs substantially from ecumenical goals and concerns in that its goal is not "visible unity" of the Christian churches, but "reconciliation" between Jews and Christians, who remain at once bound by common origins and distinct as peoples of God until the end of time.

The Commission for Religious Relations with the Jews, therefore, does not function under the rubric of the Pontifical Council for Interreligious Dialogue in the Holy See, but, rather, is attached to the Council for Christian Unity. Yet it is independent of it, lest any conclude that this commission is an agent for proselytizing. As the pope put it during his 1986 visit to the Great Synagogue of Rome, "The Jewish religion is not 'extrinsic' to us, but in a certain sense is 'intrinsic' to our own religion. With Judaism, therefore, we have a relationship which we do not have with any other religion. You are our dearly beloved brothers and, in a certain way, it can be said that you are our elder brothers."

The pope's understanding of the intimacy and distinctiveness of the Jewish-Christian relationship can be considered a normative teaching of the magisterium and has now found its way into the universal *Catechism of the Catholic Church*. Citing *NA* and Good Friday prayer, the *Catechism* states that "the Jewish faith, unlike other non-Christian religions, is already a response to God's revelation in the Old Covenant" (§ 839).[6]

Echoes of the Dialogue: Local and Universal Statements

Such an "echo effect" between Catholic documents can also be seen in the relationship of statements issued by local Episcopal conferences (the organization of bishops in a nation) and statements of the Holy See. Thus, to interpret the latter it is often helpful to examine the former. For example, the 1973 statement of the French bishops, mentioned above, was the first to raise the theological implications of the rebirth of a Jewish state in the land of Israel. The U.S. bishops' 1975 Statement on Catholic-Jewish Relations distilled the fuller reflections of the French bishops and added a caveat reflecting the American experience of certain millennial evangelical claims: "Appreciation of this link [between the People and the State of Israel] is not to give assent to any particular religious interpretation of this bond." The 1985 Vatican *Notes on the Correct Way to Present Jews and Judaism in Preaching and Catechesis* repeats the U.S. bishops' statement almost verbatim and, unusually, footnotes their statement explicitly. The terms "link" and "bond" are important, since they are used primarily for the sacrament of matrimony, which Catholic teaching considers unbreakable. In 1993 the Vatican signed the historic "Fundamental Agreement" with the Jewish State, noting in its preamble the implications of the diplomatic agreement for the larger effort for reconciliation between the Catholic Church and the Jewish People.[7]

The 1985 Vatican *Notes* goes in unprecedented depth into a number of theological issues, such as typology, affirming it as a valid approach to scripture on the one hand, yet relativizing it on the other by noting that it "only manifests the unfathomable riches of the Old Testament, its inexhaustible content." Similarly, the 2001 statement of the Pontifical Biblical Commission, "The Jewish People and Their Sacred Scriptures in the Christian Bible," expands this statement by acknowledging the validity and significance *for Christians* of Jewish readings of common scriptural texts over the centuries and today. The Pontifical Biblical Commission states that both Jewish and Christian traditions of interpretation may be true on "analogical" or different levels of meaning. This "layering" of statements over the years illustrates what I have called the "evolution" of Catholic magisterial tradition following the Second Vatican Council.[8] It should be noted as well that this interrelatedness among various statements of the Holy See makes it difficult to interpret them in isolation from one another.

The *Notes* also makes explicit the ways in which Jewish liturgy has shaped Christian worship. Moreover, it recognizes the problematic nature of some New Testament passages, attributing these texts to the times and circumstances of the evangelists rather than to Jesus himself. The U.S. Conference of Catholic Bishops provides a framework for implementation of these two concerns regarding worship and biblical texts in two statements issued in 1988. The Committee on the Liturgy issued *God's Mercy Endures Forever: Guidelines on the Presentation of Jews and Judaism in Catholic*

Preaching, and the Committee for Ecumenical and Interreligious Affairs published *Criteria for the Evaluation of Dramatizations of the Passion*.[9]

Continuing Controversies and Further Challenges

The Holy See's *We Remember: A Reflection on the Shoah* (1998) has some ambiguous language that has raised many questions.[10] In speaking of the anti-Jewish sins of the "sons and daughters of the Church," it seems to exculpate the higher levels of ecclesial leadership. In distinguishing traditional Christian anti-Judaism from modern, racial antisemitism, *We Remember* seems to deny a causal relationship between centuries of anti-Judaism and modern antisemitism. The U.S. Bishops' Committee for Ecumenical and Interreligious Affairs, taking advantage of clarifications made by Cardinal Edward Cassidy—then president of the Pontifical Commission for Religious Relations with the Jews, under whose authority *We Remember* was promulgated—issued a resource book, *Catholics Remember the Holocaust* (1998), and then a more definitive statement, *Catholic Teaching on the Shoah: Implementing the Holy See's "We Remember."* In these monographs, the bishops make clear that all Catholics on all levels, including the popes, are to be counted among Catholics who have sinned against Jews over the centuries. The authors, however, are reluctant to say that the *church itself* has sinned because of the Catholic understanding that the church has a heavenly as well as an earthly dimension. Likewise, while maintaining the distinction between traditional Christian anti-Judaism and modern racial antisemitism, the bishops acknowledge explicitly that anti-Judaism was a major cause of the development and spread of antisemitism, though by no means the sole cause:

> But Christian anti-Judaism did lay the groundwork for racial, genocidal anti-Semitism by stigmatizing not only Judaism but Jews themselves for opprobrium and contempt. So the Nazi theories tragically found fertile soil in which to plant the horror of an unprecedented attempt at genocide. One way to put the "connectedness" between the Christian teaching of anti-Judaism (leading to anti-Jewishness) and Nazi antisemitism is that the former is a "necessary cause" to consider in explaining the development and success of the latter in the twentieth century—but not a "sufficient cause." To account for the Holocaust, one must acknowledge the historical role of Christian anti-Judaism. But Christian anti-Judaism alone does not account for the Holocaust. Semi-scientific racial theories and specific historical,

ideological, economic and social realities within Germany must also be taken into account.[11]

Many issues remain unresolved. For example, although in his public lectures Walter Cardinal Kasper, current president of the Pontifical Commission on Religious Relations with Jews, speaks of "God's unrevoked covenant with his people and of the permanent and actual salvific significance of Jewish religion for its believers," it is not clear how widely such views are shared.[12] Moreover, the implications of that acknowledgment for other aspects of the church's teaching are just beginning to be debated. The limitations of some traditional theological categories were revealed when Catholic scholars in dialogue with Jews on the national level in the United States issued *Reflections on Covenant and Mission* in 2002. Their claim that the church, which no longer officially prays for the conversion of Jews, might best leave the sacred mystery of God's will for the Jewish people in the hands of God precipitated an intense, internal Catholic discussion that continues to the present.[13]

Rome Comes to Jerusalem

Finally, the teaching role of Pope John Paul II's gestures toward the Jews deserves mention. When assessing the official teaching of the Catholic Church on relations with Jews and Judaism, it is important to consider that John Paul II is the first bishop of Rome to visit a synagogue—and the first to pray with a Jewish congregation and listen to its rabbi expound the scriptures (Gen 17, the covenant with Abraham, including the promise of the land). So, too, must people take account of his visits to Auschwitz in 1979 and to Yad Vashem (Israel's Holocaust museum) in 2000, as well as the pope's liturgy of repentance at St. Peter's in Rome on Lent's first Sunday in 2000, which expressed repentance for the sins of the church against the Jews over the centuries, culminating in the Holocaust. Addressing the Pontifical Biblical Commission at the beginning of its deliberations led to the publication of "The Jewish People and Their Sacred Scriptures in the Christian Bible" (note the pronoun "their")—the pope acknowledged that "unjust and erroneous interpretations" of the New Testament, beginning as early as the first century, had by the twentieth so "lulled the consciences of Christians" that many failed to act as Christians should act during the Shoah.

In many respects, the changes begun at Vatican II and still in progress can be captured in one poignant scene in March 2000: the once robust Pope John Paul II, now an elderly and frail man, walks haltingly to the Western

Wall in Jerusalem. Like thousands of Jews before him, he places a petition in one of its cracks—the text of his prayer of repentance prayed only weeks earlier at St. Peter's Basilica. It reads:

> God of our fathers, you chose Abraham and his descendants to bring your Name to the Nations. We are deeply saddened by the behavior of those who in the course of history have caused these children of yours to suffer, and asking your forgiveness we wish to commit ourselves to genuine brotherhood with the people of the Covenant. (Jerusalem, March 26, 2000)

Would that Jules Isaac had lived to witness this moment.

Notes

1. Claire Hutchet Bishop, "A Biographical Introduction," in Jules Isaac, *The Teaching of Contempt* (New York: Holt, Rinehart and Winston, 1964), 8.
2. Second Vatican Council, *Nostra Aetate*, number 4; hereinafter *NA*. The title comes from the opening words in Latin of the document, "In our time." Unless otherwise noted, all documents discussed in this chapter may be found in one of two volumes edited by Helga Croner, *Stepping Stones to Further Jewish-Christian Relations*, and *More Stepping Stones to Jewish-Christian Relations* (New York: Paulist, 1977 and 1985, respectively). The 1977 volume includes *Nostra Aetate*, n. 4; the 1974 *Guidelines and Suggestions;* the 1967 "Guidelines for Catholic-Jewish Relations," of the U.S. National Conference of Catholic Bishops; the French Bishops' Statement of 1973; and the 1975 Statement on Catholic-Jewish Relations by the U.S. National Conference of Bishops. The 1985 volume includes the 1947 "Ten Points of Seelisberg" and the 1985 *Notes on the Correct Way to Present the Jews and Judaism in Preaching and Catechesis in the Roman Catholic Church*. All documents cited in this chapter are available online, most readily at http://www.bc.edu/research/cjl/resources/documents/catholic/.
3. "Deicide" is the incongruous term used to ascribe collective and perennial guilt to the Jews as a whole for the death of Jesus.
4. *The Jewish People and Their Sacred Scriptures in the Christian Bible* (Vatican City: Libreria Editrice Vaticana, 2002). Also available http://www.vatican.va/roman_curia/congregations/cfaith/pcb_documents/rc_con.
5. See E. Fisher and L. Klenicki, eds., *Spiritual Pilgrimage: Pope John Paul II: Texts on Jews and Judaism 1979-1995* (New York: Crossroad, 1995); and Fisher and Klenicki, eds., *Pope John Paul II on Jews and Judaism, 1979-1986* (Washington: National Conference of Catholic Bishops Committee for Ecumenical and Interreligious Affairs, and New York: The Anti-Defamation League of B'nai B'rith, 1987).

6. *Catechism of the Catholic Church* (Collegeville: The Liturgical Press, 1994).

7. See Eugene J. Fisher and Leon Klenicki, eds., *A Challenge Long Delayed: The Diplomatic Exchange between the Holy See and the State of Israel* (New York: Anti-Defamation League, 1996).

8. See Eugene Fisher, "The Evolution of a Tradition: From *Nostra Aetate* to *The Notes*," in International Catholic-Jewish Liaison Committee, eds., *Fifteen Years of Catholic-Jewish Dialogue* (Libreria Editrice Vaticana, 1988), 239-254.

9. Bishops' Committee on the Liturgy, *God's Mercy Endures Forever: Guidelines on the Presentation of Jews and Judaism in Catholic Preaching;* and Bishops' Committee for Ecumenical and Interreligious Affairs, *Criteria for the Dramatizations of the Passion*, Edición Bilingüe (both Washington, D.C.: National Conference of Catholic Bishops, 1988).

10. Commission for Religious Relations with Jews, "We Remember: A Reflection on the Shoah," in Secretariat for Ecumenical and Interreligious Affairs, *Catholics Remember the Holocaust* (Washington, D.C.: United States Catholic Conference, 1998), 47-56.

11. Secretariat for Ecumenical and Interreligious Affairs, National Conference of Catholic Bishops, *Catholic Teaching on the Shoah* (Washington, D.C.: United States Catholic Conference, 2001), 10.

12. Cardinal Walter Kasper, "The Jewish-Christian Dialogue: Foundations, Progress, Difficulties and Perspectives," Israel Museum, Jerusalem, November 21, 2001. See http://www.bc.edu/bc_org/research/cjl/articles/kasper_21_Nov_01.htm.

13. For "Reflections on Covenant and Mission," see http://www.bc.edu/research/cjl/meta-elements/texts/documents/interreligious/ncs_usccb120802.htm. Debate about seeking to convert Jews may be found in *America* 187/12 (October 21, 2002); cf. Avery Cardinal Dulles, "Covenant and Mission," and Mary C. Boys, Philip A. Cunningham, and John Pawlikowski, "Theology's Sacred Obligation: A Reply to Cardinal Dulles," available at http://www.americamagazine.org/gettext.cfm? articleTypeID=1&textID=2545&issueID=408.

Further Reading

Bernadin, Joseph Cardinal. *A Blessing to Each Other: Cardinal Joseph Bernadin and Jewish Catholic Dialogue*. Chicago: Liturgy Training Publications, 1996.

Secretariat for Ecumenical and Interreligious Affairs, National Conference of Catholic Bishops. *Catholic Teaching on the Shoah: Implementing Catholic Teaching on the Shoah*. Washington, DC: United States Catholic Conference, 2001.

———. *Catholics Remember the Holocaust*. Washington, DC, United States Catholic Conference, 1998.

Willebrands, Johannes. *Church and Jewish People: New Considerations*. New York: Paulist, 1992.

22
CHAPTER

Revising Christian Teaching: The Work of the Christian Scholars Group on Christian-Jewish Relations

Alice L. Eckardt

O UR CHRISTIAN Scholars Group on Christian-Jewish Relations draws upon the legacy of many scholars in its quest to give depth and breadth to the renewal of Christianity's relationship to Judaism. Although established in 1969 as the "Israel Study Group," our founding members had been involved in this work since the early 1940s.[1] Yet, the real pioneer within the Christian community, Dr. James Parkes, came not from North America but from across the Atlantic.

Parkes encountered endemic European antisemitism through his work with three international Christian student movements from 1923 through the 1930s in Britain and on the continent. He also discovered the German theological tendency to keep social action and politics totally separate from faith and the church. When Hitler and the National Socialist Workers Party achieved political power in 1933, Parkes needed financial help to support university students exiled from Germany. He met with two British Jews, Simon Marks and Israel Sieff, to ask for their monetary help, which they gave generously.

Parkes had already recognized that a great deal of research and work needed to be done on the long history of relations between Christians and Jews, as well as deeply embedded church teachings, if any significant change in Christian faith and action were to occur. So he approached Sieff to ask for his financial support in undertaking this task. Sieff asked, "How long do you think the work will take?" Parkes had no idea what kind of answer Sieff wanted, but he said what he believed to be true: "About three hundred years." Sieff laughed, and said, "Good, I am prepared to help you. Had you said 'twenty-five years' or 'my lifetime,' I would have told you to go away because you did not understand what you were talking about."[2] A few months after this conversation, the Nazis attempted to assassinate Parkes; he survived only because his attackers marked the wrong man.

The Christian Scholars Group realizes just how right Parkes and Sieff were in their sense of the lengthy commitment required of Christians. This came home to me in a vivid way in 1979, forty-six years after Parkes's conversation with Israel Sieff. A Jewish survivor, Eli Zborowski, invited three Protestant theologians—Robert McAfee Brown, my husband Roy Eckardt, and me—to join him (and the photographer accompanying him) in visiting the Polish Catholic family who had hidden him, his mother, and his younger brother and sister for eighteen months during World War II in their small home in Zarki.[3]

When we arrived we discovered just how small the house was and how very close the neighboring houses were. Not only did faces peering over the fences show hostility, but the local police insisted on taking the photographer and our friend Eli to the station while inquiries were made about them. A local Communist official quickly arrived at the cottage, asking her own questions. Yet our simple Catholic hostess, Maria Płaczek, greeted us with joy and generous hospitality. Rather plaintively, she asked us why her neighbors should hate her so much for having sheltered Jews during the terrible war years. She was, after all, only doing what her Lord Jesus Christ taught her: to care for those in need. Even so, she and her husband knew they had risked not only their own lives but that of their young child, Jadwiga, as well.

As recently as 2002 a documentary called *The Secret* told the story of adult Poles discovering only in recent years that their blood parents, whom they had never known or could no longer remember, were Jews—not the Catholic "parents" they had known and loved all their lives. In the process of reclaiming their Jewish identity, they faced hostility from the community.

These incidents, which occurred over a seventy-year span, are but three illustrations of the deep-seated anti-Judaism entrenched in Christian life. Those committed to transforming Christian theology must confront almost two thousand years of church history that has denigrated the Jewish people and denied the continuing validity and vitality of their faith. For example, in the years immediately following World War II, the churches were painfully slow to acknowledge the role that Christian teaching had played in the catastrophic destruction of two-thirds of Europe's Jewish population (one-third of the world's Jewish population). Nor were the churches prepared to recognize that this murderous campaign posed a serious challenge for a supposedly Christian civilization. They were unmindful of the theology and ethics of churches that on the whole had led clergy and members of the Christian faith communities to tolerate or acquiesce in governmental steps that led to genocide. The roots of the "teaching of contempt" for Judaism and its people (*adversus Iudaeos*) within all of Christendom are so deeply planted that their eradication requires enormous diligence, wisdom, and perseverance.

The Postwar Awakening of the Churches

Several church pronouncements issued in the immediate postwar years revealed that the churches had not grasped the full implications of their complicity in the Shoah. In Western Germany the Protestant Evangelical Church issued three documents (1947, 1948, 1949) that, while confessing to antisemitism and submission to state demands, nevertheless reiterated the old negative portrayal of Jews. The documents even blamed the Jewish people for their own destruction: By crucifying its Messiah, Israel had counteracted its election and rejected salvation, becoming "a warning instance of divine judgment." Its only hope, therefore, "lay in conversion to Christ." Jewish mass deaths in the gas chambers were seen as a consequence of God's wrath against the disobedience of the Jewish people. Such statements revalidated the new "true" Israel—Christianity—while once again invalidating the "old," false faith of Judaism.[4]

When the World Council of Churches held its first full-scale assembly in 1948 in Amsterdam, it rightly decried antisemitism and the "extermination of six million Jews," and confessed the past role of the churches in fostering an image of Jews as the sole enemies of Christ. Yet, it still saw no problem with continuing to stress that the churches' God-given mission was to convert Jews to Christianity. It apparently did not see the contradiction in the negation of Judaism that such a position represented.

Gradually, however, new perspectives developed. Some German theologians took offense at German anti-Judaic interpretations of the Shoah, and began to reconsider long-established assumptions about Jews. Thus, the Synod of the Evangelical Church in Germany issued a statement in April 1950 that initiated the laborious rethinking of that church's theology. In the statement, the synod affirmed that God's covenant with his chosen people Israel remains in effect; and it confessed to being "accomplices in the outrages" perpetrated against the Jews "through neglect and silence." It asked all Christians to renounce and resist all antisemitism, to protect Jewish graveyards, and to meet Jews and Jewish-Christians in brotherhood (and sisterhood). Nevertheless, it still looked forward to the "day of fulfillment" when Christians "with the redeemed Israel may extol the victory of Jesus Christ."[5]

Some signs of awakened awareness were to be found outside Germany three years earlier, in two largely ignored international gatherings of Jews and Christians. An International Conference of Jews and Christians representing their various religious communities met in Oxford in 1946 and issued a statement recognizing the "dignity, rights, and duties of man [and woman]" that "derive from his [their] creation by God and his [their] relation to God." A second report pointed out that antisemitism is a "special case requiring special treatment" insofar as "an attack on Jewry is an attack on the fundamental principles of Judaism and Christianity on which our ordered human society depends." It called for an early emergency conference to deal specifically with antisemitism.[6]

This emergency conference was held at Seelisberg, Switzerland, at the end of July 1947. The Christian participants wrote an "Address to the Churches," which focused on the "outburst of antisemitism which led to the persecution and extermination of millions of Jews living in a Christian environment." They acknowledged the continuing presence of the antisemitic poison, with its threat of extending the hate to Christians elsewhere and involving ever more humanity in "guilt with disastrous consequences." They confessed that two thousand years of preaching on Jesus' teaching about God's mercy and love of one's neighbors had not prevented Christian "hatred and distrust toward the Jews."

Their "Address to the Churches" concluded with ten statements that the conferees believed would correct "false, inadequate or mistaken" ideas in Christian preaching and teaching. The statement emphasizes the need to avoid disparaging biblical and postbiblical Judaism in order to extol Christianity; it warns against making "Jews" and "enemies of Jesus" synonymous, as if the first members of the new community were not themselves Jews, and presenting Jesus' death as solely a Jewish responsibility.[7] The so-called "Ten Points of Seelisberg" provided a conceptual scaffolding on which church leaders and scholars built in subsequent years. The writers of "A Sacred Obligation" stand on the shoulders of the Seelisberg conferees.

The Work of the Christian Scholars Group on Christian-Jewish Relations

In the following two decades some work was done by a few individual scholars and churchmen. Among these were the three founding members of the "Israel Study Group" who had lived through the war years and had been wrestling with the issues they now addressed collectively. Franklin H. Littell had been Protestant adviser to the U.S. Commissioner for Germany at the end of World War II, and worked with the German Protestant churches as they set out to renew and reform themselves after twelve years of the Third Reich's racist regime and five years of war. During the concluding years of that war and its immediate aftermath, A. Roy Eckardt had written his doctoral thesis under Reinhold Niebuhr on "Christianity and the Children of Israel." He analyzed various Christian theological positions on Jews and their connections with, or opposition to, anti-Judaism and antisemitism.[8] In the following years both Littell and Eckardt had continued their work on the theological issues related to Christian animosity toward the Jewish people and their faith. Sister Ann Patrick Ware, of the Sisters of Loretto and a member of the Faith and Order Commission of the World Council of Churches (WCC), worked from 1964 to1967 with the WCC Committee on the Church and the Jewish People to produce the "Bristol Report," a seminal study attempting to understand in a new way the relation of the church and the Jewish people within God's plan.[9] Other than Vatican II's *Nostra Aetate* in 1965 and the 1967 "Bristol Report," major church bodies were largely quiescent in regard to their relations with Jews and Judaism.

Our scholars group convened in 1969 under the sponsorship of the Faith and Order Commission, with the cooperation of the Secretariat for Ecumenical and Interreligious Affairs of the National Conference of Catholic Bishops. We understood our work to involve the rediscovery and reaffirmation of the inheritance of biblical faith we shared with Jews, and making known the richness of postbiblical Judaism to fellow Christians. We hoped our work would contribute to the refutation of the longstanding teaching that the church had replaced the Jewish people as God's chosen. This necessitated removal of the erroneous portrayal of Jews as unfaithful and accursed by God for their alleged collective responsibility for both Jesus' death and the rejection of the covenant with God. It also required acknowledgment of the suffering this teaching had brought on the Jewish people over centuries. Our scholars group believed that a new teaching of respect had to replace the old teaching of contempt if a theology of equality were to emerge. Concern for the survival of the Jewish people lies at the heart of our work. This includes commitment to the State of Israel (see Michael McGarry's chapter in this volume).

Scholarship is crucial to our identity—but scholarship in the service of building better relations between Christians and Jews. Our scholarship involves not only much study but considerable involvement in dialogue with Jews. Our meetings consist primarily of impassioned discussion of papers members take turns writing, often as a way of refining ideas for publication in journals or books. On occasion, we invite other Christian or Jewish scholars to present papers to our group. Over the years we have discussed some 165 papers exploring the Christian-Jewish relationship from many perspectives.[10] These papers are now in the archives of the Burns Library at Boston College.

Statements of the Christian Scholars Group on Christian-Jewish Relations

Although we are primarily concerned with developing our own thinking with regard to relationships between Jews and Christians, we have on occasion issued statements. In 1973 members issued a "Statement to Our Fellow Christians," specifying fourteen points that identified key issues in the Jewish-Christian relationship and their bearing on Christian faith. We made recommendations for further study and action, including advocacy of judicious interpretation of New Testament texts that portray Jews and Judaism negatively. Eighteen members signed the statement.[11] The

National Council of Churches issued the statement (without either approval or endorsement), identifying it as a "stage in a process leading . . . to a fuller theological statement."

The process of developing a fuller theological statement continues with the promulgation of "A Sacred Obligation: Rethinking Christian Faith in Relation to Judaism and the Jewish People" in 2002 and the publication of this book. "A Sacred Obligation" is the communal composition of the twenty-one members of our group, so it is not directly linked with any particular church or denomination. We believe, however, that it reflects the range of thinking that has been evolving within many churches (including those represented in our membership) in these past decades.

The many denominational and ecumenical statements prepared in the intervening years testify to this. A recent attempt to collect all the statements revealed well over a hundred from the United States, Canada, Europe, Asia, Australia, and New Zealand. The German churches alone have produced three full volumes. The chapters in this volume by Eugene Fisher and Franklin Sherman trace the principal themes in the statements.

Despite all this, the renewed thinking on Christianity's relationship with Judaism has yet to permeate the churches. A response I received to a recently published autobiographical essay, "Growing into a Daring and Questioning Faith," brought the unfinished character of our "sacred obligation" home.[12] I was asked,

> Why shouldn't Christians celebrate triumphalism based on Jesus being Messiah and Savior? The gospels are the fulfillment of prophecies of the Hebrew Testament. My disappointment with . . . the Jews is not that they promoted his crucifixion but that after the resurrection they did not recognize that he was the Messiah. This was consistent with earlier behavior in turning away from Old Testament prophets.

Such reactions led me to appreciate anew the realism of James Parkes about how long it will take to educate Christians to a more adequate understanding of our relationship to Jews and Judaism. We cannot sit back and wait: We are obliged to do this work both for the sake of justice to Jews and the integrity of Christian faith.

It is our hope that "A Sacred Obligation" will energize discussion in the churches and that this volume will provide a substantial resource for rethinking. We Christians may not face the existential problem of our survival (as do Jews), but we must not turn away from the thinking that allowed the church to compromise its moral and spiritual integrity during the Third Reich and, we now realize, during so much of the preceding centuries. We have a sacred obligation.

Notes

1. The group has undergone various changes in name and sponsorship over the years. For a brief history, see www.bc.edu/research/cjl/meta-elements/partners/CSG/history.htm.

2. James Parkes, *Voyage of Discoveries* (London: Victor Gollancz, 1969), 128–29.

3. For a full account, see *Martyrdom and Resistance* [bimonthly newspaper published by the International Society for Yad Vashem], May–June 1980, 7, 14.

4. The Oldenbourg Provincial Church, October 1947; see Richard Gutteridge, *Open Thy Mouth for the Dumb: The German Evangelical Church and the Jews, 1879–1950* (Oxford: Basil Blackwell, 1976), 301. Reich Council of Brethren of the Evangelical Church in Germany, April 1948; see Gutteridge, *Open Thy Mouth*, 301. Declaration of the Confessing Church Council of Brethren, Darmstadt, 1949; see Micha Brumlik, "Post-Holocaust Theology," in Robert P. Ericksen and Susannah Heschel, eds., *Betrayal* (Minneapolis: Fortress Press, 1999), 173-175.

5. Text in Ericksen and Heschel, 175.

6. Findings of Commission No. 2 of the International Conference of Christians and Jews, "Fundamental Postulates of Christianity and Judaism in Relation to Human Order," Oxford, 1946. The full text is available at www.iccj.org/en/?id=103. The second report is entitled "Group Tensions," Oxford, 1946.

7. "An Address to the Churches," Seelisberg, 1947. The full text is available at www.iccj.org/en/?id=102.

8. See A. Roy Eckardt, *Christianity and the Children of Israel: A Theological Approach to the Jewish Question* (New York: King's Crown, 1948).

9. See "Document 4," in Allan Brockway, Paul van Buren, Rolf Rendtorff, Simon Schoon, eds., *The Theology of the Churches and the Jewish People: Statements by the World Council of Churches and Its Member Churches* (Geneva: WCC Publications, 1988), 13–28.

10. A selection of paper topics over the years includes: "The Authority of Scripture after the Shoah"; "The Ethic, Rhetoric, and Reality of Suffering"; "The Two Covenants and the Dilemma of Christology"; "Christian Mission to the Jews in the Light of the Bible"; "The Significance of the Dead Sea Scrolls for Christian-Jewish Relations"; "The Christian Calendar and the Jewish-Christian Reality"; "Zionism: A Christian Perspective"; "The Cross: Should a Symbol Betrayed Be Reclaimed?"; "Jewish People and the Jewish State"; "Removing Anti-Jewish Polemic from our Christian Lectionaries"; "Anti-Judaism in Christian Feminist Theology: Some Good News"; "The Shoah and the Affirmation of the Resurrection of Jesus"; "Political Theology"; "Anti-Judaism in the Critical Study of the Gospels"; and "The

Challenge of Jewish Spirituality to Christian Faith." A full listing of our papers may be found at www.bc.edu/research/cjl/meta-elements/partners/CSG/history.htm.

11. "Statement to our Fellow Christians" is available at www.bc.edu/research/cjl/meta-elements/partners/CSG/csg1973.htm.

12. Alice L. Eckardt, "Growing into a Daring and Questioning Faith," in John C. Merkle, ed., *Faith Transformed: Christian Encounters with Jews and Judaism* (Collegeville: Liturgical, 2003), 17–36.

Further Reading

Eckardt, Alice L., and A. Roy Eckardt. *Long Night's Journey into Day: A Revised Retrospective*. Detroit: Wayne State University Press, 1988.

Eckardt, A. Roy. *Your People, My People: The Meeting of Jews and Christians*. New York: Quadrangle / New York Times Book, 1974.

Gutteridge, Richard. *Open Thy Mouth for the Dumb: The German Evangelical Church and the Jews, 1879–1950*. Oxford: Basil Blackwell, 1976.

Littell, Franklin H., and Hubert G. Locke, eds. *The German Church Struggle and the Holocaust*. Detroit: Wayne State University Press, 1974.

Oberman, Heiko. *The Roots of Anti-Semitism: In the Age of Renaissance and Reformation*. Philadelphia: Fortress, 1984.

Wood, James E., Jr., ed. *Jewish-Christian Relations in Today's World*. Waco, TX: Baylor University Press, 1971.

Index

About the Editor
and Contributors

Norman Beck, a pastor in the Evangelical Lutheran Church in America (ELCA), is the chairman of the Department of Theology, Philosophy, and Classical Languages at Texas Lutheran University; he also serves as the contract pastor of St. John's Lutheran Church in Denhawken, Texas. His most significant publications related to Jewish-Christian dialogue include the brief commentaries *Scripture Notes A*, *Scripture Notes B*, and *Scripture Notes C*; *Mature Christianity in the 21st Century*; *Anti-Roman Cryptograms in the New Testament: Symbolic Messages of Hope and Liberation*; and the movie script *Jesus, the Man*.

Mary C. Boys is a religious and theological educator who holds the chair in practical theology at Union Theological Seminary in New York City. Among her many publications are *Jewish-Christian Dialogue: One Woman's Experience* and *Has God Only One Blessing? Judaism as a Source of Christian Self-Understanding*. A member of the Advisory Committee on Catholic-Jewish Relations for the United States Conference of Catholic Bishops, she is a member of the Sisters of the Holy Names of Jesus and Mary. She is the recipient of a Henry Luce III Fellowship in Theology for 2005.

Rosann M. Catalano is the Roman Catholic staff scholar at the Institute for Christian and Jewish Studies in Baltimore. She has also served as an adjunct professor at the Ecumenical Institute of St. Mary's Seminary and University, and at the Weekend College of the College of Notre Dame of Maryland, both in Baltimore. A systematic theologian, she did her doctorate at the

University of St. Michael's College, Toronto; her major work was on the theology of God and the poetry of suffering in the book of Psalms.

Philip A. Cunningham, executive director of the Center for Christian-Jewish Learning and adjunct professor of theology at Boston College, is a member of the Advisory Committee on Catholic-Jewish Relations for the United States Conference of Catholic Bishops. Interested in biblical studies, religious education, and theologies of Christian-Jewish relations, Dr. Cunningham is the author of numerous articles on Christian-Jewish relations; his two most recent books are *A Story of Shalom: The Calling of Christians and Jews by a Covenanting God* and *Sharing the Scripture.* He is the editor of the recently released *Pondering the Passion.*

Celia Deutsch, a sister of Our Lady of Sion, teaches early Judaism and early Christianity in the Department of Religion at Barnard College/Columbia University. She is currently working on projects in early Jewish and early Christian mysticism. Her previous publications include *Hidden Wisdom and the Easy Yoke: Wisdom, Torah and Discipleship in Matthew 11.25-30; and Lady Wisdom, Jesus, and the Sages: Metaphor and Social Context in Matthew's Gospel.* She lives in the Midwood section of Brooklyn, where Jews, Christians, Muslims, and Hindus collaborate in building the neighborhood community.

Alice L. Eckardt is a professor of religion studies emerita, Lehigh University; executive board member of the Institute for Jewish-Christian Understanding at Muhlenberg College; and a senior associate fellow of the Oxford Centre for Postgraduate Hebrew Studies. Her books include *Long Night's Journey into Day* (coauthor); *Encounter with Israel* (coauthor); *Burning Memory: Times of Testing and Reckoning* (editor and contributor); *Jerusalem: City of the Ages* (editor and contributor).

Eugene J. Fisher, PhD, is the associate director of the Secretariat for Ecumenical and Interreligious Affairs, where he has specialized in Catholic-Jewish Relations since 1977. He has published over twenty books and three hundred articles in the field. A member of a number of learned societies, he is a consultor to the Vatican Commission for Religious Relations with the Jews and regularly represents the Holy See at international Catholic-Jewish events.

Eva Fleischner, a professor of religion emerita at Montclair State University, edited and contributed to the classic anthology *Auschwitz: Beginning of a*

New Era? She is also the author of *Judaism in German Christian Theology Since 1945* and coauthor (with Michael Phayer) of *Cries in the Night: Women Who Challenged the Holocaust.* She is the recipient of the Rose Thering Humanitarian Award from Seton Hall University, the *Nostra Aetate* Award from Seton Hill University, and the Distinguished Alumna of the Year Award from Marquette University.

Deirdre Good is a professor of New Testament at the General Theological Seminary in New York City. She is the author of *Jesus the Meek King* and the forthcoming *Mariam, the Magdalen, and the Mother.* She has published essays on Matthew, the Gospel of Philip and sacramental language, the Bible and homosexuality, and most recently on Mary Magdalene in *The DaVinci Code.*

Walter Harrelson is a professor of Hebrew Bible emeritus at Vanderbilt University Divinity School and an adjunct university professor at Wake Forest University Divinity School. He is the coauthor of two books with Rabbi Randall M. Falk: *Jews and Christians: A Troubled Family* and *Jews and Christians in Pursuit of Social Justice.* His latest book is *The New Interpreter's Study Bible.* A Baptist, his ordination is recognized by the American Baptist Churches and the Christian Church (Disciples of Christ).

Michael B. McGarry, a Paulist priest originally from Los Angeles, studied for the priesthood in Baltimore and Washington, DC, and did his graduate work in theology at St. Michael's College in the University of Toronto. He has also studied Jewish studies at the Hebrew University in Jerusalem. Author of *Christology after Auschwitz,* he serves on the Advisory Committee for the United States Conference of Catholic Bishops on Catholic-Jewish Relations. Currently he is the rector of the Tantur Ecumenical Institute in Jerusalem, where he is involved in many dimensions of the Jewish-Christian encounter.

John C. Merkle is professor in the department of theology at the College of St. Benedict/St. John's University in central Minnesota. He earned his PhD at the Catholic University of Louvain, Belgium. Merkle is the author of *The Genesis of Faith: The Depth Theology of Abraham Joshua Heschel* and the editor of *Abraham Joshua Heschel: Exploring His Life and Thought.* Most recently, he edited *Faith Transformed: Christian Encounters with Jews and Judaism.* His articles on Jewish theology and on Christian faith in relation to Judaism have been published in Europe, Latin America, and North America.

John T. Pawlikowski, a professor of social ethics at the Catholic Theological Union in Chicago and a Servite priest, has been a member of the Advisory Committee on Catholic-Jewish Relations at the United States Conference of Catholic Bishops for over twenty years. He is president of the International Council of Christians and Jews and its Abrahamic Forum. In the fall of 2004 he held the Sir Sigmund Sternberg Fellowship in Interreligious Understanding, as well as a visiting fellowship at the University of Cambridge.

Peter A. Pettit is a Lutheran pastor with a doctorate in Bible and early Judaism from the Claremont Graduate University. He serves on the Consultative Panel for Lutheran-Jewish Relations of the Evangelical Lutheran Church in America, chairs the Council of Centers for Jewish-Christian Relations (United States), and is a leader of the International Theology Conference of the Shalom Hartman Institute in Jerusalem. He is the principal author of "Facts, Faith, and Film-Making: Jesus' Passion and Its Portrayal," a study guide.

Peter C. Phan currently is the inaugural holder of the Ignacio Ellacuria, S.J., Chair in Catholic Social Thought at Georgetown University. A priest, he holds three earned doctorates and one honorary doctorate. He has published a dozen books, the latest of which is the trilogy *Christianity with an Asian Face: Asian-American Theology in the Making*; *In Our Tongues: Perspectives from Asia on Mission and Enculturation*; and *Being Religious Interreligiously: Asian Perspectives on Interfaith Dialogue*.

Jean-Pierre Ruiz teaches in the Department of Theology and Religious Studies at St. John's University in New York. He earned his doctorate from the Pontifical Gregorian University in Rome, Italy, and his research interests include biblical studies, Hispanic/Latino theology, and interreligious dialogue. A past president of the Academy of Catholic Hispanic Theologians of the United States, he is editor of the *Journal of Hispanic/Latino Theology* and an associate editor of the *Catholic Biblical Quarterly*.

Franklin Sherman was the founding director of the Institute for Jewish-Christian Understanding of Muhlenberg College and currently serves as managing editor of the international, interfaith website www.jcrelations.net. He was formerly a professor of Christian ethics and dean of the Lutheran

School of Theology in Chicago. Dr. Sherman edited the volume of *Luther's Works*, American edition, that includes Luther's writings on Jews and Judaism. He is currently editing a volume of statements on Christian-Jewish relations by church bodies and other Christian, Jewish, and interfaith organizations over the past fifty years.

Joann Spillman earned her PhD at Temple University and is a professor of theology at Rockhurst College in Kansas City, Kansas. She is the author of several articles on Jewish-Christian relations and a frequent presenter at various churches and clergy conferences in the Midwest.

John Townsend is an Episcopal priest and professor of New Testament emeritus at the Episcopal Divinity School in Cambridge, Massachusetts. His major work in Jewish studies has been to help make rabbinic literature available to college teachers of religion who have no special knowledge of Judaism. His publications include two major bibliographical articles and a three-volume translation of *Midrash Tanhuma* (Buber version) with notes.

Joseph B. Tyson is a professor emeritus of religious studies, Southern Methodist University, where he taught from 1958 to 1998. He received a PhD from Union Theological Seminary, and his major research has been in New Testament studies, the history of early Christianity, and Jewish-Christian relations. He has published numerous articles and several books, many of them on Luke-Acts, including *The New Testament and Early Christianity*, *The Death of Jesus in Luke-Acts*, *Luke-Acts and the Jewish People*, *Images of Judaism in Luke-Acts*, and *Luke, Judaism, and the Scholars*. In addition to his membership in the Christian Scholars Group on Christian-Jewish Relations, which he chaired during the writing of "A Sacred Obligation," he has been an active participant in many scholarly societies.

Clark M. Williamson is the Indiana Professor of Christian Thought, emeritus, at Christian Theological Seminary. He has written eight books about Jewish-Christian relations: *Preaching the Gospels without Blaming the Jews: A Lectionary Commentary*, *Way of Blessing, Way of Life: A Christian Theology*, *A Guest in the House of Israel*, *The Church and the Jewish People*, *A Mutual Witness*, *Interpreting Difficult Texts*, *When Jews and Christians Meet*, and *Has God Rejected His People?*